KV-198-557

The Royal Institution of Chartered Surveyors is the mark of property professionalism worldwide, promoting best practice, regulation and consumer protection for business and the community. It is the home of property related knowledge and is an impartial advisor to governments and global organisations. It is committed to the promotion of research in support of the efficient and effective operation of land and property markets worldwide.

Real Estate Issues

Series Managing Editors

Stephen Brown RICS
John Henneberry Department of Town & Regional Planning, University of Sheffield
David Ho School of Design & Environment, National University of Singapore
Elaine Worzala Real Estate Institute, School of Business Administration, University of San Diego

Real Estate Issues is an international book series presenting the latest thinking into how real estate markets operate. The books have a strong theoretical basis – providing the underpinning for the development of new ideas.

The books are inclusive in nature, drawing both upon established techniques for real estate market analysis and on those from other academic disciplines as appropriate. The series embraces a comparative approach, allowing theory and practice to be put forward and tested for their applicability and relevance to the understanding of new situations. It does not seek to impose solutions, but rather provides a more effective means by which solutions can be found. It will not make any presumptions as to the importance of real estate markets but will uncover and present, through the clarity of the thinking, the real significance of the operation of real estate markets.

Books in the series

Adams & Watkins *Greenfields, Brownfields & Housing Development*
Adams, Watkins & White *Planning, Public Policy & Property Markets*
Allen, Barlow, Léal, Maloutas & Padovani *Housing & Welfare in Southern Europe*
Ball *Markets and Institutions in Real Estate & Construction*
Ben-Shahar, Leung & Ong *Mortgage Markets Worldwide*
Barras *Building Cycles & Urban Development*
Beider *Urban Regeneration & Neighbourhood Renewal*
Buitelaar *The Cost of Land Use Decisions*
Couch, Dangschat, Leontidou & Petschel-Held *Urban Sprawl*
Couch, Fraser & Percy *Urban Regeneration in Europe*
Dixon, McAllister, Marston & Snow *Real Estate & the New Economy*
Evans *Economics & Land Use Planning*
Evans *Economics, Real Estate & the Supply of Land*
Guy & Henneberry *Development & Developers*
Jones & Murie *The Right to Buy*
Leece *Economics of the Mortgage Market*
McGough & Tsolacos *Real Estate Market Analysis & Forecasting*
Monk & Whitehead *Affordable Housing and the Property Market*
O'Sullivan & Gibb *Housing Economics & Public Policy*
Seabrooke, Kent & How *International Real Estate*
Wellings *British Housebuilders*

The Right to Buy

Analysis & evaluation of a housing policy

Colin Jones

Professor of Estate Management,
School of the Built Environment,
Heriot-Watt University

and

Alan Murie

Professor of Urban and Regional Studies,
Centre for Urban and Regional Studies,
University of Birmingham

Blackwell
Publishing

© 2006 by Blackwell Publishing Ltd

Editorial offices:
Blackwell Publishing Ltd, 9600 Garsington Road, Oxford OX4 2DQ, UK
  Tel: +44 (0)1865 776868
Blackwell Publishing Inc., 350 Main Street, Malden, MA 02148–5020, USA
  Tel: +1 781 388 8250
Blackwell Publishing Asia Pty Ltd, 550 Swanston Street, Carlton, Victoria 3053, Australia
  Tel: +61 (0)3 8359 1011

The right of the Author to be identified as the Author of this Work has been
asserted in accordance with the Copyright, Designs and Patents Act 1988.

All rights reserved. No part of this publication may be reproduced, stored in
a retrieval system, or transmitted, in any form or by any means, electronic,
mechanical, photocopying, recording or otherwise, except as permitted by
the UK Copyright, Designs and Patents Act 1988, without the prior permission
of the publisher.

First published 2006 by Blackwell Publishing Ltd

ISBN-10: 1-4051-3197-7
ISBN-13: 978-1-4051-3197-1

Library of Congress Cataloging-in-Publication Data
Jones, Colin, 1949–
    The right to buy : analysis & evaluation of a housing policy / Colin Jones,
Alan Murie.
      p. cm. — (Real estate issues)
    Includes bibliographical references and index.
    ISBN-13: 978-1-4051-3197-1 (alk. paper)
    ISBN-10: 1-4051-3197-7 (alk. paper)
    1. Housing policy—Great Britain. 2. Housing—Great Britain. 3. Home
ownership—Government policy—Great Britain. I. Murie, Alan. II. Title.
III. Series: Real estate issues (Oxford, England)

HD7333.A3J66 2005
363.5'8'0941—dc22
2005019317

A catalogue record for this title is available from the British Library

Set in 10/13 pt Trump Medieval
by Graphicraft Limited, Hong Kong

For further information, visit our subject website:
www.thatconstructionsite.com

BLACKBURN COLLEGE LIBRARY	
BB 59985	
Askews & Holts	16-Oct-2014
UCL363.585 JON	

Contents

Note

Information in tables and figures from government sources is provided with the kind permission of the Office of Public Sector Information.

1

Introduction

The year 2005 is the twenty-fifth anniversary of the introduction of the Right to Buy for nearly all local authority tenants in the United Kingdom. This book presents a wide-ranging discussion and evaluation of the Right to Buy over that 25 year period. The sale of council houses under the Right to Buy scheme was not an unprecedented step. There was a long maturation of policies for the sale of council houses in the United Kingdom and other countries had embarked upon substantial transfers of ownership of state housing to individuals. However, the Right to Buy was a flagship policy for Margaret Thatcher's Government, elected in 1979, and has emerged as the most significant act of privatisation associated with that or subsequent governments. It has changed the way housing policy operates in the UK – the way that the housing system works and the role and nature of different housing tenures – and has affected approaches to social policy more generally. While a large state housing sector has remained in the UK, it no longer accounts for almost one-third of all dwellings as it did in the 1970s, and what remains has a different reputation and image than existed in earlier phases of policy.

Twenty-five years after its introduction, the Right to Buy continues to attract controversy. The Government has reduced the financial incentives attached to the Right to Buy but there is concern about the impact of this policy on the capacity to provide housing for the homeless and those unable to afford owner-occupation. In a period of increased discussion of affordability crises and rising levels of homelessness, the Right to Buy has been regarded by some as a damaging policy, weakening the ability of Government to meet objectives relating to housing need. However, the other side of the coin is over two million households who have benefited directly from the Right to Buy and a wider number who have seen some indirect benefit.

The transfer of asset ownership from the state to individual households has been massive; perhaps not as large as was originally envisaged by the Thatcher Government, but nevertheless a major step towards creating a nation of homeowners and establishing a property owning population. The significance of the Right to Buy in the UK arises from the size of the role that the state had in the direct provision of housing, a role much greater than in many other countries. It has attracted considerable interest internationally and has been evaluated by other governments in considering their housing policy.

There are many difficulties in evaluating the Right to Buy. Looked at from the perspective of some purchasers, the policy has been a runaway success, providing access to ownership and to an appreciating asset, and opening up opportunities for mobility and choice. But this is not the experience of all of those who have bought properties, and there is a different story to tell for the next generation who have less chance of accessing high quality houses with gardens by becoming council tenants and have less opportunities for buying such properties through the Right to Buy.

This book aims to evaluate all these issues. The framework for this evaluation has three key dimensions. First, following the early analyses of the Right to Buy, there is a focus upon who benefits and upon the position of different stakeholders. The earliest assessment of the sale of council houses before the Right to Buy identified the different perspectives of tenants in different types of property, and of tenants compared with applicants for council housing (Murie 1975). It also identified the different perspectives of central and local government. It highlighted that the evaluation of this piece of social policy depended very much upon the position of the evaluator. This is what has become known as a stakeholder analysis in subsequent years. A stakeholder analysis acknowledges that the advantages and disadvantages of the policy will be experienced and perceived in different ways by different households and agencies.

Second, the evaluation considers variation according to location. House prices and housing markets vary between regions, towns and cities and within local authority districts. The benefits associated with acquiring an asset vary between different places and the impacts on communities and social rented housing also differ.

Finally, the evaluation takes account of time. There is a difference between the short term and the long term in reference to the position of different cohorts within council housing and different phasing within the operation of the Right to Buy.

This framework for evaluation relating to time, place and stakeholder is one that is of wider relevance in discussions of social and economic policy and part of the aim of this book is therefore to set out some of the general issues in evaluating policy changes and social policy programmes. There are indications of the kinds of data that need to be assembled to carry out such an evaluation. What is needed is more than a national level assessment in terms of costs and benefits; we need to consider the variations between stakeholders, places and environments.

This book then, engages with two parallel agendas: the Right to Buy itself and methods of analysis and evaluation. Chapters 2 and 3 set out the origins and nature of the Right to Buy and provide the essential background to the subsequent assessment of the impact of the policy. Chapter 4 provides a basic picture of the progress of the Right to Buy over its 25 year history and refers to variations in the progress of the policy regionally and locally. Chapter 5 considers the impact of the Right to Buy on the social housing sector. It emphasises that it is the combination of the Right to Buy and other policies introduced over the period that has changed social housing. This makes the evaluation of the Right to Buy itself problematic. Nevertheless, the Right to Buy has contributed to the change in the quality of social rented housing available for low income groups and the issues faced by managers of the social housing stock and it is possible to consider whether the idea of the Right to Buy as a successful policy is consistent with other changes that have happened in the social housing sector.

Chapters 6 and 7 consider the impact of the Right to Buy on the private housing market. Just as the policy has transformed state housing or the social rented sector, so it has also transformed home ownership and the private rented sector. For example, in some localities, former state housing is the dominant part of the private housing market. These chapters also consider the way that the Right to Buy has been exploited for profit by some privately owned companies.

The impact of the Right to Buy on different tenures is not the same as its impact on communities. Estates that were once single tenure become mixed tenure. Chapter 8 reviews the changing nature of communities within council estates, and develops the debate in relation to sustainable communities.

Chapter 9 discusses two major issues related to the management and maintenance of properties sold under the Right to Buy: the problems surrounding leasehold ownership arising from the sale of flats, and the subsequent condition of properties sold under the Right to Buy.

Chapter 10 addresses financial issues more directly. Has the Right to Buy been value for money, for example? The viewpoints of tenants of both local authorities and central government are considered. The chapter also looks at the financial consequences using discounted cash flow analysis.

Chapter 11 sets the UK experience in an international perspective. It compares the UK with three other state housing models – the transitional economies of central and eastern Europe where the sale of properties has been associated with political change; China and other east Asian countries where state intervention has directly sponsored home ownership; and finally countries which have been much more circumspect in selling state or social rented housing (the Netherlands is the prime example referred to here). Reference is also made in this chapter to public housing in the USA and the factors contributing to its residual character.

The final two chapters summarise the preceding analyses. Chapter 12 brings together the conclusions of the book's chapters and considers outcomes for different stakeholders, key consequences and issues associated with the Right to Buy and its relevance to the current housing policy context in the UK. Chapter 13 discusses how the Right to Buy stands up to scrutiny in terms of current concerns about affordability and modernisation, considerations related to equity, and the pattern of incentives and choices emerging. It considers the future of the policy itself and reflects on some wider related debates: privatisation as social policy; the nature of the housing market and emerging approaches to the welfare state to which home ownership is more central than in the past.

2

A Policy for its Time

The right for council tenants in Great Britain to buy the house they lived in was established in the Housing Acts of 1980. It is regarded as a 'flagship' policy, typifying and signalling the shift in the approach of the Government associated with the Prime Ministership of Margaret Thatcher. The Conservative Government that came to office in 1979 is regarded as having embarked on a radical agenda to reshape the politics and economics of the United Kingdom. Deregulation and privatisation were key elements of this. They fitted with a 'New Right' agenda to reduce the role of the state and to change patterns of accountability and control in the economy. Part of the agenda of reducing the role of the state was to reduce municipal influence and to attack the practices and traditions embodied in the public sector, including the influence of trade unions and what were seen as vested interests associated with public sector provision.

In retrospect, the sale of council houses has been the most important privatisation of all those introduced by the Thatcher Government. There have been other higher profile privatisations (gas, water, electricity and the telephone service) which generated higher levels of capital receipts for short periods of one or two years, but the sale of council houses has been a steady earner for the Exchequer over a period of 25 years.

While it is reasonable to present the Right to Buy in this context, and to suggest that it formed a significant part of a New Right agenda, it is important to recognise that the policy has deeper roots in debates about housing provision, especially in England. This chapter is concerned with tracing the longer origins of the Right to Buy, and connecting this with debates about the development of the public sector housing tradition in the United Kingdom. The essential argument is that the origins of the Right to Buy do not lie in the New Right debate, but in a longer debate about different forms of tenure, and the appropriate level of state intervention in housing provision (Murie 1975). It is argued that the growth of public sector housing in the UK was always contested. There were always resisters as well as enthusiasts and there were always suggestions that housing built by the state need not continue to be owned, controlled or managed by the state. There are examples of the sale of state housing throughout the inter-war years and after 1945. By the mid 1960s, the voices in favour of selling council housing were more prominent.

In early phases of the development of council housing the extent of housing shortages, the severity of housing problems, the fear of social disruption associated with inadequate housing, and the crises created during and immediately after the two World Wars, all lent strength to arguments in favour of investment in public sector housing. There was a strong case for developing a high quality, state owned housing sector that would perform better than the private sector in general and certainly better than the private landlord, the latter being the main provider of working class housing in all parts of the UK. Throughout this period, it was possible to support the growth of council housing at the same time as supporting the growth of individual ownership. This was because both could grow at the expense of a poorly managed and difficult to defend private rented sector. Those who favoured the growth of a property owning democracy did not all see council housing as a significant barrier.

By the 1970s this position had changed. The private rented sector had diminished in size and there was less scope for the continuing expansion of the other two tenures at the expense of private renting. It became harder to be in favour of the growth of both council housing *and* home ownership. At the same time, the development of housing finance and taxation and of organisational arrangements favouring home ownership (building societies, estate agents, lawyers and others in related businesses) began to create a different political environment and housing industry. Voices proposing the sale of council housing became stronger. By the mid 1970s, the resistance of the Labour Party to the sale of council houses was weaker as its identification of home ownership as the natural form of tenure was articulated. At the same time, the frustrations of Conservatives at the ability of local government to resist the tide of change, and their desire to find new ways to facilitate the sale of council houses, had become stronger. The willingness to breach principles of local autonomy and local democracy by demanding that local authorities sell council houses became more strongly expressed. There is also no doubt that some of the electoral calculations made by the Conservative Party in this period saw merit in breaking up the concentrations of council house ownership which was seen to underpin the Labour Party's electoral support in cities:

'freeing' the council tenantry would make them more likely to vote Conservative.

The debate over council house sales has a long history but it was toward the end of the 1970s that a number of different influences made the policy an acceptable one. It fitted with the electoral, political and economic ambitions of a new government. It fitted with the thinking of the New Right, although it did not originate from it. It was a policy which had found the right time, and which was therefore adopted with enthusiasm. Indeed, it may be argued that it was adopted with unreasonable enthusiasm as the terms of sale were not favourable to the exchequer or local government – the levels of discount introduced with the Right to Buy could be argued to have been unnecessarily high. It smacks more of a political and electoral agenda than one rooted in sound public finance considerations or market principles. This was a general issue with privatisations in the UK in the 1980s. There was a continuing debate about whether the prices determined for the sale of public assets undermined their value and therefore delivered a windfall gain to purchasers. However, in the case of other privatisations, the process of arriving at a price for sale was a different one. It partly reflected the approach that had been adopted under earlier policies, but also reflected the concern of Government with ensuring that the policy was a success as measured by the volume of sales that resulted.

These issues are discussed further in later chapters and the debate about the mechanisms and impacts of the Right to Buy are central to the discussion. In this chapter, our intention is to set out more fully the origins of the Right to Buy, the precursors of the policies embodied in the Housing Acts of 1980 and the previous debates about the sale of council houses, as well as providing some background to the growth of the council housing sector and patterns of tenure change in the UK. These are fundamental to the discussion and evaluation of the Right to Buy.

It is because of the size of the public sector housing stock in the United Kingdom, its control principally by local authorities, and its high quality and desirability that the Right to Buy has been such an important and significant policy. Without an understanding of the nature of the council housing sector and the debates around the sale of council houses, the consideration of more recent history is detached from its historical roots. We set out below the origins of council housing and a broad summary of the growth of council housing through the period to 1979. Following on from this, we present an account of the political debate on the sale of council houses in the period from 1945 to 1979.

The origins and development of council housing

By international standards the United Kingdom in 1980 had a large public sector housing stock. This was the product of a long tradition of state intervention in the building and management of housing and a choice to use local government as the principal provider of subsidised housing. Leaving aside the planned economies of central and eastern Europe, the UK had adopted a distinctive approach to housing. It had not followed the minimalist, residual welfare housing model associated with the USA and its state housing was not social housing in the sense of being targeted at those in social need. Rather, it was public housing designed for anyone with a housing need.

At the same time it had not followed the tradition associated with much of western and northern Europe of voluntary and not for profit or co-operative housing provision. By 1980 council housing in the UK catered for almost one in three households and consisted mainly of houses with gardens, built to high specifications over the previous 60 years. The greatest growth had occurred in the period since 1945.

Accounts of the development of state intervention in housing in the UK usually start with descriptions of the urban squalor associated with the industrial revolution (see Merrett 1979). Population growth, migration and rapid industrialisation were not sufficiently catered for by managed town expansion. The earliest interventions to deal with the threat to the general health of the whole population, to productivity and to social cohesion were public health measures. By 1890 a reformed local government system had wide ranging public health powers. The earliest housing legislation (the Lodging Houses Act 1851) provided local authorities with very limited power in relation to housing provision. Subsequent legislation enabled local authorities to clear and improve individual slum dwellings and then areas of unfit dwellings, but the period before 1919 is marked by a reluctance to envisage a permanent role for the government in housing. Local authorities did not respond enthusiastically to the powers they were given and mostly remained opposed to direct provision and rate-funded subsidy. Without local tax subsidy local authorities could only meet the costs of building activities by charging rents in excess of what the poorly housed could afford. Legislation was permissive and unsupported by Exchequer subsidies.

By 1914 only 24 000 dwellings had been built by local authorities and, without subsidy to bring rents within the reach of lower income households, direct public provision made little real impact. The period from

1915 was one of more dramatic change. The introduction of rent control in 1915 further undermined a private rented sector that had already seen a withdrawal of investment by landlords who had found better opportunities for investment in alternative markets. The reluctance of the private sector to invest in good quality housing coupled with the fear of political and social unrest because of inadequate housing provision and excessive rents changed the politics of housing policy.

Exchequer subsidy for council housing was introduced in 1919 and transformed the financial environment for local authorities' building activities. Lloyd George's pledge of 'homes fit for heroes to live in' is the most quoted slogan associated with social reconstruction after World War I. Historians discuss the pledge not just in terms of political opportunism but also of the threat of industrial and political unrest both during war time and after, with demobilisation of the armed services. The housing programme was at the heart of social reform policy. While 'we must have habitations fit for the heroes who have won the war' (Lloyd George quoted in Gilbert 1970), the housing programme was also influenced by other factors. The Prime Minister stated in 1919 'even if it cost a hundred million pounds, what was that compared to the stability of the state' and the threat posed by Bolshevism (Rodger 1992). The parliamentary secretary to the local government board stated 'the money we are going to spend on housing is an insurance against Bolshevism and Revolution' (Ibid).

Although the response to the threat of social unrest was a pledge to improve housing, the policies developed to put that into practice were seen as transitional and temporary. Successive pieces of legislation in the inter-war years changed the levels and targeting (from general housing needs initially to slum clearance) of subsidy for council housing but did not remove it. While rent controls in the private rented sector were eroded over the same period they also were never abolished.

A decline in private renting occurred throughout the UK. Where, in 1915, 90% of households were living in the sector, by 1938 only 58% of dwellings in England and Wales were owned by private landlords. Thirty-two per cent of dwellings were owner-occupied and 10% publicly owned. Over 50% of owner-occupied dwellings in 1938 were pre-1914 dwellings and as many as 1 million rented dwellings were sold to owner-occupiers between 1919 and 1938. Although the stock of council dwellings built in the slum clearance drive of the 1930s was generally inferior to dwellings built under earlier legislation, it was superior to 'reconditioned' private housing which has mostly since been demolished.

By 1938 some 1.1 million council dwellings had been built. This represented 10% of the housing stock. Given the condition of housing stock, the slogans concerned with homes fit for heroes and the early targets for council house building (half a million dwellings in three years), this represented only a small achievement over 20 years. In the same period it was owner-occupation that had expanded most dramatically. New building for owner-occupation in the period accounted for 1.8 million dwellings. In addition 1.1 million properties had passed from private renting to owner-occupation. New building by private landlords and other organisations accounted for 900 000 dwellings – not far short of the figure for local authorities. The declining importance of private renting was accelerated by sales to owner-occupiers. It is relevant to note that throughout this period legislation enabled the sale of council houses to owner-occupiers and that a small but significant number of sales were completed. The conviction that there was a large and permanent role for council housing was not universally accepted.

The outbreak of war in 1939 and the change of government in 1945 altered the debate considerably. Wartime controls, damage and redeployment of resources for the war effort caused a deterioration in the housing situation. By the time of the general election of 1945, a series of temporary and emergency measures had been taken to address the crisis. The emergency housing programme relied on local government to carry out the building and maintained control over private building. Differences between the political parties over the respective roles of public and private sectors were starting to become apparent, and continued to affect policy development after 1945.

Nye Bevan, as Labour Minister of Health in 1945, justified the emphasis on council housing in terms of the ability to plan and mobilise resources as well as social objectives. He stated:

'Before the war the housing problems of the middle classes were, roughly, solved. The higher income groups had their houses; the lower income groups had not. Speculative builders, supported enthusiastically, and even voraciously, by money-lending organisations, solved the problem of the higher income groups in the matter of housing. We propose to start at the other end. We propose to start to solve, first, the housing difficulties of the lower income groups. In other words, we propose to lay the main emphasis of our programme upon building houses to let. That means that we shall ask local authorities to be the main instruments for the housing programme.' (House of Commons 1946)

Bevan went on to comment on the problems caused when local authorities only built houses for lower income households while private speculators built houses for higher income groups:

'You have castrated communities. You have colonies of low income people, living in houses provided by the local authorities, and you have the higher income groups living in their own colonies. This segregation of the different income groups is a wholly evil thing, from a civilised point of view. It is condemned by anyone who has paid the slightest attention to civics and eugenics. It is a monstrous infliction upon the essential psychological and biological one-ness of the community.' (House of Commons 1946)

Local authorities were to be encouraged to build for higher income groups and make use of diversified designs linked to the different needs of people at different stages of the family cycle. The principles of planning, priority for letting and diversification in local authority activity necessitated severe restrictions on building for sale. Building for private ownership was restricted by licence. Although the Government rejected municipalisation of property in the private rented sector, rent restrictions retained the range of control over the housing stock.

At this stage in the construction of a housing policy, party differences of approach were evident. When a Conservative spokesman stated in 1946 that 'from the point of view of the country, it matters not one jot whether the houses are for sale or to let so long as houses are forthcoming' (Murie 1975), his remarks had been prefaced by doubts at the over-reliance on local authorities which were not staffed, designed or organised to licence or build.

By 1948, as local authority building completions increased, private completions remained low and even declined. Local authority completions rose from 3364 in 1945 to 190 368 in 1948, compared with the previous high point of 121 653 in 1939. Dwellings built between 1945 and 1951 were built to a standard in excess of those recommended by the Dudley Committee in 1944. In 1948 one quarter of the cost of post-war council houses was attributed to these improvements in size and amenities. The average area of a three-bedroom house in 1946–51 was 37% greater than in the period 1934–39. However, between 1949 and 1953 the average floor space of three-bedroom dwellings fell by 13%. The Labour Government in 1951 had promoted reduction in 'circulation space' and subsequent policy reduced living space and equipment. As a result dwellings built by local authorities in the 1950s were considerably smaller than and not so well equipped, for example in kitchen storage space, as those built in the late 1940s. Only after the publication of the Parker Morris report in 1961 did average dwelling size begin to increase again (Merrett 1979).

After 1945, the Conservative Party adopted the slogan 'a property owning democracy' and their policy promised 'to increase home owning as part of their plan to create a property owning democracy: widening the scope for the private builder and lowering costs' (Hoffman 1964). Private property was 'an equipoise to political power' (MacLeod & Maude 1950) and people found 'satisfaction and stability in the ownership of property, especially of their own homes and gardens' (Conservative Party 1949). Harris (1973) has interpreted the reformulation of policy within the Conservative Party between 1945 and 1951 as an attempt to adopt alternatives to 'nationalisation' and 'public ownership'. In constructing such policies housing was of major importance and on taking office in 1951 the Conservative Government immediately committed itself to a shift in policy.

In 1951, Mr Harold Macmillan, the new Minister of Housing and Local Government, stated:

> 'there will always be a very large number of people in this country who are compelled to, or want to, live in rented houses; but there will also be, I hope, a growing number of people who both want to own their own houses and may be enabled by various means to do so. Since it is part of our philosophy that a wide distribution of property rather [than] its concentration makes for a sound community, we shall pursue this aim wherever it is appropriate and can be done with due regard to the interests of those who need to live in rented houses. I shall hope soon to give local authorities guidance in this matter, both in respect of the building of new houses for letting and for sale, and in respect of the sale of existing houses to the people.' (House of Commons 1951)

This Conservative Government achieved new building targets of 300 000 dwellings a year by raising subsidy levels under the Housing Act 1952, by setting higher targets for local authorities and by encouraging private building. Increased local authority building was also facilitated by a reduction in standards. This, added to the relaxation of building licensing followed by its abolition in 1954, the return to a slum clearance policy in 1956–57 and the changes in housing finance and rent control between 1954 and 1958, formed the basis of the Conservative attitude towards housing policy until 1964. Government shifted the emphasis towards slum clearance, conservation and rehabilitation. It also set an objective to promote building for owner-occupation as one of the best forms of investment and because 'of all forms of ownership, this is one of the most satisfying to the individual and the most beneficial to the nation' (MHLG 1953).

The expansion of owner-occupation would enable local authorities to concentrate on slum clearance and would reduce their role and the burden of housing subsidies. In 1954 Macmillan said:

'Local authorities and local authorities alone can clear and rehouse the slums, while the general housing need can be met, as it was to a great extent before the war, by private enterprise.' (Speech to the Urban District Councils Association, June 1954, quoted in Samuel *et al.* 1962)

This return to the pre-war role of local authorities formed part of a 'market' philosophy in housing. The temporary and extraordinary shortages occasioned by war had been remedied and the problems remaining were seen to reflect a misallocation of resources rather than actual shortage. The market was seen as the best mechanism to reallocate and local authority action was only needed to meet the peculiar circumstances of slum clearance. Arguments urging 'realistic' or 'economic' rents in the public sector, and the removal or reduction of subsidies, were based on the assumption that 'better use' of the stock would result. The arguments were not solely based on economic assumptions and the long established antagonism against council housing continued:

'The council house system today is morally and socially damaging and I think we ought to do something about this nuisance during the life of this parliament.' (Enoch Powell, quoted in Samuel *et al.* 1962)

After 1955, in spite of increased slum clearance activity (29 000 dwellings in 1955 rising to 71 000 in 1964), new building by local authorities declined, but the phase of policy after 1956 merits some further attention. This was the period of the high rise housing experiment which has generally proved damaging to the council housing sector. The Housing Subsidies Act of 1956 reduced local authority building for general needs but encouraged multi-storey building. Subsidy levels were increased for blocks of flats even though the increased construction costs in high-rise building more than outweighed other savings. While the proportion of approved tenders for blocks of flats of five storeys or more averaged 6.9% annually from 1953 to 1959, this rose to 25.7% in 1966 but then fell to 9.8% in 1970. A gas explosion which caused five fatalities and the collapse of part of the Ronan Point flats in London in 1968 ended the enthusiasm for high rise schemes. While tenders for flats in high rise blocks

declined, tenders for dwellings in blocks of less than five storeys rose from
27% in 1967 to 38% in 1970 (Cooney 1974).

At this stage the Labour Party, with its stronger identification with council housing, was hedging its bets. During the general election of 1964 some
86% of Labour election addresses referred to 'home ownership' compared
with 57% of Liberal and only 33% of Conservative addresses (Butler &
King 1965). The elections of 1959, 1964 and 1966 seem to offer some
contrast with the view that the Conservative Party was the party for
owner-occupation. In 1966, 74% of Labour, 46% of Liberal and 40% of
Conservative election addresses mentioned home ownership (Butler & King
1966). It is difficult to sustain a view that the parties' attitudes to owner-
occupation differed in principle. The difference lay rather in what steps
were considered justifiable to achieve the objective and in the not unrelated aspect of attitudes towards local authority housing and the private
landlord.

In 1964, the new Labour Government identified its 'primary job' as building houses to rent, and some 50% of new building was intended for
letting by local authorities. The balance between building for letting and
building for owner-occupation was based on 'acute social need' and consideration of demand for purchase. The Labour Government attempted
to reduce the impact of uncertainty regarding interest charges on house
building by revising the subsidy system and from January 1969 Parker
Morris space and heating standards became mandatory. This led to
some increase in dwelling standards. Increased subsidy costs came under
pressure as economic problems prompted reduced targets for building and
public expenditure.

It is in this period that major changes in tax relief subsidy to owner-
occupiers occurred. Merrett (1982) identifies the origins of tax relief for
payments of interest associated with owner-occupiers' house purchases
and argues that before 1939 tax liability, and therefore tax relief, was
limited to higher income groups. In addition, in the period up to 1963,
the average owner-occupier's Schedule A taxation offset any tax relief on
interest repayments. Only with the abolition of Schedule A taxation in
1963 and the increasing extension of tax liability down the income scale
did the value of tax reliefs increase. These reliefs were extended in 1965,
when capital gains from the taxpayer's sole or main residence were
excluded from the new tax on capital gains, and in 1969, when tax relief
on interest paid on loans used for the acquisition or improvement of
property was retained when other loan interest payment tax reliefs were
abolished. These changes maintained or improved the fiscal advantages

of the owner-occupier in a period when subsidies to council housing were radically changed and, in the 1980s, dramatically reduced.

After 1964 council house sales emerged as a major aspect of council housing policy. By 1980 what has become labelled 'privatisation' in housing had become dominant and any hesitations connected with local autonomy and local needs had been over-ridden. The Conservative Party's policy toward council housing after 1964 was characterised by concern to avoid subsidising those not in need, to avoid proposals to sell at current market value and to avoid a situation in which local authorities were building more houses than was justified by the number of families in genuine housing need. It could be argued that the prime threat to the development of a 'Tory' society was 'the extension of state monopoly landlordism' (MacGregor 1965) and proposals to give council tenants the right to buy their houses were presented as a way of breaking up 'huge municipal domains' (Howe 1965). While these sentiments predate the Thatcher Government of 1979 the authors were to reappear as ministers in that Government.

On its return to office in 1970, one of the first actions of the Conservative Government was to remove the restrictions on council house sales introduced in 1968. Council houses sales became part of a new policy package designed to reduce the distorting effect of public intervention on the housing market. Rent levels and house prices were to be determined by the forces of supply and demand save where local scarcities unreasonably inflated rents. Protection for those unable to afford market prices was to be offered through rent rebate and allowance schemes. The principal vehicles for these policies were the Housing Finance Acts of 1972 and the 'fair rents policy' and 'return to the market' they embodied. If rents in the public and private sectors were allowed to rise to their 'natural' level (but not a level inflated by scarcity) better use of the housing stock would result. The Housing Finance Acts of 1972 removed local authority discretion in setting rents and granting rebates. In England and Wales council rents were to be linked to the 'fair rents' introduced for private tenancies by the Rent Act 1965. Linked with the increase in rents a new mandatory national system of rent rebates for council tenants was introduced. The legislation of 1972 marked the most complete change in policy since the introduction of Exchequer subsidies in 1919. However the policy package did not have the effects intended. Rather than freeing the market and releasing the natural forces of demand and supply, an increase in house prices and rise in interest rates led to a slump in private building. Not only were fewer tenants coming forward to buy their existing houses but fewer households of all types were willing and able to buy. The effective demand for house purchase had declined and local authority house waiting lists had lengthened alarmingly. The number of house completions in 1973 was 294 000 – the lowest figure since 1959.

Among the earliest actions of the minority Labour Government elected in 1974 were a series of measures which abandoned the Conservatives' approach. They repealed the Housing Finance Act, took development land into public ownership, and provided additional funds for municipalisation, building for sale by local authorities and municipal house building. Consistent with this, advice on the sale of houses in the new towns and by local authorities was changed. All of these actions could be represented as logical and necessary steps to increase building output. They also reflected and were affected by the general economic situation which did limit local programmes. The continued support for owner-occupation and for the measures embodied in the Housing Act 1974 demonstrate a consensus between the parties. However, the particular components of the Labour strategy and the emphasis within it reflected long established views about policy, in contrast with fundamental elements in the Conservative Government's policy between 1970 and 1974 and in contrast with the proposals contained in the Conservative Party's manifestos at both of the general elections of 1974. There were also differences over the expansion of council housing. One simple example illustrates this. Local authorities in the first year of the Labour Government bought over 9000 new houses from private developers. In addition to this, municipalisation of older houses represented an important extension of the public sector. The contrast with Conservative policies was marked. Conservative spokesmen argued that when no other buyer existed there might be an argument for local authority purchase, but 'there is no compelling reason why the houses should remain Government owned thereafter', and that tenants should be enabled to purchase the houses. The general effect of these early Labour policy measures was a significant increase in public sector housing starts, municipalisation and subsidy to the public sector.

In the general election of October 1974 housing policies were prominent. The Conservative spokesman on the environment, Margaret Thatcher, promised 9% mortgage interest rates, the abolition of rates and a bill to enforce the sale of council houses. In the midst of talk about 'coalition' these promises were stated to be non-negotiable. Legislation was to be passed to give council house tenants of three or more years' standing the right to buy at one-third less than market values, with a five year pre-emption clause. No reservations referring to rights of appeal, dwelling type, area or 'needs' were included. The package of housing promises was de-nounced by Labour politicians as an attempt to buy votes and as 'midsummer madness' which would add 5 pence in the pound to income tax. At a time when there were 30 000 unsold newly built houses there was no reason to believe that council tenants would buy, even with a considerable reduction in price. Furthermore, such purchase would decrease rather than increase the demand for new houses. The Right to Buy as offered in 1974 failed to appeal sufficiently to the electorate and Labour won the election.

In the period 1973/4 to 1978/9 public expenditure on housing grew by 7% but the fastest growing element within this expenditure was subsidy. Although housing expenditure retained its priority, the pattern of expenditure within housing, especially when tax reliefs are taken into account, was haphazard and regressive. The Secretary of State for the Environment set up a major review of housing finance but before this was completed housing expenditure had been cut in the budget of 1975 and concentrated in 'stress' areas (1976). Expenditure cuts in December 1976 were connected with borrowing from the International Monetary Fund and a stricter system of public expenditure control linked to cash limits and annual allocations of loan sanction for capital expenditure.

The Government's Housing Policy Review of 1977 was widely regarded as a conservative document indicating that Labour's support for home ownership and acceptance of a more limited role for council housing was complete. The Green Paper *Housing Policy* declared that 'for most people, owning one's house is a basic and natural desire' (DoE 1977a). A consensus had developed in which the major political parties competed to be regarded as the party for owner-occupation and in which there was little priority or policy for council housing.

Tables 2.1 and 2.2 indicate the major components of change in the structure of the housing stock in Britain. The period since 1914 has been marked by three major trends in housing tenure: the decline of private renting; the growth of owner-occupation and the growth of council housing. New building for private rental has been negligible since 1938 but even in the inter-war years was outweighed by sales into owner-occupation. These transfers from private renting to owner-occupation continued in the post-war period and losses to private renting as a result of demolitions and changes of use were a major additional element in 1960–75.

New building and transfers between tenants have contributed most significantly to the growth of owner-occupation. Only in 1938–60 (and especially in 1945–51) was new building principally in the public sector. As a result the numerical growth of council housing in that period was the highest, both absolutely and in comparison with the growth of home ownership. The growth of council housing almost offset the decline of private renting in both 1960–75 and 1975–81. However, in the early 1970s high rates of council house sales and of slum clearance involved

Table 2.1   Components of change of housing stock by tenure: England and Wales 1914–81 (millions).

	Owner occupied	Local authorities and new towns	Private landlords and miscellaneous	Total
1914–38				
New building	+1.8	+1.1	+0.9	+3.8
Purchases(+) or sales(−)	+1.1	*	−1.1	0
Demolitions and changes of use	*	*	−0.3	−0.3
Net change	+2.9	+1.1	−0.5	+3.5
1938–60				
New building	+1.3	+2.3	+0.1	+3.7
Purchases(+) or sales(−)	+1.5	+0.2	−1.7	0
Demolitions and changes in use[a]	−0.1	*	−0.4	−0.5
Net change	+2.7	+2.5	−2.0	+3.2
1960–75				
New building[b]	+2.6	+1.6	+0.3	+4.5
Purchases(+) or sales(−)	+1.1	+0.1	−1.2	0
Demolitions and changes of use	−0.2	−0.1	−0.8	−1.1
Net change	+3.5	+1.6	−1.7	+3.4
1975–81				
Net change	+1.2	+0.3	−0.4	+1.1

* Negligible.
[a] Includes 0.2 million destroyed by air attack.
[b] Includes conversions.

Source: DoE (1977b) Housing Policy Technical Volume Part 1 p. 39 and estimates for 1975–81 from figures in Hansard vol. 5, no. 108, 21.5.81 cal. 120, Department of Environment Housing and Construction.

a substantial net decline of rented housing. By 1979 rented housing was again in decline – more as a result of low rates of building and of council house sales than of either slum clearance or losses to private renting. By 1980 this combination resulted not just in a decline in renting but also in a decline in council renting for the first time since 1919. By 1993, completions of council housing were lower than achieved during World War II and between 1997 and 2003 remained lower than any year since 1919.

Towards privatisation of council housing

Throughout the growth of council housing since 1919, governments have encouraged the expansion of individual ownership through various mechanisms, and individual home ownership has grown more dramatically than

Table 2.2   Completions of local authority dwellings in Great Britain 1920–2003.

Year	Completions	Year	Completions
1920	576	1962	116 424
1921	16 786	1963	112 780
1922	86 579	1964	141 132
1923	67 062	1965	151 305
1924	19 586	1966	161 435
1925	23 862	1967	181 467
1926	49 508	1968	170 214
1927	83 948	1969	162 910
1928	120 492	1970	157 026
1929	69 677	1971	134 000
1930	73 268	1972	104 553
1931	63 996	1973	88 148
1932	79 013	1974	103 279
1933	68 156	1975	129 883
1934	72 343	1976	129 202
1935	57 326	1977	119 644
1936	70 486	1978	96 215
1937	87 423	1979	74 412
1938	92 047	1980	76 997
1939	121 653	1981	54 888
1940	60 926	1982	33 200
1941	20 122	1983	32 805
1942	5985	1984	31 593
1943	4095	1985	26 085
1944	4922	1986	21 547
1945	3364	1987	18 789
1946	25 013	1988	18 997
1947	97 340	1989	16 542
1948	190 368	1990	15 686
1949	165 946	1991	9651
1950	163 670	1992	4141
1951	162 584	1993	2076
1952	186 920	1994	1869
1953	229 305	1995	1445
1954	223 731	1996	862
1955	181 331	1997	468
1956	154 971	1998	428
1957	154 137	1999	165
1958	131 614	2000	302
1959	114 324	2001	480
1960	116 358	2001	331
1961	105 529	2003	286

Source: Merrett 1979; Wilcox (various).

has council housing. Throughout this period there have also been demands for council houses to be sold. The most important nineteenth century housing legislation required that council-built dwellings in redevelopment areas should be sold within ten years of completion. In the inter-war years powers to sell dwellings with ministerial consent existed and were used, albeit on a small scale. Sales had to be carried out at the best price obtainable.

It was not until the 1960s that council house sales became a major issue in political debate and housing policy action; not until the 1970s that mandatory action was contemplated; and not until the 1980s that legislation providing tenants with a right to buy was placed on the statute book. Since 1945 the debate on council house sales was consistently conducted along party political lines. Although it became a more prominent debate after the 1960s the difference of view was long established. The Conservative Party consistently pressed for sales and gradually moved to support for a Right to Buy. The Labour Party, from a refusal to contemplate any council house sales (in 1945–51), came to accept the general stance of the Conservative Party until, following their election failure of 1983, Labour ceased to oppose the policy. The history of council house sales prior to the Right to Buy has been presented elsewhere (Murie 1975) and the following account is based on this work.

During World War II restrictions on the sale of rented property were accompanied by a refusal to grant consent to the sale of council houses. This refusal was maintained by the Labour Government after 1945 on the grounds that 'in present circumstances it is considered that as many houses as possible should be kept available for letting by local authorities' and that 'where public money and public facilities have been found to provide houses for letting to those in the greatest need, I do not consider that those houses should now be sold to others merely because they have the money to buy them' (House of Commons Debates, 1947–48, vol. 445, col. 1167); or 'it is contrary to the Government's policy to agree at the present time to the sale of council houses in view of the importance of ensuring that as many houses as possible are available for letting to persons most in need of them' (House of Commons Debates, 1948–49, vol. 468, col. 186).

The Government continued to refer to keeping as many houses as possible available for letting to those in need. In 1951 the Minister for Local Government and Planning added that 'this means selling public property to private people, and on the whole I think that is objectionable and would arouse resentment from those on waiting lists for housing' (House of Commons Debates, 1950–51, vol. 489, col. 2132).

In sharp contrast to the position of the Labour Party, Conservatives argued that council house sales should be permitted on various grounds, from 'there are hundreds of local authority tenants who would like to buy the house in which they live', to 'the potential reduction in rates and taxes or the relief of local authorities', and the state's local indebtedness (House of Commons Debates, 1945–46, vol. 427, col. 1423). The Conservative Party was committed to the relaxation of licensing and the encouragement of council house sales. The newly elected Conservative Government in 1952 issued a general consent which enabled local authorities to carry out sales and notify the Minister only on completion. This general consent was justified by the Government on grounds wider than those of housing need or housing policy. Harold Macmillan, the Minister of Housing and Local Government in the new Government, stated:

> 'we wish to see the widest possible distribution of property. We think that, of all forms of property suitable for such distribution house property is one of the best.' (House of Commons Debates, 1951, cols. 2227–2354)

The general consent was, however, restrained. It did not urge local authorities to sell and simply provided a clear framework for sales where local authority and tenant desired this. The Housing Act 1952 removed the requirement that local authorities selling houses had to obtain the best price, and provided powers for the local authority to limit resale price for a period of five years and to reserve to itself a right of pre-emption in the event of any proposal to resell or lease within five years. Sale prices for houses completed before 1945 were to be not less than 20 times the net rent and, for houses completed in or since 1945, not less than the all-in cost of the dwelling.

The general consent remained unchanged until 1960. Its impact was limited and the issue was defused by the lack of response to the policy. In March 1953 Harold Macmillan stated that 'owing to the time taken by legal and other formalities the number of actual sales completed is at present negligible' (House of Commons Debates, 1953, vol. 513, col. 642). In October 1954 it was reported that about 2440 council houses had been sold, and in May 1956, 5825.

This rate of progress was slower than many desired. Although in 1953, 60% of local authorities were estimated to be willing to offer houses for sale and 20% were undecided, the slow progress with sales caused some advocates of a policy of council house sales to find fault with local authorities. In 1955 the Minister of Housing was asked to take steps to ensure that 'most local authority house tenants are granted the rights, with proper safeguards for the councils concerned, to purchase the house which they occupy'. Many backbenchers held the view that 'it is unfortunate that in many cases people living in certain local authority areas have not the opportunities which are often given to people living in joint areas' (House of Commons Debates, 1953, vol. 522, col. 191–2). However, the view that the local authorities should properly decide remained dominant.

It appears to have become accepted that the slow rate of progress with council house sales had explanations other than local authority intransigence. Figures for sales were regularly reported. Ministers did not consider it necessary to issue a further Circular encouraging local authorities to sell council houses (House of Commons Debates, 1955–56, vol. 543, col. 83) and denied that there was confusion on the issue (House of Commons Debates, 1958–59, vol. 604, col. 26–7; vol. 610, col. 25). By 1958 some 31% of local authorities in England and Wales had sold dwellings (House of Commons Debates, 1958, vol. 591, col. 997). Demand seems to have been the limiting factor, and indeed Ministers suggested that 'the increasing number of houses being built by private enterprise and sold reduces the number of people who wish to buy council houses.' (House of Commons Debates, 1955–56, vol. 544, col. 204). They also explained that 'many more local authorities have approved the policy of selling council houses, but there has been no demand for purchase' (House of Commons Debates, 1958, vol. 591, col. 997).

The Housing Act 1961 was accompanied by a revised general consent for council house sales. The new Circular governed sales until 1967 and made some important modifications to previous procedures to prevent sales at unreasonably low prices and bring pricing processes into line with those for compensation. Some 16 000 council houses were sold between 1957 and 1964. This was low compared with the growth of municipal housing or the expansion of owner-occupation. The new Labour Government of 1964 identified a larger role for local authorities in house building but did not choose to withdraw or revise the general consent issued in 1960. Labour was actively in favour of sales in new towns in order to achieve objectives of social and economic balance and had brought in leasehold reforms, giving leaseholders the right to purchase freeholds or extend leases by 50 years. These and other considerations made it undesirable to prohibit council house sales. In addition, in 1965 the volume of council house sales was insufficient to threaten the Government's housing programme or to merit actions which would further reduce local autonomy at a time when such reduction would provoke complaint. Local government opinion of the general consent may have been further influenced by their composition and whether they were in urban areas where housing need was felt to be most acute. Labour control of these authorities declined significantly, however, between 1966 and 1969 and the number of completed sales shot up due to increased Conservative influence.

The Labour Government between 1964 and 1967 reluctantly accepted local authorities' wish to sell council houses stating that authorities 'should have regard to the value of the capital asset of which they are disposing' (House of Commons Debates, 1965, vol. 715, col. 39). By 1967 their reluctance was becoming more marked. The Minister for Housing and Local Government stated that in general local authorities 'ought not to sell their houses where there is still an unsatisfied demand for houses to let at moderate rents and where they intend to continue a substantial programme of building houses to let' and the encouragement of home ownership was desirable but was 'primarily a matter for the private sector to deal with' (House of Commons Debates, 1967, vol. 740, col. 1336). The Government's desire to avoid a complete ban on sales and to adopt a flexible approach was difficult to achieve. Newly won Conservative majorities in many cities had led to changes in local policy which directly contradicted the Minister for Housing and Local Government's stated principle, the main examples being Birmingham and London. In Birmingham the

Table 2.3   Sales of dwellings by public authorities (England and Wales) 1960–80.

Year	Local authorities	New towns
1960	2889	280
1961	3795	353
1962	4404	657
1963	3673	485
1964	3817	465
1965	3590	779
1966	4906	919
1967	4867	630
1968	9979	455
1969	8590	504
1970	6816	551
1971	17 214	3438
1972	45 878	16 079
1973	34 334	7497
1974	4657	745
1975	2723	227
1976	6090	84
1977	13 022	367
1978	30 045	374
1979	41 660	813
1980	81 465	4231

Source: Housing and Construction Statistics, HMSO Quarterly.

Conservative-led council suggested that 'during the long years of social-ist control in the City of Birmingham, the building of new houses for sale has reduced to a mere trickle and that it is necessary now to restore a proper balance.' In these circumstances and in view of the 'widespread desire for extra home ownership' a policy of council house sales was 'right and proper' (House of Commons Debates, 1967, vol. 743, col. 203). How-ever, this stance was not consistent with Labour Government policy, con-cern with households on the waiting list or the serious housing shortage in the city.

A new Circular introduced in 1967 was a response to the rise in sales in certain areas. It unequivocally expressed ministerial opposition to sales in areas with a pressing social need for rented housing, but nevertheless renewed the general consent. The terms were changed and for the first time required sale prices to be based on market valuations. Because of problems with making valuations and restrictions on resale, authorities could reduce values by up to 20% below vacant possession market value provided no loss on the sale was incurred.

Neither these new pricing arrangements nor the views expressed in the Circular restricted the local enthusiasm for sales and it was at this stage that Labour MPs began to press the Minister for Housing and Local Govern-ment to prevent or limit council house sales. The Minister replied in terms similar to those used previously. In June 1967 he stated 'I deprecate the sale of council houses if the sale of them affects the waiting lists and reduces the stock of available houses' (House of Commons Debates, 1967, vol. 748, col. 1397). Such a view was bound to draw Conservative comment and their spokesman Geoffrey Rippon stated 'if the Council is satisfied that there is a legitimate demand for council houses to be purchased' the Minister should not 'thwart the electoral will' (House of Commons Debates, 1967, vol. 748, col. 1397).

This line of argument was less likely to influence a decision than 'any substantial erosion of the housing stock in areas where there is still a long waiting list for accommodation at reasonable rents'. Consequently, the Minister for Housing and Local Government reported in November 1967 that he had 'asked the Greater London Council, Birmingham and the other major towns which are embarking on this policy for monthly reports on the progress which is made' (House of Commons Debates, 1967, vol. 755, col. 214). Although it was expected that there would be fewer sales in 1967 than there had been in 1966, the level of sales had reached a point incompatible with the stated position of the Government and it was attract-ing adverse comment within the Labour Party.

In 1967 a motion at the Labour Party Conference expressed concern about the 'sale of council houses by Tory controlled authorities in many areas where there is still an unsatisfied demand' (Labour Party 1967). The Minister of Housing and Local Government maintained that it was desirable to retain the general consent both because it was wrong to interfere with local authorities and because there were cases where sales were justified. However, he went on to say, 'It would not surprise me if a lot of local authorities were praying for the Minister to . . . get them off the hook for what in many cases is an embarrassing electoral commitment.' (Ibid).

However, party concerns led to the issue of a new Circular (42/68) limiting sales in the major conurbations. The consistently repeated view was that council house sales were not an intelligent method of encouraging owner-occupation and that the policy was financially and socially unwise if pursued unchecked. It was maintained that the mass sale of council houses would seriously affect the ability of local authorities to meet housing need as this depended on a regular supply of relets as well as on new construction. In 1968, through the Circular, the general consent was renewed with a quota system limiting the proportion of municipal stock to be sold annually in the major conurbations.

The stance of the Conservative Party remained sharply different. Sir Keith Joseph at the Conservative Party Conference of 1967 stated that the sale of council houses had been a success but 'we must not regard it as the limit of our ambitions for altering local authority housing' (Conservative Party 1967). Not surprisingly the new Conservative Government in 1970 removed the restrictions on sales introduced in 1968 and reverted to the terms of the 1967 Circular, in line with a pledge in the 1970 election manifesto that 'we will encourage local authorities to sell council houses to those of their tenants who wish to buy them' (Conservative Party 1970). This was designed 'to encourage the spread of home ownership and to increase the opportunities for tenants of council houses to own the houses in which they live.' The Minister for Housing and Construction believed 'that those people in bad housing conditions and on housing waiting lists will benefit more from what is being done as a result of Circular 54/70 than by waiting for existing tenants to vacate their homes.' (House of Commons Debates 1970, vol. 803, col. 1340–1). Sales would release resources and so help people still on the housing list.

Consistent with this, much of the earlier caution over both purchase prices and restrictions was put aside. Increasing reference was made to the right to buy and decreasing reference to safeguards for the local authority. In addition, local authority representatives were demanding an increased discount for purchasers (see Conservative Party 1972; 1973; House of

Commons Debates, 1970; 1973). At the 1971 Conservative Party Conference, the Minister for Housing and Construction announced his willingness for Birmingham as well as Manchester to sell at a 30% discount
instead of 20%. Commenting on allegations that some Labour councils
were breaking faith with tenants when reversing sales policies the
Minister replied that the electoral process was a better method of pre-
vention than his interference with local government. However, he also
stated, 'I have a little list of Tory authorities which refuse to sell council houses', and hoped that this list would be shorter in the next year
(Conservative Party 1971).

The whole tenor of debate had changed considerably from that of the 1950s
and early 1960s. It was to change further with disappointment at progress
with this and other housing policies after the initial interest of 1970–72,
which included a growth in the number of council houses sold from under
7000 in 1970 to nearly 46 000 in 1972. The decline from this peak after
1972 inevitably aroused comment within the Conservative Party. At the
Party Conference in 1972 it was urged that councils which refused to sell
to their existing tenants must be compelled to do so, at current prices,
with an appropriate allowance for the years of tenancy and a restriction
before resale would be permitted.

At the same conference, the Secretary of State for the Environment claimed
that the provisions of the new rent rebate scheme and the opportunity of
purchasing homes at a 20% discount on the market price were of great
benefit to council tenants. He deplored:

> 'those Tory councils which, from what I believe is normally bad advice
> of their officials, do not offer the prospect of owner-occupation to the
> tenants. I deplore also those socialist councils which, out of political
> doctrine, wish to keep council house tenants as tenants and do not wish
> them to own their own houses.'

He went on to claim 'we are beginning to succeed' and pointed to the
'good news' that in the first half of 1972 nine times as many council houses
had been sold as in the same period of 1970. This, however, was
'nowhere near enough' and Labour councils should be confronted with
tenants 'deploring the manner in which they have been deprived of this
very basic right'.

If the number of council house sales was to be a measure of success
in housing policy it was likely that consideration would be given to
methods of boosting figures. The general consent was extended to

Scotland, and departmental Circulars were increasingly admonitory. Permission to increase the discount on purchase price was given and the Housing (Amendment) Act 1973 enabled the Secretaries of State for the Environment and for Wales to authorise or require local authorities to control resale for a period of over five years. This last provision was intended to remove objections which were based on the fear that purchasers would make a quick profit after buying houses.

It is probable that, despite these changes, the general rise in house prices had taken the value of dwellings beyond a level which many remaining tenants wishing to buy could afford or were willing to pay. The figures for council house sales were also, no doubt, being held down by the unwillingness of many local authorities to incorporate sales policies into their housing programmes.

Criticism of such local authorities, both Labour and Conservative controlled, was regularly linked with suggestions that Government should make it obligatory for local authorities to facilitate tenant purchase. By 1973 it was clear that any traditional reluctance to interfere with local autonomy, within either the Ministry or the Conservative Party, was wearing thin. The Conservative Party Conference was told that the enforced sale of council houses with discount, together with the Housing Finance Act, could form a basis for election victory.

The Conservative Party election manifesto of February 1974 included a commitment that, 'subject to the right of appeal to the local authority on clearly specified grounds, we shall ensure that, in the future, established council tenants are able, as of right, to buy on reasonable terms the house or flat in which they live.' Although the manifesto did not state on what grounds appeals would be made, it is clear that the intention was to limit the autonomy of local authorities. It was stated that the number of new home-owners would have been still larger had certain councils not opposed the sale of council houses to those council tenants who were willing and able to buy them with the help offered by the Government. Frustration, or concern, at the failure to maintain sales at a high level, was apparently widely felt within the Conservative Party and merited a considerable change in the approach to local government. By 1973, the number of sales was failing in spite of Government policy. This cannot be attributed simply to local authority obstruction. Indeed, the fall was marked in new towns where there was no discretion in implementing policy.

The newly elected Labour Government in 1974 did not adopt the policy of Right to Buy but nor did it rescind the general consent to council house

sales. The Conservatives in the general election of October 1974 reiter-
ated the promise of legislation to give council tenants of three or more
years' standing the right to buy at one-third less than market value, with
a five year pre-emption clause. The Labour Government contented itself
that it had in March 1974 reissued the general consent with a stern refuta-
tion of its predecessor's advice but with no change in the terms to be
followed. The Government's complacency in this was, no doubt, affected
by the dominance of Labour groups in the large urban authorities. However, as local electoral fortunes changed, Conservative councils began to
implement policies within the terms of the general consent but yielding
increasing numbers of sales. By 1977 sales were higher than those that
had led to the quota system nine years before, and in 1978 they more than
doubled to the third highest figure ever. Only in March 1979 did the
Government intervene to restrain this development with a revised general
consent preventing sales of empty houses and restricting sales to sitting
tenants to those of two years' standing.

Conclusions

The background to the development of council housing and housing
policy in Britain has been the need to subsidise housing costs in order to
achieve objectives relating to the supply of dwellings and their standards.
The growth of council housing through the twentieth century has been
an important factor changing the social and political environment in Britain.
The establishment of council housing as a major tenure form was not
a result of any general acceptance of the desirability of state-provided
housing. The collapse of investment by private landlords and the destruc-
tion and disruption occasioned by two world wars increased the role of
council housing beyond the intentions of the policies which enabled its
growth.

The expansion of council housing consistently formed only part of a wider
restructuring of the housing market. The period of growth of council housing was also a period of growth of owner-occupation. Throughout most
of the period the preoccupation of governments was to facilitate private
rather than state-controlled production and consumption of housing.

Over sixty years of investment by local authorities has radically changed
the face of British towns and cities. Municipal enterprise has produced a
variety of dwelling types. Even in the early years of council development,
experimental dwellings involving non-traditional building techniques
and different estate and planning layouts meant that the public sector

was by no means uniform. Some dwellings were built to higher standards under more generous subsidy schemes (the Wheatley and Bevan Acts) while others are associated with lower standards or prefabricated building methods (especially slum clearance building both before and after World War II). While the fashion for high rise building in the 1960s was regarded by some as 'delegitimising' council housing and damaging its public support and appeal, there were other elements in diversity which played a part. Early, unmodernised, purpose built dwellings, slum dwellings acquired for clearance, conversion or improvement but used (perhaps after limited patching) pending such treatment, various prefabricated and non-traditional dwellings with design faults, dwellings in isolated locations or on stigmatised estates, were all parts of the council housing sector and affected its public image and popularity. It was variety and differentiation which marked council housing rather than uniform unpopularity. The bulk of council dwellings had been built to a high standard and provided tenants with housing they were very satisfied with. The high rise building was a metropolitan image and did not apply in the vast majority of areas. In most towns council housing consisted of traditional houses with gardens and the image of council housing was not that of the ghetto for the poor and the newcomer.

If council housing had developed a more complicated image which varied from locality to locality it had also changed its financial and social base. It was no longer a heavily subsidised or privileged sector. As council housing aged or matured so the structure of debt matured and opportunities for cross-subsidisation became more important. As funding took this into account and as income maintenance arrangements and rent rebates developed, council housing became less exclusively for the affluent, employed sections of the working class and those able to pay high rents. Indeed, as private renting declined, council housing progressively took on its role as the source of housing for the marginalised poor.

These features and the limited rights of council tenants formed the basis of criticism that, although council dwellings were generally of a high standard, the quality of service in terms of rights, representation and influence was remarkably low. While legal remedies for the grievances of private tenants accompanied rent control and especially rent regulation in the 1960s, council tenants had no such remedies until the limited measures in the tenants' charter under the Housing Acts 1980. The quality of service in terms of aid and advice, repairs and maintenance, and community facilities was generally poor for council tenants. If council housing was regarded as a flow of services, rather than just a physical entity the 'delegitimation' of council housing was endemic.

The high rise building phase can also be referred to in stressing the influence and interests of private sector builders in council housing. Council housing has been largely built by the private sector throughout its history. This privatisation in production affected its costs and determined the technology adopted. Since its inception there have been pressures to fully privatise the production of council housing and to privatise its use through sale. Pressures for privatisation were not new phenomena.

The 60 years of growth of council housing were more notably the years of growth of owner-occupation. Home ownership became the dominant and normal tenure; has developed as an industry with major interests relying on it; has achieved a status which leaves it too powerful for political 'interference' and is suggested by some to have contributed to real changes in political and class attitudes in society. Its growth has represented a social revolution and a significant restructuring of private enterprise and capital. During this period of restructuring – the withdrawal of private renting and its replacement by individual ownership backed by the home ownership 'industry' – municipal activity played a critical role in maintaining production and standards, in managing the transition, and in compensating for the dislocation and disruption associated with such a transition. Through the period of transition few saw what was happening. Some were concerned with temporary dislocations, some with re-establishing the traditional norm, some with building socialism, some with building barriers against socialism, some with social and environmental engineering and so on. Only crises associated with war created real shortages and problems which were generally acknowledged.

Even in these periods the consensus over how to proceed was limited. The growth of council housing had always been accompanied by an orchestra of opponents and denigrators and claims that the free market could do better. Such views were difficult to support in the face of historical evidence but had greatest weight in periods when the threat of civil disorder or the power of organised labour were weakest, when unemployment was highest, when housing problems were less severe and when the private market ideology was most strongly represented in parliament. The periods of residual policy when support for council housing was lowest or when the role of council housing was most limited (say to slum clearance) broadly coincided with such a perspective. Such underlying factors operated to predispose governments to a more substantial attack on council housing than had occurred previously.

Between 1952 and 1970 some 61 000 public sector dwellings had been sold to sitting tenants in England. The early 1970s saw much higher rates of sale as Government encouragement coincided with Conservative control of key local authorities and with a favourable economic environment. Changes in the economy and in political control at local and national levels affected the subsequent pattern, and by the end of the decade 210 000 dwellings had been sold to sitting tenants. The figures for England and Wales prior to 1979 showed that the peak year for sales of dwellings by local authorities was 1972 with almost 46 000 dwelling sold. In 1973, this figure was 34 000 dwellings. These figures are high compared with those which were achieved under the Right to Buy in the period after 1990 and they indicate the importance of acknowledging that sales were occurring under discretionary policies with much lower levels of discount and with almost no flats available for sale.

By the 1970s owner-occupation was the majority tenure but could no longer expand at its established rate through new building and transfers from the much diminished private rented sector. For the first time support for the expansion of home ownership and council housing were in conflict. The political ideology of radical and Thatcherite Toryism and the pressures from its economic policy makers coincided to produce a more concerted and in that sense a new attack on council housing. Proposals for the privatisation of council housing formed part of a wider attempt to reduce public expenditure through the sale of assets and to facilitate the provision of services through private rather than public capital. At the same time the encouragement of home ownership continued to be a major feature of policy and was extended through a variety of special schemes including building for sale, sales of land, improvement for sale, homesteading, mortgage guarantees and shared ownership.

3

The Right to Buy in the UK 1980–2005

The Conservative Government elected in 1979 changed the approach towards council housing from one of residual neglect and disinterest to one of aggressive restructuring. The success of the Conservative Party electorally was widely associated with the main plank of their housing policy – the introduction of a statutory Right to Buy for council tenants.

The Right to Buy did not introduce the sale of council houses for the first time and on coming into power in 1979 the Conservatives replaced the existing Circular providing a general consent for the sale of council houses. A new Circular encouraged such sales and increased the discounts that should be provided to the levels that would subsequently be embodied in the Housing Acts of 1980. The success of this Circular was apparent in the high rate of sales achieved in 1979 and 1980, but the innovation in 1979 was the pursuit of legislative action to introduce a Right to Buy – a Conservative commitment since 1974. Any hesitation about local autonomy, or housing need, or the terms of sales, had been overcome.

In considering the aims of the Right to Buy it is important to refer back to the Conservative manifesto of 1979 and the statements made at the stage of introducing legislation. The manifesto referred to housing under the heading 'Helping the Family' and devoted one and a half pages to housing – more than to social security, education, health and welfare or the elderly and disabled. The issues referred to were principally about ownership and the sale of council houses and no reference at all was made to investment in new building, improvement, homelessness or housing need. Helping people to become home owners was designed to support family life. The paragraphs referring to the sale of council houses were preceded by the comment, 'To most people ownership means first and foremost a home of their own'. The difficulties of raising a deposit and affording purchase were referred to and wider taxation and economic policies were designed to address this. At the same time the manifesto stated, 'as it costs about three times as much to subsidise a new council house as it does to give tax relief to a home buyer, there could well be a substantial saving to the tax and rate payer.' In relation to the sale of council houses specifically, the manifesto stated:

> 'Many families who live on council estates and in new towns would like to buy their own homes but either cannot afford to or are prevented by the local authorities or the Labour Government. The time has come to end these restrictions. In the first session of the next Parliament we shall therefore give council and new town tenants the legal right to buy their homes while recognising the special circumstances of rural areas and sheltered housing for the elderly. Subject to safeguards over resale, the terms we propose would allow a discount on market values reflecting the fact that council tenants effectively have security of tenure. Our discounts will range from 33% after three years, rising with length of tenancy to a maximum of 50% after 20 years. We shall also ensure that 100% mortgages are available for the purchase of council and new town houses. We shall introduce a right for these tenants to obtain limited term options on their homes so that they know in advance the price at which they can buy while they save their money to do so. As far as possible we will extend these rights to housing association tenants. At the very least we shall give these associations the power to sell to their tenants. Those council house tenants who do not wish to buy their homes will be given new rights and responsibilities under their own Tenants' Charter.' (Conservative Party 1979)

The Right to Buy was seen as an end in itself. It was a mechanism for increasing owner-occupation and for responding to the desire of some tenants to own their properties. It was not a means of achieving any other housing objective and the response to questions from the Environment Committee during its inquiry into the sale of council houses in 1979 and 1980 was largely to brush aside other issues. The issues about the loss of relets, the financial implications of the policy, or whether or not the policy would contribute to the development of welfare housing, were almost dismissed. These concerns, from the Government's perspective, missed the point and the simpler intent of the policy.

When it was introduced in 1980 the Right to Buy provided a new framework for the sale of public sector housing in Britain. It did not introduce council house sales, rather it replaced previous powers that allowed local authorities to sell properties but did not require them to do so and it introduced more generous terms for purchasers than had previously been allowed. Consequently it introduced a higher volume of sales at a higher discount rate and more widely available to tenants. In the lead-up to the legislation of 1980 a number of considerations lay behind the decision to extend the discretionary powers of Government that had existed for a long time and to introduce a Right to Buy programme that would limit local discretion. Some of these considerations were directly related to the way in which local authorities exercised discretion – there was a view that they did not recognise the desire of tenants for home ownership and the restrictions placed on sales were based on doctrinaire and party political judgements rather than the interests of tenants. At the same time the Right to Buy policy formed part of a strategy to alter local authority housing and attack paternalism and poor management. The aim was to encourage an increase in home ownership and to increase the opportunities for council tenants to own the houses in which they lived. There was a belief that this would not have any adverse impact on other tenants or on the operation of the housing market.

The drafting of the Housing Act 1980 represented a determined attempt to ensure that neither the aspirations of tenants wishing to buy nor those of Conservatives with respect to council house sales could be frustrated by local opposition or lethargy. The new mechanism to achieve privatisation in housing was in the Housing Act 1980 in England and Wales and the Housing Tenants Rights Etc. (Scotland) Act 1980. This involved major changes in policy and practice towards council house sales. The principal elements and innovations in the new legislation were as follows:

- A statutory Right to Buy replaced local discretion and applied to almost all secure tenants with three years' tenancy and to almost all properties where the landlord was a council, new town, non-charitable housing association or other public sector body (with the exception of some dwellings for the elderly or disabled and some other lesser categories).
- A statutory procedure for sale was laid down to limit local variation over implementation of the Right to Buy.
- Strong powers were established for the Secretary of State to monitor and intervene in local administration of the scheme.
- A new basis for establishing the price at which sales would occur was established. This was based, as under discretionary policies, on valuation less fixed rates of discount. These were now to be linked to

the number of years of tenancy in any council or other relevant dwelling. The discounts were those introduced in the general consent of 1979 and rose from 33% (for three years' tenancy) by 1% for each additional year of tenancy up to a maximum of 50%.

- Discounts were to apply even where no pre-emption clause or other restriction existed. The only disincentive to early resale related to repayment of discount (reduced by 20% of the total for every complete year of residence) if resale occurred within five years.
- Detailed procedures in relation to valuation, appeal against valuation, cost floors and maximum discounts were generally regarded to have been very favourable to the potential purchaser rather than the landlord.
- The scheme included the legal right to a mortgage and the powers of the Secretary of State to determine procedures (for example multiples of income and age limits for mortgage qualification) to govern local implementation; and the freezing of valuations and a deferred purchase scheme under which the Right to Buy could be carried out at the current price for up to two years.
- In designated rural areas a locality condition or pre-emption clause could be adopted and purpose-built elderly persons' housing was excluded from the Right to Buy.

Other than these exclusions the scheme was designed to be inclusive. The new policy package was uniform. It applied to flats as well as houses, although there had been very little experience of selling flats under discretionary policies. The scheme was highly publicised and made more attractive by the expectation that rents would continue to rise. After some initial nervousness on the part of building societies and other lenders, these institutions adopted the Right to Buy with enthusiasm and more than nine out of every ten sales under the scheme were financed with private sector loans.

This (plus other factors) had the effect of giving expansive powers to the Secretary of State to influence local action and to maximise incentives to purchase. Since the implementation of the Housing Acts these powers have been consistently used. As is indicated later in this book the nature of central monitoring and intervention have significant implications for central–local relations. The Housing Acts represented a thoroughly centralist, compulsory approach to policy implementation and the Housing and Building Control Act of 1984 reinforced this by increasing discounts for council house sales and consolidating policy. Under the impact of these Acts and the policies being pursued at the time in relation to rents, subsidies, public expenditure and housing investment, the nature and role of council housing changed and attitudes which have been associated with council housing since its inception continue to be modified. At the same time, as subsequent discussion will suggest, the capital receipts associated with council house sales and privatisation have become more important.

Financial considerations

The Housing Act 1980 and the changes in public expenditure accompanying it marked a substantial change in policy. Council housing moved into a period of numerical decline for the first time and a subsequent dramatic reduction in subsidies meant that local authorities and most tenants no longer benefited from Exchequer subsidies. The conventional image of council housing developed in the previous 50 years was increasingly inaccurate.

The policies pursued by the Conservative Government in respect of public expenditure, taxation and housing legislation had changed considerably. The planned reduction in housing public expenditure between 1980/81 and 1983/84 was 48%, accounting for 75% of the planned total reduction in Government spending over the period. Housing's share of total public expenditure fell from 7% in 1978/79 to 3% in 1980/81 and was planned to fall further to a little over 2% by 1985/86. No other programme was to be so heavily cut and the House of Commons Environment Committee considered that the 'Government's medium term strategy of reducing public expenditure thus relies principally on the achievement of the planned reduction in housing expenditure' (House of Commons 1980).

Housing was to decline from a major to a minor programme and immediate cuts in investment programmes resulted in a sharp decline in council house building programmes to the lowest peace time levels since the 1920s. Initially both private sector completions and improvement activity were also at a low level and the recovery in these areas did not occur until after 1982. After 1982 the level of council house building remained low and the emphasis in investment activity was on the private sector and owner-occupation. The major elements of policy towards council housing supported this emphasis. Sharp, real increases in rents enabled a reduction of Exchequer subsidy and increased the attractiveness of council house purchase. Unprecedentedly high rates of council house sales contributed to financial changes which were the most dramatic since the introduction of Exchequer subsidy in 1919. The majority of local authorities by 1983/84 were no longer in receipt of Exchequer subsidy and in many areas rents and income-related subsidies were more than covering the costs of providing council housing. In 1981/82 the sale of council houses formed by far the largest single element in the Government's programme of disposal of assets.

The reductions in Exchequer subsidies facilitated by these changes were not accompanied by any parallel review of subsidies to owner-occupiers. As a result the subsidies received by owner-occupiers in the process of purchase began to pull away from those received by tenants. In 1978/79 Exchequer subsidies plus rate fund contributions for council tenants in England totalled £1386 million while the total subsidies for option mortgages plus mortgage tax relief for owner-occupiers was £1299 million. By 1981/82 these figures were £896 million and £1495 million, respectively. The average subsidy per council dwelling in 1981/82 was £241 (including rebates) or £183 (excluding rebates) while the average subsidy from tax relief on mortgage interest and option mortgages was £285.

Developments in the Right to Buy

In the period following 1980 a number of important modifications were made to the Right to Buy by Conservative Governments. These are summarised in Box 3.1. Key elements were intended to increase the generosity and attractiveness of the Right to Buy and thus to increase house sales:

- increasing the eligibility for the Right to Buy to all tenants with two years' tenancy or more (rather than the three years or more at the outset);
- extending the maximum discount to 60% for houses (rather than 50%);
- introducing higher differential discounts on flats: 44% after two years' tenancy, rising by 2% per year to a maximum of 70%;
- reducing the period of discount repayment from five years to three;
- changing the maximum discount and cost floor rules.

Against this background the Labour Party in opposition's initial commitment to remove the Right to Buy was replaced by acceptance and even enthusiasm.

Box 3.1   The changing face of the Right to Buy: principal legislative changes

Before 1980
- Discretionary powers available to local authorities to sell council dwellings with the consent of the Minister responsible under that legislation.

Housing Acts 1980
- Introduction of statutory Right to Buy for all secure tenants;
- statutory procedure for implementation discount linked to length of tenancy, 33% for three years' tenancy rising by 1% per year up to maximum of 50%;
- right to a mortgage from the local authority.

Housing and Building Control Act 1984
- Extended scope of the Right to Buy to 50 000 additional tenants (tenants of county councils, more dwellings for the disabled, successors);
- eligible to buy after two years' tenancy (250 000 tenants affected);
- minimum discount 32% rising to 60%;
- right to purchase a shared ownership lease.

Housing Act 1985
- Consolidated Right to Buy legislation.

Housing and Planning Act 1986
- Higher, differential discounts on flats: 44% after two years' tenancy rising by 2% per year to a maximum of 70%;
- period for discount repayment reduced from five years to three.

Housing Acts 1988 and 1989
- Detailed amendments to the Right to Buy.

Leasehold Reform, Housing and Urban Development Act 1993
- Rent to Mortgage scheme replaced the Right to Buy on shared ownership terms.

Housing Act 1996
- Statutory purchase grant for housing associations;
- removed right to a mortgage.

Statutory Instruments: No. 2997 1998 (England) and No. 292 (Wales)
- Limited the maximum discounts available in England and Wales to between £22 000 and £38 000 – varying them by region in England;
- specified the period of time used in the calculation of costs incurred as ten years (instead of eight years).

Housing (Scotland) Act 2001
- Extended across the social rented sector as part of a common set of tenants' rights;
- restricted the Right to Buy for new tenants;
- established procedure to suspend the Right to Buy in designated areas.

Housing Act 2004 (England)
- Extended the qualifying period for potential buyers from two to five years;
- extended the period after sale when discount may have to be repaid from three to five years;
- additional measures related to sales where there were plans for demolition, agreements to sell to a third party and resale within ten years.

Modifying the Right to Buy

The election of a Labour Government in 1997 did not result in any immediate modification of the Right to Buy and the Government confirmed its support for the policy. However, over time, there was a series of incremental changes in England and a more thorough review of policy in Scotland. In England, the new Labour Government reviewed the scheme as part of a comprehensive spending review, stating that it remained strongly committed to promoting sustainable home ownership and it wished the Right to Buy scheme to continue with tenants having the opportunity to buy at generous discounts. At the same time the Government was concerned with improving value-for-money, resulting in modifications to the cost floor rules to include repair and maintenance costs as well as other costs incurred over a ten year period and changes to the maximum discount arrangement.

In July 1998 the Department of the Environment, Transport and the Regions issued a consultation paper seeking views on changes to the discount arrangements for the Right to Buy in England (DETR 1998a). Following consultation the DETR announced in December 1998 that it would be changing the structure of Right to Buy discounts (Housing Order 1998). The changes came into effect on 11 February 1999. Prior to that date the policy operated with a maximum discount of £50 000. The discount available to tenants applying to exercise their Right to Buy on or after that date became subject to lower cash limits. These differed between regions broadly in line with property valuations. The highest ceiling was consequently in London (£38 000) and the lowest in the north-east (£22 000).

These changes did not remove the concerns about the continuing impact of the Right to Buy and the years up to 2005 saw a concerted campaign to amend the policy, with particular regard to three areas:

- The impact of continuing Right to Buy sales on local housing needs and the supply of affordable housing, resulting in demands to reduce (or remove) the discount and other privileges or incentives to buy.
- The impact of abuses which had aroused controversy and led to the commissioning of research by the Office of the Deputy Prime Minister (ODPM). The research, carried out by Colin Jones, is referred to elsewhere in this book.
- The impact and costs arising from the Right to Buy applications triggered by plans for the demolition or major restructuring of estates could considerably impede progress.

The response to these concerns was a further selective reduction in the maximum discount in the south of England in 2003. In nine local authority areas in the south-east region and in all except two London boroughs the maximum discount was set at £16 000 rather than the regional norm of £38 000. One further adjustment to the Right to Buy designed to address rural housing affordability problems was the introduction of restrictions on the resale of Right to Buy homes in the seven National Parks in England, the 37 Areas of Outstanding Natural Beauty and 35 areas which were designated as rural for this purpose.

The Housing Act 2004 introduced a variety of new provisions about housing in England, including changes in the Right to Buy scheme. These changes were designed to curb abuses by property developers and tenants. Ironically the legislation and the policy at the time were also preoccupied with a crisis of provision of affordable housing, especially in the south and east of England – parts of the country which had been particularly affected by the Right to Buy.

The changes to the Right to Buy scheme operated from 18 January 2005 were as follows:

- The initial qualification period was extended from two to five years for new tenancies.
- The discount repayment period was extended from three to five years with a discretion not to require the repayment of discount where to do so might lead to hardship.
- The amount of discount to be repaid if the property was sold within five years would be a percentage of the market value when it was resold disregarding the value of the improvements made by the owner of the property.
- If the landlord intended to demolish a property, the Right to Buy could be suspended when an initial demolition notice had been served by the landlord and ended when a final demolition notice had been served.
- Tenants who agreed during the discount period to sell their home to a third party at a later date must repay some or all of their discount, as if they had actually sold their home at the time of the agreement. This change also applies to tenants who applied for the Right to Buy prior to 18 January 2005 but where the agreement to sell to a third party was made after that date.
- Owners who wish to resell their home within ten years of it having been sold under the Right to Buy must first offer it at market value to their former landlord or to another body prescribed by the Secretary of State.

- Landlords could serve a notice after three months requiring a tenant to complete their Right to Buy purchase replacing the existing requirement to do so after 12 months.
- Landlords must give their tenants information on the costs and responsibilities of home ownership.
- Tenants would no longer be able to apply for the Right to Buy on rent/mortgage terms after 17 July 2005.
- Jurisdiction in respect of appeals by tenants against being denied the Right to Buy on the grounds that their homes were particularly suitable for occupation by elderly people transferred from the Secretary of State to the Property Tribunal service.

Wales

In Wales the framework for the Right to Buy continued to be set by legislation determined by the UK Parliament. After similar consultation as for England the maximum discount was reduced by the Welsh Office to £24 000 in 1999. Since the establishment of the Welsh Assembly it only has the right to set the maximum discount via an order. In 2003 the Assembly exercised this right and the maximum discount was reduced to £16 000. This figure was chosen as equivalent to that for the right to acquire by housing association tenants. It is not clear what initiated this change but it occurred almost at the same time as the reduction in maximum discounts in pressured local authorities in England.

The modified Right to Buy in Northern Ireland

As with other regions there are distinctive features of the housing market and the process of council house sales in Northern Ireland. All public sector housing was brought together under the ownership of the Northern Ireland Housing Executive (NIHE) in 1972 prior to any extensive sales programme. The NIHE embarked upon a house sales programme in 1976 and has continued to operate that programme since. Since the introduction of the more generous House Sales Scheme in 1979, over 80 000 NIHE properties have been sold. Although it has not strictly operated the Right to Buy, and there was no tenancy qualification period – in Northern Ireland tenants were eligible to buy as soon as they became tenants – the adjustments in the Northern Ireland sales scheme have otherwise been broadly in line with those of the Right to Buy. Northern Ireland benefited from much greater sustained investment since the 1970s than other parts of the UK (DoE 1995; Paris 2001). The poorest quality properties and most of the multi-storey properties in the Housing Executive stock were demolished. A higher proportion of the stock has been built since the 1970s.

This and the low rates of construction in the inter-war years in Northern Ireland mean that the Housing Executive stock tends to be more modern with higher standards of maintenance, repair and management than elsewhere in the UK. At the same time the prices of private sector properties in Northern Ireland have generally lagged behind those of other regions of the United Kingdom.

After 1 September 2002, some adjustments were made to the House Sales Scheme in Northern Ireland including the introduction of a tenancy qualification. Applicants must have been tenants for at least two years before they can apply to buy their homes. A maximum discount of £34 000 was introduced for all applications received after 1 September 2002 and there were some other detailed adjustments related to joint purchase, the exclusion of buildings for older persons, antisocial behaviour, development land and some administrative and technical changes.

The modernised Right to Buy in Scotland

The 2001 Housing (Scotland) Act passed by the Scottish Parliament was the first opportunity for the Labour/Liberal Government to modify the Right to Buy. The changes introduced as part of the 2001 Housing Act have been dubbed by the Executive as the 'modernised Right to Buy' and followed a consultative Green Paper, *Better Homes for Scotland's Communities* (Scottish Executive 1999). This acknowledged there was a need to modernise the Right to Buy to achieve a better balance between the interests of the individual, the landlord and community. Even so, the modernised Right to Buy was extended across the social rented sector as part of a common set of tenants' rights within a single standard secure tenancy for all social sector tenants, introduced at the same time. Those tenants who already had the Right to Buy had their existing rights ring fenced so the changes therefore applied only to new tenants.

The Executive's thinking behind the modernised Right to Buy was partially set out in a paper by MacLennan *et al.* (2000). First, they argued that the Right to Buy had been operating in isolation from other policy instruments and in some instances possibly at variance to them. Second, in comparison with other policies such as cash incentives for tenants to move elsewhere to buy it was an expensive policy. Third, they accepted that the policy might cause problems in some areas. Their conclusion was that the Right to Buy needed to be 'rebalanced rather than removed' to meet the aspirations of both low income households and the objectives of communities.

The Right to Buy for existing tenants remained unchanged except that there were increased constraints on applications. The Right to Buy could be refused if tenants had any rent, council tax or water and sewerage charges arrears or were subject to eviction orders. The changes incorporated in the legislation extended the Right to Buy to other social landlords but the main provisions of the modernised Right to Buy meant that new tenants had a different set of rights in relation to purchase of the home they lived in. This involved:

- an increase in the qualifying period to five years rather than the two previously;
- discounts that started at a lower level (20% rather than the previous 33% or 44% for flats) and rising by 1% a year to 35%, subject to a maximum £15 000 (current average discount is just over £20 000);
- the differential rate of discount between flats and houses no longer applying to new tenants;
- establishing a procedure for designation of 'pressured' areas where the modernised Right to Buy would be suspended.

The procedure for 'pressured' areas merits more detailed discussion. Section 45 of the Housing (Scotland) Act 2001 inserted new sections into the 1987 Act which allowed Scottish Ministers to designate any part of a local authority's area as a 'pressured area' following a proposal submitted by the local authority itself. The broad effect of designation would be to suspend the Right to Buy for certain tenants living in the area for a period of up to five years.

The policy objective behind these provisions was to establish a mechanism for safeguarding the continued availability of social rented housing where the Right to Buy could otherwise lead to serious shortages. The guidance set out details to be followed for designation.

The criteria for designation as a pressured area
Two specific criteria must be taken into account by Scottish Ministers in considering proposals. These are that the need for social rented housing (i.e. houses provided by the local authority or housing associations) in the area in question is or is likely to be substantially in excess of the social rented housing; and that this situation is likely to be exacerbated by tenants in the area exercising their Right to Buy.

The shortfall referred to in the first of the two criteria may be a current shortfall or one that is expected to arise in the future.

It is necessary for both criteria to be met. Scottish Ministers only have authority under the Act to designate areas where they are satisfied that these criteria apply.

The effect of designation as a pressured area

The effect of the designation is to suspend the Right to Buy for those who became tenants in the area on or after the introduction of the Scottish secure tenancy for that landlord (30 September 2002 in most parts of Scotland). Those with tenancies created before this (except tenants of housing associations with assured tenancies who do not have a preserved Right to Buy) will not be affected by the suspension if they had the Right to Buy before the introduction of the Scottish secure tenancy.

The suspension will be for a period of five years or less but it is open to local authorities to propose a further designation. The suspension has no effect on notices to purchase under the Right to Buy which have been served prior to the designation of the area as a pressured area even if this application is still being processed by the landlord.

Selection of areas and consultation

It is for local authorities to make proposals for the designation of pressured areas and the Scottish Executive expect local authorities to take account of their local housing strategies and to be consistent with the local housing strategy or the draft housing strategy if it has not yet been finalised.

The 2001 Act allows local authorities to propose the designation of any part of its area providing the specified criteria are met. Although the precise boundaries must be a matter for local determination, the Scottish Executive view is that the aim should be to identify recognised localities or neighbourhoods. In most circumstances, relevant areas are likely to be a contiguous group of houses, but this is not a statutory requirement and there may well be cases where an alternative approach is appropriate.

There is a statutory duty on local authorities, before submitting proposals in respect of specific areas, to undertake wide-ranging consultations with every housing association with houses in the proposed area, bodies representing the interests of tenants or other residents living in the area and any other persons as the authority think fit. Consultations should be conducted before finalising proposals for pressured areas and should be about the need for a designation as well as amendments relating to the details of the boundaries and timing. In addition to consulting groups of tenants and residents, local authorities should also ensure that all individual tenants affected are informed of the proposal and its likely effect on them, and given an opportunity to offer and seek further information.

Submission of proposals to the Scottish Executive

The guidance details the information that local authorities who wish to put forward proposals for the designation of pressured areas should submit to the Scottish Executive. This includes maps of the boundaries of the proposed area; details of the number, type and size of local authority and housing association houses within the proposed designated area; an estimate of the initial number of tenants whose right to buy will be suspended as a result of the designation; the period (not exceeding five years) proposed for the designation; information on the consultation undertaken identifying the organisations and persons consulted together with a summary of their responses; and sufficient information to allow Scottish Ministers to satisfy themselves that the statutory criteria for designation are met. This is likely to include evidence of a substantial shortfall in social rented accommodation in relation to need, evidence of pressure in the private sector arising from the demand by households for the available private housing stock and evidence on the impact of the Right to Buy on the shortfall of social rented housing in relation to need.

Assessment and confirmation of proposals

Following receipt of proposals for a designation, the Scottish Executive will check to ensure all the necessary information has been submitted and, providing this is the case, it will ask Communities Scotland, a national housing agency, to carry out an assessment of the proposals. In the light of this assessment Scottish Ministers will decide whether to make the designation and will confirm the boundaries of the pressured area, specify the date on which the designation takes place, and specify the period for which it has affect.

If Scottish Ministers decide not to approve the proposals, the Scottish Executive will write to the local authority explaining the reasons for this decision.

Action by local authorities following designation

Once an area has been designated, the local authority should publicise the decision and its effect. There is a statutory duty on landlords (both local authorities and housing associations) under section 23(5) of the 2001 Act to notify the tenants directly affected that the designation has been made and of the effects of the designation on their right to buy.

Once the designation has been made, both local authorities and housing associations as landlords are placed under a statutory duty by section 23(4) of the 2001 Act to notify prospective tenants of houses in the area of the designation and its implications.

If the local authority wishes to amend or revoke the designation during the specified period, it should write to the Scottish Executive with the details of the proposed amendment or revocation and the reasons for proposing this. In this event Scottish Ministers will consider the proposals and decide if the designation should be amended or revoked in line with the local authority's proposals. If necessary, they will issue a revised designation for the remaining period of the designation or written confirmation that the designation is to be revoked from a specified date. Local authorities will need again to ensure that tenants and other interested parties are fully informed.

Where local authorities wish to propose a further designation for all or part of the area that was originally designated they will follow the same process of consultation and submission as summarised above.

By the time of the general election of 2005 a number of applications had been made or were in preparation but none had been approved.

Increasing complexity

The policy changes set out above have incrementally introduced complexity into the Right to Buy. What started off as a simple scheme with a uniform set of rules and regulations has become more complicated. There are different discount levels for flats and houses. There are different maximum discounts for different regions and selective variations for particular local authorities. There are complex arrangements for taking into account the cost floor. In Scotland there are differences between different cohorts of tenants although fewer differences according to whether the landlord is a local authority or housing association.

The complications around the Right to Buy have not arisen simply because of amendments to the legislation but arise because of other measures that have developed alongside it. Some of the complexities which have emerged from parallel policy streams can be summarised briefly:

1. **Charitable housing associations**
   The legislation of 1980 excluded charitable housing associations from the Right to Buy.
2. **The development of assured tenancies in the housing association sector**
   As the Right to Buy only applies to secure tenancies, the switch to

assured tenancies effectively created a new and growing class of tenants who are not eligible for the Right to Buy.

3. **Stock transfers and preserved Right to Buy**

   Where public sector landlords transfer their stock under large-scale voluntary transfer or other arrangements all tenants who transfer have a preserved Right to Buy even though their tenancy becomes an assured tenancy with a market rent. Where the transfer has occurred to a charitable association, the preserved Right to Buy will still exist.

4. **Stock transfers and later cohorts of tenants**

   Where public sector landlords transfer their stock under large-scale voluntary transfer or other arrangements, any new tenants are assured tenants without the Right to Buy or preserved Right to Buy.

5. **Alternatives to the Right to Buy**

   Charitable housing associations increasingly look to voluntary equivalents to the Right to Buy – perhaps partly to fend off demands for the extension of a statutory right.

   - Legislation in 1980 provided the basis for a Home Ownership for Tenants of Charitable Housing Associations (HOTCHA) scheme. Broadly, this gave qualifying tenants the opportunity to buy a property on the open market at a reduced cost.
   - A Do-It-Yourself Shared Ownership scheme (DIYSO) was also introduced allowing tenants to select a home and buy it on a shared ownership basis.
   - HOTCHA operated between 1984 and 1988 and was replaced by the Tenants Incentive Scheme (TIS) introduced in 1990. This scheme applied to all registered housing associations, charitable and non-charitable, and involved making cash incentives available to existing housing association tenants to enable them to purchase on the open market. Again, the scheme was a voluntary one with all registered associations eligible to participate in it and with the Housing Corporation paying an allowance to cover associations' administrative costs and to meet the tiers of payment. Unlike the Right to Buy, TIS was extended to assured tenancies. It did not apply to sitting tenant purchase, but rather to the purchase of another property. The amount of cash incentive payable was dependent on geographical location.
   - TIS and DIYSO were replaced by a simplified low cost home ownership scheme based on Homebuy in Wales which only applies in areas with a shortage of social housing.
   - In 1996 two further schemes were introduced: the Voluntary Purchase Grants (VPG) scheme and the Right to Acquire (RTA). The VPG Scheme did not confer a statutory right or duty, but enabled housing association tenants to purchase the home they live in at a flat rate discount equivalent to TIS. Unlike the Right to

Buy, charitable as well as non-charitable associations were eligible. As with HOTCHA and TIS, housing associations bid to the Housing Corporation for the funding to make participation possible.

- The RTA also introduced in 1996 is mandatory and confers a right on certain tenants to acquire their home through a statutory purchase grant system. It applies to all new build and rehabilitation for rent schemes that received Social Housing Grant and all tenanted property transferred to a registered social landlord from a public sector landlord on or after 1 April 1997. The grant is at a flat rate with no sliding scale of discounts related to length of tenancy.

Tenants' rights in the UK are now fragmented and confusing, relating to:

(1) the type of property that the tenant lives in;
(2) who their landlord is;
(3) what the history of ownership and tenancy has been;
(4) the country, region, type of region (urban or rural, whether pressured areas status applies), and even local authority lived in; and
(5) what costs have been incurred.

As the pattern of new building and stock transfers (especially in England) has steadily reduced the number of council tenancies, so the number of tenants with the Right to Buy has declined. In effect stock transfer in England and Wales (but not Scotland) involves a reduction in the Right to Buy, not instantly but progressively as tenants with the preserved Right to Buy are replaced by assured tenants with no Right to Buy. As the balance between secure tenancies and assured tenancies shifts, so the more complicated arrangements that may apply in assured tenancies begin to replace the entitlements under the Right to Buy. The largest group of tenants in the social rented sector continue to have the Right to Buy but what this is worth varies according to property type and region, in addition to being related to individual circumstances and the individual value of the property. A diminishing number of tenants who have transferred from local authorities to another landlord have the preserved Right to Buy.

Other tenants in the social rented sector have rights that are based on very different formulae. TIS, the Right to Acquire scheme and the VPG all involve flat rate cash entitlements, although these vary by region. While TIS was a portable scheme, VPG and RTA relate to the property in which tenants live. The arrangements under the Starter Homes Initiative (2001) and Key Worker Living Initiative (2004) provided particular opportunities for some households. These initiatives were targeted at specific categories of key workers and first time buyers. Proposals in 2005 to extend the Homebuy scheme to tenants in the social rented sector would further add to the complexity of the alternative incentive schemes available to different households.

Conclusions

Twenty-five years after the introduction of the Right to Buy it continues to be a significant policy and political debates around it are as likely to propose its extension to housing associations as to propose its further weakening. Its abolition seems unlikely because this would invite a populist political storm but also because there are concerns about potential claims under the Human Rights Act. The simplicity of the Right to Buy has changed and the complexities described above are a potential source of confusion. At the same time the wider policy context within which it operates has changed with Government more fully committed to the idea of a property owning welfare state than even under the Governments of Margaret Thatcher.

The 2005 Labour Government was more enthusiastic than ever in promoting home ownership but it was at the same time expressing concerns about affordability, key worker housing needs and the problems experienced in rural areas. Having rejected the Conservative Party's arguments for extending the Right to Buy in England to housing association tenants, Government was contemplating new measures to address affordability including increased investment in the provision of social rented housing.

The Right to Buy, an essential part of 'Thatcherism', continued to flourish under 'Blairite' New Labour and the Labour/Liberal administration in Scotland. Some changes have emerged slowly and there are common threads in the reasons for these changes. This is particularly reflected in the reductions of discount and measures to address both abuse of the policy and adverse consequences. However, the rebalancing measures introduced in the Scottish 'modernised Right to Buy' seem timid in comparison with England and Wales. Reductions in the incentives to purchase under the Right to Buy only applied to new tenants and the pressured area designation process is slow and cumbersome. In comparison the cash limitations introduced on discounts for all tenants in England in 1999 and the further reforms in 2003 seem bolder. In both cases the measures taken can at best only preserve the status quo (and even this is unlikely), and not redress the past impact of the Right to Buy on access to housing. All of the changes may be too little and too late. They do not propose to revive council or social rented housing through reinvesting to change the image and residualisation of the tenure.

4

Unequal Opportunities, Time and Place

This chapter is concerned with the pattern of sales of council houses under the Right to Buy over the period since 1980, and it addresses the uneven impact at a regional and local authority level. Descriptive statistics of the pattern of sales, not surprisingly, show a fluctuation over time and variation according to place. The discussion that follows considers the significance of this and the evidence about the differential pattern of sales between property types. It also considers the characteristics of purchasers.

The pattern of sales underpins the discussion in subsequent chapters about the impact of sales on the social housing sector, the private housing market, communities or estates and different groups of tenants, but the initial perspective provided is one of unequal opportunities. Tenants who were in the right place at the right time have been able to take advantage of an opportunity to buy below the then market price, and buy a dwelling that has subsequently appreciated massively in value. The Right to Buy has for this group provided a pathway to home ownership and wealth that was not previously available.

For other households in the same generation and with the same length of tenancy, the opportunity was much less attractive. Rather than living in a dwelling that would appreciate in value they were located in a part of the market that was less buoyant or in types of property that were less attractive, or less in demand. In some cases tenants purchased properties that had design faults or were flats or other properties which became difficult to sell on because lenders were unwilling to provide mortgages for a future purchaser.

These unequal opportunities are compounded if we then look at households that bought the right property, but at the wrong time. They bought attractive properties, but at the peak of the market in a period when property values subsequently failed to rise. These purchasers were not necessarily disadvantaged in an absolute sense; because of the discount they are likely to have avoided negative equity, but in relative terms they did not fare as well as purchasers who bought at a more opportune time. If we take this one stage further, there are tenants who, because they were not in the right place at the right time, became tenants after stock transfer, and were not eligible for the Right to Buy, or were unable to obtain a transfer to the kind of attractive property that had provided such a good opportunity for other tenants.

These kinds of differences led to the Right to Buy being described as 'a lottery'. Where you lived, when you bought, how long you had been a tenant, what the property was and other factors determined the benefits that were gained. A more critical perspective might argue that there is a clearer generational pattern to this than is implied in the term 'lottery'. A generation of council tenants who entered the tenure in the early post-war years had often experienced long waiting times before they were able to access housing. They often moved initially to less attractive housing and waited for transfers to move them to the most desirable properties; but it is this generation that was then in a position to take maximum advantage of the Right to Buy. They were in the best properties and were entitled to the highest levels of discount. In contrast, the generation of households entering the social rented sector after the 1980s entered into a less varied and less attractive tenure where some of the best properties had been sold off. They were more likely to be allocated to flats or less desirable houses. They were less likely to be able to transfer to better properties. There was a greater likelihood that their landlord was a housing association and they would not have the Right to Buy. They were also more likely to be affected by reduced discount entitlements. Even amongst this later generation, there were unequal opportunities. Some benefited from the Right to Buy, and others benefited from much improved management and maintenance and higher levels of investment in social rented housing, but the generational effect should not be overlooked.

The starting point for the Right to Buy

Discussions of the origins of the Right to Buy have emphasised the high level of state owned housing in the United Kingdom. In addition, the tradition of provision of social rented, non-profit or decommodified housing in the UK had been associated with provision by local authorities. Other countries with substantial social rented sectors are more likely to have adopted an arm's length organisation more similar to housing associations in Britain.

The years 1979 and 1980 were the peak years for council housing in the UK and it accounted for some 32% of all dwellings. Prior to the introduction of the Right to Buy there were some 6.5 million dwellings in the public sector, housing almost a third of households in the UK. Only 2% of households were in a small but expanding housing association sector and 10% in a private rented sector with a long standing pattern of decline. Unlike the municipal or social rented sectors in many other countries, local authority and other public sector housing was not a marginal sector catering for a small, poor minority. Local authorities dominated the rental sector. In 1979, 71% of all rental dwellings were in the municipal sector. By 1989, after eight years of the Right to Buy and the sale of some 1.6 million dwellings, local councils still owned 69% of dwellings in the rental sector. This is because over the same period the housing association sector had only experienced modest growth and the private rented sector had continued to decline. This pattern changed through the 1990s. Local authorities still dominated the rental sector but their share declined to 43% by 2003 when the housing association sector accounted for 24% of all rented dwellings.

Table 4.1 indicates the tenure structure of the different parts of the United Kingdom in 1981 and compares these with later years. In the UK in 1981 29% of the housing stock was in the ownership of local authorities and new towns and some 2% was owned by housing associations. The largest tenure was home ownership, accounting for 58% of the stock. The highest rates of home ownership were in Wales (62%) and England (60%), with Scotland significantly behind with 36% of the stock in home ownership and 52% owned by local authorities. By 2001 this position had changed considerably. The owner-occupied sector had expanded by at least 10 percentage points everywhere and the expansion had been 27 percentage points in Scotland.

The council housing stock in 1980 was a varied one. However, the 6.5 million dwellings in the stock were predominantly traditionally built houses with gardens with a smaller proportion of flats and even fewer high rise blocks. Local authorities had built popular dwellings to high standards and they were maintained at high levels. The quality of what was offered under the Right to Buy was generally very high and the popularity and value of the housing stock was also high. For tenants in such good quality dwellings the opportunity to purchase at a substantial discount was attractive. The research evidence suggests that the households living in the best

Table 4.1   Dwellings by tenure (%).

	1981	1991	1995	2001	2003
England					
Home ownership	59.8	67.3	67.4	69.8	70.8
Local authority rented	26.6	19.8	17.6	13.3	11.4
Privately rented	11.3	9.8	10.8	10.2	10.2
Housing association	2.3	3.1	4.2	6.7	7.6
Scotland[a,b]					
Home ownership	36.4	52.4	56.9	63.4	64.3
Local authority rented	52.1	37.8	32.6	24.0	22.0
Privately rented	9.7	7.1	7.0	6.7	7.5
Housing association	1.8	2.6	3.5	5.9	6.2
Wales[c]					
Home ownership	61.9	70.7	71.1	72.2	73.1
Local authority rented	26.4	18.8	17.1	14.8	13.7
Privately rented	9.6	8.2	8.3	8.7	8.8
Housing association	2.2	2.4	3.4	4.3	4.4
Northern Ireland					
Home ownership	54.1	65.6	68.5	72.6	75.3
Local authority rented	37.9	29.3	25.8	19.4	16.3
Privately rented	7.6	3.5	3.5	5.2	5.1
Housing association	0.6	1.9	2.2	2.9	3.3
UK					
Home ownership	57.6	66.3	66.7	69.4	72.3
Local authority rented	29.2	21.4	19.1	14.5	13.0
Privately rented	11.0	9.3	10.1	9.7	10.1
Housing association	2.2	3.1	4.1	6.4	7.4

Source: Wilcox (various).

Notes:

See www.scotland.gov.uk/Publications/2005/05/23152516/25353

Estimates for Scotland from 2001 onwards are based on the 2001 census and are not strictly comparable (see notes and definitions).

[a] 2003 – Provisional.

[b] Stock transfers took place for Dumfries & Galloway, Glasgow and Scottish Borders from April 2003. Estimates for 2003 will reflect this change of tenure.

See www.wales.gov.uk/keypubstatisticsforwales/content/publication/housing/2004/whs2004/whs2004-ch1/whs2004-t1-2.xls

[c] Dwelling stock estimates for Wales, by tenure, at 31 December 2004.

properties were often those who qualified for high levels of discount. They were households in the middle of the family lifecycle, in their 40s and 50s. More affluent tenants qualified for the largest discounts and these applied to the best quality dwellings. The formula generated high levels of sale, especially amongst this group of tenants and among the better quality properties (Forrest and Murie 1990a).

The progress of the Right to Buy

At the time that the Right to Buy was introduced there was very limited evidence as to what its effects would be. There was an assumption that pent up demand existed, especially in areas where discretionary powers to sell houses had not been used; but there was also uncertainty over the willingness of financial institutions to provide loans for a Right to Buy purchase (House of Commons 1980). Although the new legislation provided a right to a local authority mortgage, the impact remained uncertain. The only robust indicator of what might happen under the Right to Buy was provided by evidence about the operation of discretionary house sales policies. There was systematic but limited evidence on this issue provided from the research programme at the Centre for Urban and Regional Studies, University of Birmingham (Murie 1975; Murie, Niner & Watson 1976; Niner 1976; Forrest & Murie 1976) and some limited reference elsewhere. Where opportunities to buy had existed the tenants who bought tended to be in the better properties and to be longer established tenants who had often lived in more than one council property and had moved through transfers within the sector to a home they were attached to and wanted to continue to live in. They were most often in their 40s and 50s and in employment although there was also a significant number of older tenants who bought with a guarantee from other members of their family.

In retrospect the assumptions about the impact of the Right to Buy based on this evidence have been remarkably accurate. The characteristics of purchasers under the Right to Buy were consistent with those identified in studies of discretionary house sales. However, there was scepticism about how far these studies would indicate the likely long-term effect. Discretionary policies had not included the sale of flats, had involved much less generous discounts and had not been accompanied by the publicity and the national exposure of the issue. At the same time some commentators assumed that there was a finite limit to the uptake of the Right to Buy related to incomes or other characteristics of tenants.

Twenty-five years later there is more evidence on which to base a discussion of the Right to Buy. There have been a series of studies funded largely by central government and other studies in England, Wales, Scotland and Northern Ireland. There is international experience of the impact of similar privatisation schemes. All of this enables reference to a much more robust evidence base.

Table 4.2 and Figure 4.1 provide details of the progress of council house sales in the UK. Between 1979 and the end of 1995 there were over 2.2 million

Table 4.2 Public sector dwelling sales into home ownership 1979–2003.

	Scotland	England	Wales	Northern Ireland	Great Britain	UK
1979	1010	41 313	1220		43 543	
1980	6127	83 559	2080	473	91 766	92 239
1981	10 749	104 904	8850	6504	124 503	131 007
1982	14 140	207 841	16 933	6199	238 914	245 113
1983	17 949	149 710	9887	5367	177 546	182 913
1984	16 173	113 418	6531	5665	136 122	141 787
1985	14 963	98 787	6086	4330	119 836	124 116
1986	14 106	95 223	5761	3660	115 090	118 750
1987	19 391	103 287	6109	2802	128 787	131 589
1988	31 930	149 960	10 012	3000	191 902	194 902
1989	39 335	159 291	13 077	4340	211 703	216 043
1990	33 213	106 389	6805	4474	146 407	150 881
1991	23 349	61 162	3913	3290	88 424	91 714
1992	24 110	52 600	2920	3234	79 630	82 864
1993	20 303	53 424	2918	3710	76 645	80 355
1994	21 699	54 352	3437	4608	79 488	84 096
1995	17 335	43 861	2862	4595	64 058	68 653
1996	13 594	40 095	2815	4755	56 504	61 259
1997	17 410	39 875	2632	4665	59 917	64 582
1998	14 976	39 846	2613	4907	57 435	62 342
1999	14 257	50 435	3454	4395	68 146	72 541
2000	14 962	53 962	3497	4526	72 421	76 947
2001	14 139	50 214	3389	5555	67 742	73 297
2002	17 147	58 526	4302	5011	79 975	84 986
2003	17 550	70 848	6906	6054	95 304	101 358
Total	449 917	2 082 882	139 009	106 119	2 671 808	2 777 877

Source: DoE housing and construction statistics 1979–89, 1984–94 and 1986–96; Wilcox 2004.

Note: Figures include sales by housing associations and by Scottish Homes. Figures after 1996 refer only to sales recorded as under Right to Buy except in Northern Ireland where they are estimates of sales under the house sales scheme.

Thousands of dwellings

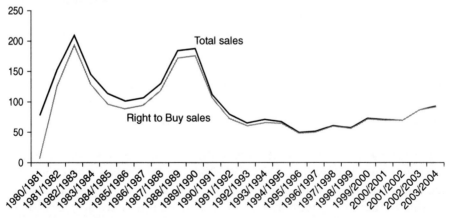

Figure 4.1 Social housing sales: sales of local authority dwellings for owner-occupation in Great Britain, from 1980/81.

Source: Housing activity (P1B) returns.

house sales recorded by local authorities, new town corporations and housing associations in the UK, although these figures do not relate solely to the Right to Buy. However there is a problem in the available data on the Right to Buy which makes it more appropriate to refer to the larger figure. Under the legislation local authorities were not obliged to carry out sales using the Department of the Environment's forms and some authorities which have sold properties on terms identical to the Right to Buy have not recorded all of these as Right to Buy sales. Consequently the official figures on the Right to Buy itself and those produced in some compendiums of data (e.g. Wilcox 2002) underestimate the real number of Right to Buy sales to sitting tenants. Table 4.2 includes all sales to home owners up to 1996. Thereafter the figures relate solely to Right to Buy sales. These involve sales by local authorities, new towns and housing associations and they include sales to sitting tenants and to other home owners. Sales to other home owners include sales of vacant dwellings but, as Figure 4.1 shows, these declined in importance in later years.

The data presented shows that sales rose dramatically in the early years of the Right to Buy and peaked in 1982. This reflects both the pent up demand from areas where discretionary sales had not operated and new demand generated by the new terms for sale and the publicity associated with the new legislation. Following this, sales fell to a relatively low figure in 1986 before rising to a new peak in 1989 – slightly lower than that of 1982. Subsequently sales fell back to a new low level in 1995/96 and remained low in 1996/97 before rising steadily to 2003/04 at which point they were at a higher level than at any time since 1990/91.

In the early years of the Right to Buy sales in Scotland rose more slowly than in England and Wales. Conservative-controlled local authorities in England had already embarked upon the equivalent of the Right to Buy through the general consent which had introduced the same terms for sales in June 1979. Sales rose rapidly to a peak in England whereas elsewhere they were slower to increase and did not achieve such a high level. The less buoyant market conditions existing from the early 1980s onwards affected the rate of sale under the Right to Buy.

An explanation for this second surge in Right to Buy sales is merited. Some commentators had assumed that the Right to Buy was a spent force by the mid 1980s and regarded it as unlikely that a revival would take place. As this is the view commonly expressed by commentators in 1997 it is important to consider why it proved incorrect at an earlier stage. It is difficult, however, to isolate the factors leading to the revival. One factor in particular, the increased level of discounts for flats, was not likely to

Table 4.3 Houses and flats as percentage of all Right to Buy sales 1980–95.

	England		Scotland	
	Houses	Flats	Houses	Flats
1980			88.3	11.7
1981	98.0	2.0	88.6	11.4
1982	97.2	2.8	86.8	13.2
1983	93.4	6.6	86.5	13.5
1984	94.3	5.7	87.2	12.8
1985	92.4	7.6	84.6	15.4
1986	91.0	9.0	84.5	15.5
1987	90.0	10.0	75.3	24.7
1988	82.6	17.4	69.2	30.8
1989	79.0	21.0	65.4	34.6
1990	74.3	25.7	58.1	41.9
1991	73.2	26.8	58.7	41.3
1992	74.4	25.6	61.1	38.9
1993	79.8	20.2	62.9	37.1
1994	82.9	17.1	64.9	35.1
1995	78.7	21.3	64.7	35.3

Source: DoE, housing and construction statistics 1979–89, 1984–1994 and 1986–96.

be repeated. If the revival of sales after 1985 was largely attributable to this, then it would be reasonable to assume that no similar revival is likely to occur subsequently. The evidence for this presents difficulties. There was an increase in the sale of flats (see Table 4.3). However this increase was not sufficient to account for the surge in sales generally. It would appear that the factors contributing to this revival are associated more with changed economic conditions and with housing market trends. The coincidence of improved economic circumstances, higher unemployment and rising incomes with the housing market boom (with substantial gains to be made through home ownership) would appear to explain the surge in sales in the late 1980s. Analysis of sales by house type shows a consistent surge in each case.

When sales increased again after 1996/97 there were some factors similar to those of the 1980s. Rising employment, increased affluence and the booming home ownership market attracted more people to buy properties. In addition to this there was a series of public debates about revising the Right to Buy that undoubtedly encouraged some people to bring forward plans to buy. They thought – misguidedly – that the policy was about to be changed to revoke the Right to Buy. A key element in this was the publicity surrounding the change in maximum discount level in 1998 and the media attention given to various statements of Ministers related to the Right to Buy over succeeding years. All of these elements can be seen as having been effective contributors to increasing the rate of uptake of the Right to Buy. Sales rose steadily from 1995 to 2003 throughout the UK but particularly in England and Wales. Changes to discounts were, however, affecting the rate of sales by 2005.

Regional patterns

The rate of sales completed varied significantly between the different parts of the UK. In England the northern regions lagged behind and the south-east and south-west consistently had the highest rates of sale. Scotland lagged so far behind that MacLennan (1983) suggested that the Scots were sales-resistant and Foulis analysis (1985) also accepted a view that the underlying demand for house purchase in Scotland was lower. Subsequent analysis showed that these assumptions were not accurate. The second surge of sales was more marked in Scotland and in the northern regions of England and there was some levelling up of regional differences. Sales reached a low point in 1996 but, perhaps stimulated by the UK general election, rose again to a minor peak in 1997. Subsequently, sales have reached a plateau of 13–14 000 sales per year. The recent rise in house prices has stimulated an increase in sales activity with sales in 2002 rising to almost 16 000, a five-year high.

In retrospect the Scottish position would appear to be more strongly influenced, both by changes in discount arrangements (Scottish purchasers are more likely to live in flats), and also by the experience of economic change and recovery through the 1980s. The picture presented for Great Britain is dominated by that of southern England. The northern regions of England and Scotland show a different profile (Table 4.4). This suggests that pent up demand was the significant factor in sales. At least in some regions we cannot attribute the major surge in sales to pent up demand.

All the regions of England show two peaks of sales. However, the regions form four groups in terms of the pattern of sales over time:

(1) In the north, north-west and east Midlands there were two pronounced peaks, with that of the early 1980s higher than that of the late 1980s.
(2) In the west Midlands and Yorkshire and Humberside a very similar pattern exists although the second peak was nearly as high as the first.
(3) In the east sales did not fall as markedly between the two peaks.
(4) In the south-east, Greater London and the south-west sales again did not fall as markedly between the two peaks and the second peak was higher than the first.

Table 4.4 All sales by region 1979–95.

	Sales 1979/80 to 1985/86	Sales 1986/87 to 1989/90	Sales 1990/91 to 1995/96
East Midlands	67 324	42 579	18 652
East	86 830	52 279	68 615
Greater London	82 242	87 241	64 169
North	50 768	29 974	27 136
North-west	90 025	48 986	41 428
South-east	109 999	92 058	105 867
South-west	622 052	43 340	41 151
West Midlands	83 553	54 701	44 887
Yorkhire and Humberside	64 517	50 255	35 209
Scotland	55 991	75 930	113 117
Wales	49 547	33 652	21 672
Northern Ireland	28 538	18 276	19 437

Source: ODPM.

It is apparent from this data that the different pattern of sales between Scotland and England does not represent the only variation in rates of sale. The northern regions of England show a pattern more like that of Scotland than of the southern regions of England in the early 1980s. However, they do not follow the Scottish surge of sales in the late 1980s. In view of the second surge in sales it is also wise to be cautious about attributing the first surge to pent up demand. Changes in policy and prices for purchase appear to have had an impact but employment, incomes and confidence in the economy are also important in the explanation of trends (Foulis 1985; 1987; Murie & Wang 1992).

In Northern Ireland the pattern of sales was more comparable with that for the north of England. Sales peaked in 1981 and remained high until 1985. They fell away steeply to 1988 before rising to a second peak in 1990. A third peak of sales in 1994 and 1995 were above those of any year since 1984. In Wales sales followed a similar pattern, although the 1982 peak was not sustained as long. A second peak in 1990 saw sales slightly below those of 1982.

Table 4.5 refers to sales under the Right to Buy in England for the period 1979–2004. The comparable figure for stock sold in Scotland is 37%. The lowest rate of sale has been in the north-west, followed by London.

Table 4.6 sets out the rate of depletion of the social rented housing stock in the regions of England and in Scotland. The higher rate of depletion in Scotland is evident for the 1990s while in England it was the high selling

Table 4.5   Right to Buy sales as a proportion of the original stock in regions of England.

	Right to Buy sales 1979–2004	% of 1979 'stock'*
North-east	142 857	35.8
North-west	191 592	27.6
Yorkshire and Humberside	184 933	32.0
East Midlands	153 065	36.1
West Midlands	202 436	33.5
East	178 831	34.2
London	270 981	30.6
South-east	198 486	32.0
South-west	135 588	35.2
England	1 658 769	32.4

Source: ODPM.

* Numbers of sales in the period 1 April 1979 to 31 March 2004 as a percentage of stock at 1 April 2003 plus sales between 1 April 1979 and 31 March 2003.

Table 4.6   Regional annual stock depletion rates.

	1990–93	1993–95	2003–04
North	1.2	1.2	3.84
Yorkshire and Humberside	0.8	0.7	3.6
East Midlands	1.1	1.1	2.8
East	1.8	1.9	1.97
Greater London	0.9	0.9	2.56
South-east	1.8	1.8	1.87
South-west	1.6	1.6	1.73
West Midlands	1.0	1.0	3.25
North-west	0.8	0.7	3.24
Scotland	2.5	2.2	2.92

Source: ODPM.

south-east and south-west that had the high depletion rates. The rate of sale in 2003/04 has resulted in a more rapid depletion of the stock, especially in the lower selling regions. The 2003/04 figures are based on Right to Buy sales as a percentage of council housing stock in previous years and overestimate depletion rates as a result.

Local variations in rates of sale

Research on the sale of council houses has consistently shown major variations in rates of sale between local authorities. Early on, this may have been due to the reluctance of local authorities to sell and to administrative and political delays. Legislative and administrative action was taken by central government to minimise these delays and beyond the first phase of sales it cannot reasonably be argued that variations in sales are attributable to these. As with the regional figures, the evidence from local variation is that differences in economic circumstances, the nature of council housing within the district, the relative attractiveness of council housing compared with other alternatives, price and dwelling type factors, local housing market conditions and price levels all impact on the rate of sale. An analysis carried out in 1985 suggested that price and property types were particularly important when accounting for variations in the volume of sales (Dunn *et al.* 1987).

Analysis carried out in the early years of the Right to Buy showed that the highest selling local authorities were smaller, rural district councils and the lowest selling authorities were large, urban authorities, in particular in inner London and the north-west of England (Forrest & Murie 1984a; 1984b; 1990a). These studies note that the data for London was affected by the exclusion of properties sold by the Greater London Council before transfer to Borough Councils but the inclusion of transferred stock (and sales from this) after transfer. This has the effect of understating the rate of sale in London Boroughs receiving transferred stock.

Figure 4.2 sets out the proportion of social housing stock sold to sitting tenants in England. The statistics used here are those of all sales to sitting tenants and include the sales recorded for housing associations since 1989. Without including these figure the rate of sales in stock transfer districts will terminate when stock transfer occurred and we have attempted to provide a more accurate picture of the relative rate of sales at a district level by including this data.

The picture emerging has clear elements to it. The highest rates of sale are in two belts, one across the south and one across the north of England. There are also some strong rates of sale in shire districts in all regions except for Yorkshire and Humberside. The lowest belt of sales covers the Pennines from the Mersey to the Humber and north of these. There are relatively low rates of sales in the West Midlands and Tyneside.

By the end of 2001/02, 20 local authorities in England had sold less than 20% of their stock and 39 had sold 40% or more. Variation within regions was greater than that between them. No authority in Yorkshire and Humberside (and only one each in the West Midlands and north-east) had sold 40% or more of its stock. The variation in the rate of sales was

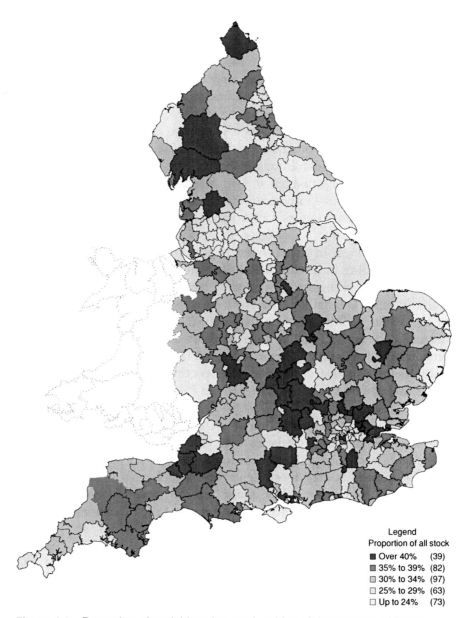

Figure 4.2   Proportion of social housing stock sold to sitting tenants 1979/80 to 2001/02, by local authority districts and unitary authorities in England.

Source: Centre for Urban and Regional Studies, University of Birmingham.

Table 4.7 Right to Buy: the highest selling local authorities in England 1979–2004.

Region	Highest within region
East	Forest Heath (48%)
East Midlands	Corby (49.9%)
London	City (59%)
North-east	Berwick (47.4%)
North-west	Eden (57.7%)
South-east	Crawley (53.5%)
South-west	Torridge (46%)
West Midlands	North Warwickshire (46%)
Yorkshire/Humberside	Richmondshire (47.7%)
Other local authorities with over 45% sales	
North-west	South Lakeland (49.4%)
East	Harlow (46.9%)
	Stevenage (46.4%)
	Castle Point (45.3%)
South-west	Teignbridge (45.9%)
North-west	Carlisle (45.7%)
North-east	Alnwick (45.7%)
South-east	Cherwell (45.4%)

Source: ODPM.

greatest in London and the south-east of England. In London six boroughs recorded less than 20% of their stock sold; 20 less than 30%; and 13 (including the City of London) over 30%. In the south-east outside London three districts recorded less than 20% of their stock sold; 19 less than 30%; and 48 more than 30%. The impact of the Right to Buy has been to increase the relative concentration of rented housing in London and to increase the contrast between the tenure structure in London and in the south-east.

By the end of March 2004, 70 local authorities in England had sold more than 40% of their stock and 17 had sold over 45%. This latter group are listed in Table 4.7. The list includes new towns but is dominated by shire districts.

The pattern of sales outlined above has held true. Although in the second peak of sales there was a different pattern this was not so different that rank orders of highest and lowest sellers were radically changed. As in England there was a significant variation in sales at a local level within Scotland, Wales and Northern Ireland. Consequently localities in these countries appear throughout the distribution and are not all clustered together.

As noted earlier there are some problems with the data on sales of properties which make it difficult to separate out Right to Buy sales from all sales. In the data recorded for some local authorities Right to Buy sales are extraordinarily low and it is apparent that administrative practice records sales in different ways. For example, by the end of 1995 Fenland had 3.3% of Right to Buy sales but 39.4% of sales overall and Redbridge had 0.4% of Right to Buy sales and 44.4% overall. Because of this problem with the data it is more appropriate to refer to all sales. We know that in the vast majority of local authorities sales were dominated by the Right to Buy and in a small number, notably Wandsworth and Westminster, discretionary sales which were outside the terms of the Right to Buy were significant.

By the end of 1995 in Scotland when local government was reorganised, the highest rates of sale were achieved in the five new towns and in Badenoch and Strathspey (48.8%), North-East Fife (42.7%) and Stewartry (40.8%). The lowest rates of sale were in Glasgow (16.6%), Inverclyde (17.6%) and Motherwell (19.8%). In Wales the highest rates of sale were in Taff-Ely (45.5%) and Port Talbot (45.4%), and the lowest rate of sale was in Rhondda (17.4%), followed by Swansea (25.1%). In Northern Ireland within the Northern Ireland Housing Executive the same kind of variation existed. Belfast with 19.8% of sales had the lowest rate of sale.

Properties sold

The properties sold under the Right to Buy and earlier sales under discretionary powers do not represent a cross-section of dwelling types. They were disproportionately more attractive, better quality and larger houses with gardens and were houses rather than flats (Forrest & Murie 1984a; 1984b; 1990b; Foulis 1985; 1987). A study in England carried out in 1985–86 (Kerr 1988) found that three-bedroom, semi-detached houses were heavily over-represented among sales. Whereas more than half the sitting tenant purchasers had bought semi-detached houses, only a third of the remaining public sector tenants lived in such dwellings. Conversely, only 3% of purchasers had bought flats but almost a third of tenants in the sample lived in such dwellings. There were fewer sales of acquired properties, of properties in less popular estates and of small dwellings.

The analysis by Holmans (1993) of the labour force survey and rating records suggested that, by 1991, 44% of semi-detached family houses had been sold in England compared with 18% of smaller terraced houses and only 7% of flats. Sales of flats increased after higher discounts were introduced for them in 1986. While flats remained heavily under-represented in the overall total of sales, by the 1990s they accounted for over a quarter of all disposals in England. This pattern of sales considerably changed the profile of the council housing stock in England. The proportion of public sector tenants living in flats increased by 5% between 1981 and 1993. These figures were more dramatic for local authorities with high levels of flats. Households on the waiting list for council housing are now much more likely to be offered a flat than in the past and the contrast between home ownership and council housing has become more pronounced in terms of dwelling type.

The pattern of change was also illustrated by Birmingham where council housing had become more concentrated in certain parts of the city. The early progress of council house sales generated a zonal pattern, with most sales in a middle ring and fewer sales in the inner city and peripheral estates, but the longer term pattern was more of a patchwork, with differences related to property type, construction date and estate reputation. Within this patchwork, the proportion of dwellings in the more popular, leafy, suburban council estates of houses and gardens built to traditional styles that had been transferred to owner-occupation was substantial.

In Scotland, sales of flats had always been proportionately higher than in England arising from their greater number in the public sector stock. However, a similarly dramatic increase was apparent with flat sales accounting for around one in ten sales in the early 1980s and four in ten by 1990. Sales of flats in Scotland continued at a relatively high level and by mid-1995 accounted for 28% of all sales to sitting tenants where the dwelling type of the property was recorded (Scottish Homes 1996).

In Northern Ireland between 1979 and 1992 only 3% of dwellings sold were flats and maisonettes although these properties accounted for a fifth of stock in 1992 (NIHE Research Unit 1992). Subsequent work indicated that sales had been concentrated in post-war pre-1971 terraced houses, in provincial towns and rural locations. There were considerable variations in the rates of sale at district level, but there was a consistency in the pattern. The highest rates of sales were in the South region while Belfast generally showed the lowest sales (McGreal *et al.* 2004).

Purchasers and choices

Since the Right to Buy was established there have been a number of studies that have examined the characteristics of households buying under the scheme. Despite the essentials of the Right to Buy remaining unchanged over the 25 years, the nature of the choices facing households has changed (see Chapter 10). The decision to purchase is very different today from what it was in 1980 in terms of the economic and housing market contexts. Similarly the housing market of the 1990s was very different again, being strongly influenced by falling house prices and the prevalence of negative equity at the beginning of the decade. The demographic profile of council tenants has also changed over time and this must have an impact on the types of households who purchase (see Chapter 5).

During the early years of the Right to Buy a profile of a typical buyer emerged in a series of studies (Kerr 1988; Lynn 1991; Forrest & Murie 1984a; 1984b). This was a household in work, in the middle of the family life cycle, with two or more adults and with one or more earners in white collar, skilled or semi-skilled occupations. Put negatively, those who were not buying were the youngest and oldest, the unemployed, female-headed households, lone parent families and those in the lowest paid and un-skilled jobs (see Table 4.8). In most areas there was a coincidence between those groups with least bargaining power in the labour market and those in the least desirable parts of the council stock – flats and maisonettes and houses on the least popular estates. Those households have least incentive to buy and least resources to do so.

Kerr's study (1988) in England found that buyers' incomes were on average about double those of tenants. The young and the elderly, households with pre-school children and single person households were significantly under-represented among purchasers. Kerr also found that the main reasons for not purchasing were 'being too old or having insufficient incomes' or were associated with living in a flat rather than a house. Holmans's later study (1993) found a similar profile. Purchaser households were typically married or cohabiting couples aged from 45 up to retirement age. He also found a striking contrast between tenant purchasers and council tenants as a whole. Purchaser households were considerably more likely to be multiple earner households with a male head in full time employment.

Almost a decade later a study by Jones and Murie (1999) considered buyers who had bought in the period 1992–95 in two localities, Birmingham and Croydon, during a relative low point in the housing market cycle but at a time when resales where becoming more common (see Chapter 5). The study found that dwelling types and sizes associated with new buyers were very similar to those in the past. Flats formed 9% of dwellings sold in Birmingham and 12% in Croydon and the dominant group of properties sold were three-bedroom, semi-detached or terraced houses. When comparing the new buyers with those in earlier periods, the most striking

Table 4.8 The Right to Buy before 1986: council tenants and council dwelling purchasers compared.

	Tenants	Purchasers
Sample no.	971	1031
	%	%
Age of head of household		
16–24	6	–
25–34	15	11
35–44	13	26
45–54	12	27
55–64	21	23
65–74	20	10
75+	12	2
Household type		
One adult	27	5
Two adults	29	27
Small family	19	16
Large family	10	12
Large adult household	15	40
Marital status		
Married	56	86
Single	11	3
Widowed	22	7
Divorced/Separated	12	4
Pensioners		
Single pensioners	18	3
2+ persons, all pensioners	11	5
No pensioners	56	76

Source: Kerr 1988.

difference is that purchasers in the period 1992–95 included a much higher proportion of people with short periods of tenancy and young households.

In Kerr's study referring to pre-1986 sales only (Table 4.8), 11% of heads of households were aged under 34 and 7% of households had held the tenancy less than five years. The comparable figures for Birmingham almost a decade later are 19% and 34% and for Croydon 17% and 24% (Table 4.9). In the Birmingham sample the proportion of older households and those with tenancy periods of 20 years or more was much lower than in earlier studies. Only 17% of purchasers had been tenants for 20 years or more compared with 46% in Kerr's study. In Croydon the comparable figure was 37%. In Birmingham 30% of purchasers were aged 55 or over, compared with 35% in Kerr's study and 36% of new buyers in Croydon.

Table 4.9   Comparison of buyers in 1980s and early 1990s.

	All buyers pre 1986	New buyers	
		Birmingham	Croydon
No. of bedrooms			
1 or 2	20	30	28
3	76	61	69
4+	4	9	4
Age of head of household			
16–24	–	19	17
25–34	11		
35–44	26	29	24
45–54	27	21	24
55–64	23		
65–74	10	30	36
75+	2		
Length of tenancy			
Less than 5 years	7	34	24
5 years less than 10	15	18	15
10 years less than 15	16	16	9
15 years less than 20	15	14	15
20 years less than 25	14	13	21
25 years less than 30	14		
30 years or more	18	4	16

Source: Kerr 1988; Jones & Murie 1999.

The implication is that as the Right to Buy matured younger households became more strongly represented. By the 1990s, households buying through the Right to Buy were no longer exclusively long established tenants attached to their home and wanting to secure their future in it and reschedule payment for it. Rather, they included a significant group with shorter periods of tenancy and less attachment to the home and neighbourhood. For this group the Right to Buy offered a different opportunity – that of providing the asset base to enable residential movement. For this group the damaged reputation of council housing, poor services and facilities on estates and the relatively limited opportunities to move to better housing within the council sector were also likely to be a significant influence.

Not every household had a member in employment at the time of house purchase; about a third of households did not, but the working situation of these purchasers (except for those over 55 years of age) showed some fluidity. For 17% of households work situations had changed. Of those who were working when they bought 7% were not working by the time of interview. This included people from all age groups, although 50% were aged 55 or over. Of the total, 10% of households had not been working when they bought the house but were working now. These were not all younger households and included six (23%) persons aged 65 or more. At the time respondents bought the property 4% were long term sick or disabled, 3% were unemployed and 15% were retired. The others were all in paid employment or looking after the home or family.

New buyers in the Jones and Murie (1999) study indicated a stronger preference for moving from their address in the near future than was reported in the previous study (Kerr 1988). A total of 53% in Birmingham and 49% in Croydon said they would like to move from their address in the near future, compared with 41% in the earlier study. A small minority had considered moving prior to purchasing. There was a clear relationship with age and affluence in the desire to move. Of the under 35s 75% said they would like to move but the same was true of only 33% of those aged 55 or over. The relationship with position in the family cycle was much stronger than that with income. Although the lowest income group was the least likely to wish to move, the moderate income group was more intent on moving than the highest income group.

The reasons for wanting to move were mainly push factors. Almost a third, 32%, referred to a deterioration in the area. The next most cited reason was a positive one – wanting more space, more bedrooms or a house rather than a flat or bungalow (24%). However, if all of the factors associated with location are combined, these are much more significant than concerns about gardens, the size of property or internal dwelling arrangements and improvements. A smaller proportion of people offered reasons for moving which related to changes in their personal and family circumstances.

A study by Jones (2003) provides an insight into a later cohort of Right to Buy purchasers. It comprised household surveys from 2002 of Right to Buy applicants and purchasers of approximately three years' standing in Birmingham, Leeds, the outer London borough of Havering and the inner London boroughs of Camden and Lambeth. These Right to Buy applicants were purchasing near the peak of a house price boom. The results presented here primarily relate to the applicants although reference is made to the (existing) owners.

In demographic terms, Right to Buy purchasers are predominantly households with four members or fewer: the most common family type is a two parent family with children at school. The most likely time for tenants to purchase is between 35 and 45 years of age, with over half of all applicants

Table 4.10   Age of applicants by area.

Age	Area					Total
	Camden	Lambeth	Havering	Birmingham	Leeds	
18–24	5	4	1	3	4	17
25–34	23	22	21	23	18	107
35–44	34	41	37	27	32	171
45–54	14	22	8	15	20	79
55–64	11	5	7	12	13	48
65–74	5	4	6	11	7	33
75+	3	1	12	6	5	27
Not stated			1	1		1
Total	95	99	93	98	99	484

Source: Jones 2003.

Table 4.11   Household type of applicants by area.

Type	Area					Total
	Camden	Lambeth	Havering	Birmingham	Leeds	
One adult under 60	17	16	5	13	9	60
One adult aged 60 or over	7	5	11	13	4	40
Two adults, both under 60	5	10	6	8	13	42
Two adults, at least one aged 60 or over	1	3	7	9	9	29
Three or more adults aged 16 or over	15	9	8	2	18	52
1 parent family, with at least one child under 16	12	23	20	24	11	90
2 parent family, with at least one child under 16	37	32	34	25	34	162
Other	1	1	2	4		8
Not stated					1	1
Total	95	99	93	98	99	484

Source: Jones 2003.

and owners aged 25–44 (see Table 4.10). One parent families and the retired represent almost 20% and 10% of purchasers, respectively (Table 4.11). An indication of the stage in the family cycle of purchasers can be gauged from changes to their household composition. In the last three years, 7% of applicants have had a new baby whilst at the other end of the cycle 2% have seen an older child leave home and 5% have had a death in the family. There is a similar incidence of life events for owners: 6% have had a birth in the family, 3% have experienced an older child leaving home and 3% have suffered a death in the household since they purchased.

Table 4.12 Social class of applicants by area.

	Area					Total
	Camden	Lambeth	Havering	Birmingham	Leeds	
A	1					1
B	6	12	1		3	22
C1	32	40	19	16	25	132
C2	28	16	29	29	33	135
D	18	20	25	21	31	115
E	10	11	17	32	7	77
Not stated			2			2
Total	95	99	93	98	99	484

Source: Jones 2003.

Key
A   Professional etc. occupations
B   Managerial and technical occupations
C1 Skilled non-manual occupations
C2 Skilled manual occupations
D   Partly skilled occupations
E   Unskilled occupations

The socioeconomic characteristics of purchasers also demonstrate a range of circumstances. Almost three-fifths (59%) of households have a full or part time worker and a further 10% are (both) retired. More than one in ten (11%) of households have a member who stays at home to look after the family and in 4% of cases the household is entirely composed of long term disabled adults. With a further 6% who are unemployed there is a high proportion, a third of households, with no economically active members, much higher than the 1990s study. Decomposition of these statistics to the individual case study finds that Birmingham has the lowest percentage of households with a member employed (47%) and the highest percentage of economically inactive (45%). In contrast Leeds has the least economically inactive (22%) and the highest in employment (71%).

Table 4.12 does not reflect the variation in the demographic profile and economic circumstances of these households, but shows that more than half (55%) of applicants and 61% of owners fall into either C1 or C2, namely the lower middle class and skilled working class, split broadly equally between the two. Almost a quarter of applicants (24%) are social class D, the partly skilled working class, and 16% are social class E, those in unskilled occupations. The figures are lower for these latter groups amongst owners. The distribution of social classes broken down for each of the areas reveals that the highest proportions of social classes A and B are in inner London. Social classes C1 and C2 represent more than half of both samples in each area except Birmingham where the majority of applicants are in classes D and E.

Reflecting their occupations, Right to Buy purchasers are generally on incomes below the national average, even those in work. Over half (54%) of applicant households have a gross income less than £16 000 and one in five (20%) have a gross income over £26 000. Owners generally have higher gross incomes with only 38% of households with less than £16 000 and 32% above £26 000. The vast majority (77%) of one parent family applicants have incomes less than £16 000. Over a quarter of applicants are on income support or housing benefits, with the highest percentage of these to be found in Birmingham (45%). Two-thirds of retired applicants are receiving benefits and these households account for almost a third of applicants in receipt of these benefits. The equivalent figure for owners at the time they bought their home is less, just 7% on income support or housing benefit. Again the highest percentage (11%) on income support or housing benefit is in Birmingham.

When the Right to Buy was originally introduced nearly half of purchasers had lived in their home for 20 years (Kerr 1988), but by the early 1990s this period had been reduced substantially (Jones & Murie 1999). Almost one in five applicants (19%) in a later study (Jones 2003) had lived for less than four years in their current home. This pattern is broadly similar across the case study areas, ranging from 26% in Havering to 8% in Lambeth. Although the mean number of years of residency is highest in Leeds and Birmingham at 11.8 years, and above 10 years in all areas, it is probably lower than in previous studies. The most likely time to buy is between six and ten years although 18% of applicants have lived in their home for over 20 years (Table 4.13). The provincial cities have higher percentages of this latter group, 25% and 21% of applicants in Birmingham and Leeds respectively. Two person and one person families comprise 74% of all those who have applied within four years, and 62% of those who applied between four and six years.

A high percentage of households that have moved to their present home in the last four years had been statutorily homeless prior to moving to their current accommodation in inner London. Although the actual numbers are small, 31% of recent movers in Lambeth and Camden had been accepted as homeless. The figures are lower in the other study areas but these numbers show how it can be relatively quick for people to move from being homeless to being home owners under the Right to Buy. In some cases households may have accumulated debt and other problems that can make it difficult to obtain a mortgage from a high street lender.

Table 4.13   Length of residence of applicants by area.

	Area					Total
	Camden	Lambeth	Havering	Birmingham	Leeds	
Under 6 months		1			1	2
6–12 months	1	1	3	2	2	9
1 up to 4 years	20	6	21	15	17	79
4 up to 6 years	16	16	17	16	9	74
6 up to 10 years	21	31	20	22	24	118
10 up to 20 years	21	33	14	18	25	111
20+ years	15	11	17	25	21	89
Not stated	1		1			2
Total	95	99	93	98	99	484

Source: Jones 2003.

The most important trigger factors for applicants were the right time in the family cycle (34%), national economic factors (30%) and domestic finances (23%). Children offering finance is the most important trigger factor for 8% of all applicants (23% of retired households). Just over one in five (22%) applicant households are planning to buy their homes with financial support from relatives. Three-quarters of applicant households receiving help from relatives do not have the relatives living with them. Where the relatives that are giving financial support are not living with the Right to Buy applicant 17% are expected to live there in the future. Of the 36% of relatives providing financial aid, 19% have an agreement to become owners in the future (before the death of the Right to Buy purchaser), 4% have an agreement to have a share in the house when it is sold (before the Right to Buy purchaser's death) and 28% will inherit the property.

Three-fifths of retired households are receiving help in this way from relatives, as are a quarter of one parent families. A third of households with incomes below £16 000 are receiving such help. Similarly two out of five retired owner households are receiving help from relatives but only one in ten single parent families. Just over a quarter (27%) of households with incomes below £16 000 are receiving such help.

Like the case study evidence of the 1990s, many of these Right to Buy purchasers expect to move house shortly. Just over a third of the owners expect to move in the future, virtually all to buy a home elsewhere. Of the total owners 7% expect to move within a year and a further 11% in between one and three years. This expected mobility is greatest in Havering where more than half expect to move, and least in Camden. In comparison, less of the applicants surveyed, but still one in five, expected to move prior to purchase. These figures are lower than found in the 1990s but this may be because of the tightness of the market caused by the housing price boom. The numbers are still significant and the motivations behind this decision have important consequences for the impact of the Right to Buy. This issue is taken up in Chapters 5 and 6.

A review of these studies over three decades reveals that the stereotypical purchaser in the 1980s of an older couple, over 45 years of age, with grown up children and at least one member in full time employment is no longer accurate. Today's Right to Buy purchasers are generally younger than those of the 1980s but not than those of the early 1990s and the most common household type is a two parent family with children at school. However, there is a much more eclectic collection of households than those buying in the mid 1990s. Household incomes are generally low and most purchasers are drawn from the lower middle class and the skilled working class. Some applicants such as single parents and the retired are on state benefits and some depend on relatives for financial support – 13% of Right to Buy sales are funded in this way and children offering finance can be a key trigger in the decision to buy. Some of this support is on the understanding of (future) residence and subsequent ownership/ inheritance.

The predominant occupations of Right to Buy purchasers are subject to variable incomes, for example through more susceptibility to unemployment, and as a result such households may have had debt and housing problems, even homelessness, in the recent past. Looking down the income spectrum many of the households attracted to the Right to Buy are not necessarily served by the standard mortgages available. Some tenants may require 'sub-prime' finance because they cannot certify their income, have County Court Judgements against them or have significant arrears. A new industry has grown up of firms offering services and mortgage advice to applicants in the Right to Buy process. The varied economic standing of the potential pool of Right to Buy purchasers, with people moving in and out of poverty, implies that it is not possible to think in terms of a finite lower income bound to the demand for the Right to Buy. Studies in different regions and localities show a similar pattern related to age, household structure and occupation. Summarising this data, Forrest and Murie (1990a) indicated that buyers are drawn disproportionately from households in work, in the middle of the family life cycle, with one or more earners, with two or more adults and in white collar, skilled or semi-skilled occupations.

The prominence of purchasers with shorter tenancies, along with the intro-duction of a maximum discount rule, means that the extent to which there has been discount beyond that needed to achieve sales (deadweight) under the Right to Buy is not evident. A higher rate of sales is being achieved with a lower rate of discount. It makes more sense in terms of value for money. However, in terms of agendas targeting long established tenants who have been paying rent but have nothing to show for it, the pattern is less justifiable. Increasingly, the tenants benefiting from the Right to Buy have relatively short periods of tenancy and may be purchasing with a different motive. They are less likely to be buying with a view to stay-ing for a long period, if not for the rest of their lives, in a house that they regard as their home. Rather they are households who see house purchase as an effective way of organising a move on and an exit from their exist-ing house and neighbourhood (Jones & Murie 1999).

In Northern Ireland the 1992 House Sales Review (NIHE Research Unit 1992) described the typical buyer of a Housing Executive property in a way reminiscent of the research produced in England. The buyer was 'a middle-aged head of a small adult household, in full time employment, in a skilled manual occupation and earning around £100 to £140 per week. Generally the buying household will comprise of at least two earners and no pensioners'. A second emerging profile was also identified as 'a head of an elderly household, aged over 60 and wholly retired. The majority of these buyers purchased jointly with an average of one other person, possibly a child of the tenant.' The Northern Ireland research suggested that the profile of purchasing households remained broadly similar in 1986 and 1991. The most commonly quoted reason for buying was related to rent – buying was seen as cheaper than renting in the longer term.

Conclusions

Twenty-five years after the Right to Buy was introduced there can be no doubting the impact of the policy. Over 30% of council tenants have exer-cised the Right to Buy. As will be discussed later the majority of these have benefited considerably from the process. At the same time the Right to Buy has added to the process of social change and residualisation asso-ciated with council housing and contributed to the transformation of both council housing and home ownership. It can reasonably be argued that the volume of sales and capital receipts has far exceeded expectations. However the Right to Buy cannot be summed up in this way. It has oper-ated within a changing environment and it is important to consider how far it has developed in accord with this.

At this stage there are two essential elements to consider. First, the Right to Buy, as was discussed in the previous chapter, has become more complicated and now operates alongside different measures from those in place when it was introduced. Second, the agenda associated with the council housing sector has changed. From a large sector housing almost one in three of the population, marked by considerable social mix, and with concern about whether the sector provided the full range of options for more affluent tenants, the council sector, and the social rented sector more generally, in 2005 is smaller and more beleaguered. There are concerns about social stigmatisation and segregation and about the more limited opportunities available to most tenants within the sector and those seeking to enter it. It is these issues that are discussed in the following chapter.

5

Transforming Social Housing

Twenty-five years of the Right to Buy, during which more than two million council houses have been sold, has had a substantial and irreversible impact on the size of the sector. The impact cannot be seen in isolation from other housing policy changes and initiatives but the cumulative effect of sales is seen through lost relets and reduced access to social rented housing. One potential long term impact stemming from the reduced supply is a shortage of affordable rented housing, and this can be judged by the scale of homelessness over time and the experience of homeless people. Sales also change the composition of the types of housing within the sector and the opportunities for existing tenants. Consequently, the role of the sector has adapted within the housing system.

The differential pattern of sales is chronicled in Chapter 4 in terms of areas and house types. This chapter focuses on the impact of these changes on lettings and the consequences for existing and would-be council tenants. First, the chapter considers the policy context and the relationship between the Right to Buy and access to council housing. Next the chapter reviews macro trends in lettings and examines the subsequent impact on homelessness and the changing characteristics of tenants. The analysis then considers the micro detail of sales at an estate level in urban and rural areas. This latter research is based on a scrics of case studies. Finally, the chapter summarises the key impacts of the Right to Buy and reviews the role of council housing today by revisiting the original ideals.

Policy context

The role of council housing, as Chapter 2 outlines, has never been one-dimensional. At times it has been variously and simultaneously a means to address housing shortages, a demonstration to the private sector of how to build good quality housing to rent, a vehicle for rehousing people from slums that were being demolished, the main provider of houses for the working class and, after World War II, it was encouraged to take a more general role in the housing system. Even so, by the 1970s there were the beginnings of a debate about the residualisation of council housing and the increased concentration of lower income and unemployed households on certain council estates.

The period leading up to the Right to Buy during the 1960s and 1970s had already been one of great transformation for council housing with the widespread adoption of system building. Large new council estates were built in inner cities and overspill areas to replace the swathes of slums demolished by large-scale clearance programmes. These decades saw the numbers of council dwellings rise dramatically to realise politically charged building targets. People rehoused through slum clearance programmes into this new housing were now living in much better physical conditions. However, beyond this improvement in physical amenities there were concerns about the quality of this housing. By 1980 most council tenants lived in well built traditional houses.

Notwithstanding the Right to Buy, the 1980s saw the beginning of significant changes to the council housing sector. The vast council and new town house building programmes came to a halt, although they had been already stuttering in the second half of the 1970s (see Chapter 2). Strict reductions to public sector budgets in the pursuit of a monetarist macroeconomic strategy by the Conservative Government led not only to an immediate halving of the public sector house building programme but also to wider ramifications for the sector in terms of rents and subsidies. Social housing completions (including those by housing associations) have remained low ever since, mostly focusing on special needs. By 2005 the annual number of houses built by local authorities had dropped to the low hundreds for the whole of the UK, and since 1998 housing association output has averaged just over 20 000 per annum.

The Government entered into a policy of raising rents and reducing subsidies in real terms in the 1980s. Rents rose not just faster than prices but faster than earnings over the next two decades. In England an average council house rent was 6.9% of average earnings in 1981; by 1991 it had risen to 10.7% and, followed by further real increases in the next decade, the percentage rose to 13.3% in 2002. In Scotland, where an average council house rent has traditionally been slightly lower relative to earnings, the percentage similarly rose from 6% in 1981 to 9.2% in 1991 and 11.5% in 2002. The experience in Wales is slightly different: rents relative to earnings were higher in 1981, on average 9.5% of earnings. Rents rose more slowly in real terms and by 2002 the percentage in Wales had risen to 12.7%.

Rents have risen in real terms as a direct result of reduced subsidies. General subsidies to council housing (per house) from central government and rate payers fell substantially at the beginning of the 1980s and continued on a downward trend for the rest of the century. In fact the sector produced a financial surplus between 1994/95 and 2000/01. Since 2001/02 this trend has been reversed except in Wales where a council house on average still produces a financial surplus of £500. The structure of subsidies has also changed from supply subsidies on bricks and mortar to personal financial assistance for households on low incomes via housing benefit. In contrast subsidies to home ownership continued unabated until tax relief on mortgage interest was phased out in the latter half of the 1990s (see Chapter 9).

The Right to Buy and access to council housing

There has been no formal assessment of the impact of the Right to Buy by the UK or devolved governments on access to council housing. Such an assessment would necessarily involve an analysis of the impact of sales on access to council housing and the choice of lettings available. Access to council housing can be simplified as having two dimensions: access to the sector and access to good quality housing. The relative significance of these two dimensions depends on the state of local housing markets, in particular whether there is a shortage or surplus of social housing available. The changing number of households moving within the sector gives an indication of choice and the opportunities for existing council tenants.

The pattern of subsequent resales is also important when considering the impact of the Right to Buy. Arguably there is no short or medium term impact on the housing system if purchasers remain in the same house for the rest of their lives. As Chapter 4 demonstrates, initially Right to Buy purchasers tended to be older tenants who did indeed expect to stay for the rest of their lives in their home (Forrest & Murie 1984a; 1984b; Foulis 1985). This would suggest the impact of the Right to Buy on the access to housing is minimal. However, over 20 years, the characteristics of households exercising the Right to Buy has changed partly as a consequence of the changed socioeconomic demographic profile of council tenants and partly because of Right to Buy sales. Recent evidence suggests that purchasers are becoming more diverse and younger, with many expecting to move on in the housing market (Chapter 4). The implication is that the lag between a Right to Buy sale and a lost relet is now much shorter. This conclusion is tempered by a second potential impact of resales. If and when resales occur, if these homes are bought by local people who traditionally would have been housed locally by the council, then arguably there is no effect on communities where the local authority stock is relatively uniform. This latter effect is assessed in Chapter 6.

National trends in lettings

The stock of council housing has fallen by half in England although this includes demolitions and transfers of stock to housing associations. There is a cumulative loss of 131 000 housing units because of demolition between 1992 and 2003 although some of these were lying vacant or derelict, unavailable for letting. The proportion of council housing that lies empty available for letting has remained broadly constant over the last decade, varying between 1.2 and 1.6%. Annual new council lettings have fallen from 439 000 in 1982/83 to 273 000 20 years later, a fall of 166 000 or 38%. The fall in council housing lets is to some extent naturally balanced by lettings from housing associations in England which have risen from 51 000 to 136 000. Thus there has been a loss of 80 000 annual social housing tenancies since the early 1980s. In Scotland new lettings by local authorities similarly fell from 46 000 to 28 000 in the 20 years to 2003/04 (including nominations to housing associations), a cut of 39%.

Interpretation of these statistics should be undertaken with care because they are the outcome of demand and supply, but they are indicative of the scale of lost tenancies. As noted above there has been some displacement of demand into owner-occupation so these statistics cannot be seen in isolation. Another factor when judging these statistics has been a trend toward a greater rate of turnover in social housing ameliorating the loss of stock. Pawson and Bramley (2000) estimate that turnover rose by two-thirds between the early 1980s and the late 1990s. One key issue is the constraint on meeting housing need that the reduction in lets creates. There are no statistics that comprehensively address this question but it is possible to look at this by examining the statistics on lettings to existing tenants and the homeless households rehoused through new council housing lets.

The number of lettings to existing council tenants in England fell from 180–190 000 in the early 1980s to 82 000 in 2002/03, a drop of around 100 000, or more than half. Over the same period the equivalent number of housing association lettings rose from 9000 to 42 000. Overall lettings to existing social housing tenants have fallen by approximately 70 000 (36%) over the period of the Right to Buy, less than the reduction in the number of tenants. This statistic suggests that tenants' opportunities have increased but this is because of greater turnover and relates to a less attractive stock as the Right to Buy has led to much of the most attractive stock being sold off. Perhaps a better indicator of the lot of existing tenants is that they accounted for 39% of English social housing lettings in 1980 but only 30% more than 20 years on.

In comparison the number of social housing lettings to new tenants in England has fallen only marginally, from 297 000 to 285 000. These statistics should be seen in the light of an increase in households since 1981 of the order of 20%. Furthermore social trends which began in the 1970s brought changes to the overall composition of households with a growth of one person, multi-person and lone parent households, as set out in Figure 5.1. These demographic developments resulted in an increase in smaller households with consequent implications for the demand for housing.

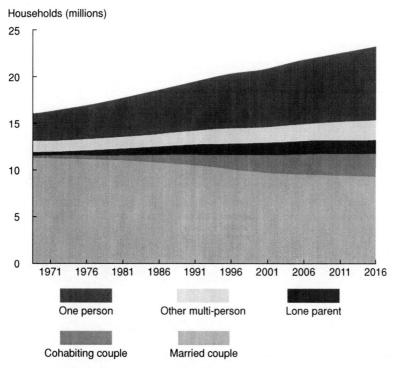

Figure 5.1   Number of households: England: 1971–2016.
Source: ODPM.

In addition over this period the proportion of new English council tenants who are homeless (i.e. are statutorily homeless and rehoused as a priority need) has increased from 19% to 34%. An even more extreme trend is seen in Scotland, from 14% to 34%. Although these figures are cyclical there is an upward trend and it means the numbers of social housing tenancies filled from normal letting in England have fallen by a fifth since 1980. These statistics suggest that access to social housing has in general become more difficult and thus there are increased housing shortages and difficulties in transferring within the sector. For example over 230 000 households in England in 2003 are on council housing registers for three-bedroom or larger properties but only 5000 socially rented homes of this size are currently built each year (Shelter 2005).

Homelessness

The number of homeless households applying to be rehoused by their local authority under their statutory duty indicates a major factor of stress on the housing system. Homeless statistics presented in Figure 5.2 show two peaks over the last quarter of a century, at the beginning of the 1990s and the early 2000s. Published homeless statistics give a breakdown of the immediate reasons why people become homeless. The most common

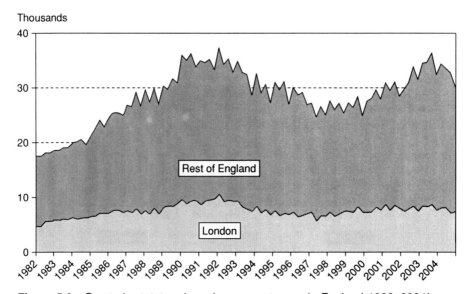

Figure 5.2 Quarterly statutory homeless acceptances in England 1982–2004*.
* Households accepted as homeless and in priority need by local authorities in England.
Source: ODPM.

Table 5.1 Homeless households in priority need accepted by local authorities: reasons for loss of last settled home.

Year	Total (thousand)	Relatives/ friends no longer willing to provide accommodation	Relationship breakdown with a partner	Mortgage arrears	Rent arrears	End of assured tenancy	Loss of other rented or tied housing	Other reasons
1997	102.0	27	25	6	2	13	9	17
1998	104.6	27	25	6	3	15	8	17
1999	105.4	28	24	5	3	14	8	19
2000	111.3	30	23	3	3	15	8	18
2001	117.8	33	22	3	3	15	7	18
2002	123.8	34	21	2	3	14	6	20
2003	135.6	36	20	1	2	13	6	22
2004	127.8	38	20	2	2	13	5	20

Source: ODPM.

reasons are friends or relatives no longer being willing or able to accommodate them or a domestic dispute between spouses or cohabitees. However, there is some variation in the incidence of these reasons between areas, for example the former accounts for just over 40% over the period of the operation of the Right to Buy, and the latter for around a quarter of homeless cases in Scotland (Jones & Leishman 2001). In England the proportion of households homeless as a result of having left relatives is generally a little lower although it has risen to almost 40% in recent years.

Given the increasing difficulties of access to social housing identified by the analysis of lettings a priori it would appear that this is a major factor in the latest rise in homelessness. To examine the causes it is useful to examine how the reasons for homelessness have changed during the recent upturn in the statutorily homeless. Table 5.1 gives a breakdown of the relative incidence for England from 1997 to 2004. From this table it can be seen that the number of households who became homeless as a result of mortgage arrears, loss of tied housing and relationship breakdown are falling in relative and absolute terms. The number of homeless households who left their home because of rent arrears or the end of a tenancy rose by the order of 42% and 28% respectively (at their peak points). The largest rises are in the numbers who have left relatives and friends, both up 84%. These households accounted for more than three-fifths of the total increase of the 35 590 in homeless households between 1997 and 2003.

These statistics point to a housing shortage but beneath these immediate reasons for homelessness are underlying causes which it is instructive to assess. The economic cycle is a potential influence and the recession of the early 1990s had a dual impact on unemployment and the housing market, and hence in a rise in mortgage defaults. A second major cause of homelessness may be simply local housing shortages as represented by the 'hidden homeless' – people forced to stay with friends or relatives. Third, there are changes to legislation which can aid or exacerbate the scale, for example the removal of security of tenure in 1989 for most new tenancies in the private rented sector and the introduction of the care in the community policy in the 1990s. To this list may be added the influence of demographic change and migration (including from abroad) on the number and type of households.

The principal influence of the economy on homelessness is poverty. This occurs both as a result of fluctuations in the economic cycle and also through fundamental structural changes in inequality. High interest rates affect affordability in the owner-occupied sector, with knock on effects on forced moves and mortgage defaults. Unemployment is linked to the economic cycle and non employment as a whole (including long term illness and retirement) has grown over the last 25 years. Unlike the previous peak in homelessness in the early 1990s when there were record levels of mortgage defaults the recent surge in homelessness has not occurred at a time of economic recession.

In many ways the position is reversed – low interest rates and consistent economic growth has stimulated demand. One of the key differences between the housing booms of the 1980s and the 2000s is that private house building did not respond by a substantial rise in output in the latest cycle. The Barker report (2004) argues that land supply constraints have restricted private sector output. While the number of new houses built seems to have kept pace with the number of new households, these national figures take no account of variations in local housing market conditions, housing quality and any deterioration in the housing stock since 1979.

The homelessness crisis of the 2000s is therefore more clearly the consequence of an absolute shortage of housing compared with the early 1990s. Affordability is a key issue for those rationed out of owner-occupation by high house prices and limited opportunities in the private rented sector. At the same time the social housing sector is now smaller than it was and this necessarily has three impacts. First, with less housing available and a statutory obligation to rehouse the homeless there is a reduction in relets for transfers and general applications. Second, the lack of social housing generally available will lead to more households facing the crisis of homelessness. Third, the lack of social housing can also mean that local

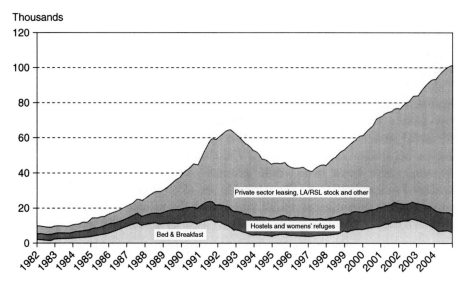

Figure 5.3 Temporary housing for statutory homeless households 1982–2004*.

* Households in accommodation arranged by local authorities in England under the homelessness provisions of the 1985 and 1996 Housing Acts.

Source: ODPM.

authorities have to seek a private sector solution to rehousing the homeless. By the end of 2004 almost twice as many homeless households (55 590) in England were temporarily rehoused in private sector accommodation as in social housing (28 920) including housing associations (Figure 5.3 provides a broad overview of trends).

In fact, in 2004, 70% of homeless households, 72 000, were rehoused in bed and breakfast hotels, hostels, women's refuges or private sector leased accommodation. Many of these households live in a series of temporary accommodation units for months, even years, in high demand areas. Very often these households live in over-crowded and poor housing conditions where they are exposed to health risks. The lack of a stable domestic environment has long term detrimental effects on children's schooling and emotional development (Shelter 2005).

Changing profile of council tenants

Twenty-five years of the Right to Buy have contributed to substantive changes to the profile of households living in the different tenures. Its impact has not only been directly, through providing a route to house purchase, but also through the constraints on opportunities to rent.There has, for example, been an increasing proportion of lettings allocated to homeless people. The overall impact can be seen most dramatically in the socioeconomic composition of households in the different tenures, and Tables 5.2 to 5.4 record the changes based on a series of Government national surveys. Before comparing these tables it is important to note two factors. First, this trend was well established before 1979 and is affected by social and economic changes, the decline of private renting and the increasing attractiveness of home ownership to middle income households. Second, there have been some general changes to society that have widened inequality. Over the period since 1980 there has been a modest move toward non-manual employment and the numbers of economically inactive rose in the 1980s but remained broadly stationary subsequently.

Table 5.2   Socioeconomic groups of heads of household by tenure in 1980.

Socioeconomic group	Owned outright	Owned with mortgage	Local authority	Housing ass'n	Private rented furnished	Private rented unfurnished	All
Professional	3	8	0	4	0	9	4
Employers/managers	10	24	3	3	4	9	12
Intermediate non-manual	4	11	2	4	5	17	6
Junior non-manual	5	10	6	7	6	18	8
Skilled manual	15	34	27	19	17	21	25
Semi-skilled manual	6	8	14	8	9	10	10
Unskilled manual	2	1	5	3	3	5	3
Economically inactive	56	4	42	52	55	11	33
Total	100	100	100	100	100	100	100

Source: General Household Survey 1980, National Housing Review.

Table 5.3   Socioeconomic groups of heads of household by tenure in 1990.

Socioeconomic group	Owned outright	Owned with mortgage	Local authority	Housing ass'n	Private rented furnished	Private rented unfurnished	All
Professional	2	10	0	0	2	8	5
Employers/managers	9	24	2	4	7	11	14
Intermediate non-manual	4	14	2	5	6	14	8
Junior non-manual	3	7	4	4	6	10	5
Skilled manual	12	30	15	12	20	17	21
Semi-skilled manual	3	7	11	10	9	9	8
Unskilled manual	1	1	4	1	3	4	2
Economically inactive	66	7	61	63	48	26	38
Total	100	100	100	100	100	100	100

Source: General Household Survey 1980, National Housing Review.

Table 5.4   Socioeconomic groups of heads of household by tenure in 2002.

Socioeconomic classification	Owned outright	Owned with mortgage	Local authority	Housing ass'n	Private rented furnished	Private rented unfurnished	All
Large employers	2	8	0	0	4	4	4
Higher professionals	3	12	0	0	7	12	6
Lower managerial and professionals	9	29	4	6	17	21	17
Intermediate	3	8	4	4	7	9	6
Small employers and own account	6	9	2	3	6	4	7
Lower supervisory	4	12	4	4	9	6	8
Semi-routine	4	8	9	11	11	4	7
Routine	4	7	10	9	6	6	7
Never worked/long term illness	0	0	3	3	2	2	1
Economically inactive	64	7	64	61	31	32	37
Total	100	100	100	100	100	100	100

Source: General Household Survey 2002, National Housing Review.

In the first decade of the Right to Buy the proportion of council tenants who were skilled manual workers fell from 27% to 15%, much faster than the national trend. This is consistent with the predominant characteristics of Right to Buy purchasers at that time. At the same time the proportion of households with an economically inactive head rose by 50%, again considerably faster than the national trend. By 1990 three-fifths of council tenants were economically inactive. There was also a small fall in the percentages of non-manual households in council housing but these households still comprised 8% of the total.

The trends since 1990 are obscured by the change in the socioeconomic-demographic classification used by the Government. However, it would seem that the trends established in the 1980s have continued. By 2002 the percentage of households with economically inactive heads had risen to more than two-thirds and there were few households with workers who might have been described as skilled or non-manual. In terms of age profile in 1981, 28% of council tenants had retired, but by 1991 this figure had risen to 40% and in 2002 it remained broadly the same (38%).

The changing age profile of council tenants is quite complex. In 1980 the dominant head of household age group was 45–64 years, accounting for 36% of the total. However by 1990, 45–59 year olds represented only 17%, at least partly because this group dominated the first wave of Right to Buy purchasers. It is important not to exaggerate this effect because the age structure of the population as a whole saw a similar but less marked trend with the respective proportions falling from 34% to 23%. In 1980 council tenants were generally older than the rest of the adult population and they continue to be. However, the proportion of tenants under 25 years old increased to 8% of the total in 2002, twice the national average and that of house buyers.

The increasing proportion of new tenants who have been provided accommodation because they were homeless (over one-third in 2004) is likely to contribute to this trend. Half of these households have dependent children and a further 10% have a household member who is pregnant. There is also a growing percentage of young people who are rehoused by local authorities as homeless following recent changes in the regulations defining priority need. The proportion of these households has risen from 3% in 1997 to 9% in 2004. In comparison the elderly account for only 3% of households rehoused as homeless.

Comparison with 1980 shows a reduced overlap between the socio-economic backgrounds of households buying with a mortgage and council tenants. The growing gulf between the two is also illustrated by the changing ratio of average incomes of home buyers with a mortgage and council tenants. In 1980 the ratio was approximately 2:1. In 2005 this figure was over 3:1. In 2002 there were over 1.8 million council tenants in Great Britain on housing benefit, approximately 57% of all tenants. Almost two-thirds (63%) of councils tenant in 2002 did not have a car, nearly twice the national average.

Local experiences

The empirical analysis so far in this chapter has been at a national level but the impact of the Right to Buy is essentially at the local level. In many ways the pattern of sales and lost lettings is most critical at the estate or sector level in an urban area or settlement in a rural area. Figures in this respect are limited to a number of case studies. This section briefly looks at the evidence on the local variations in sales and then considers the interaction between sales and lettings in more detail.

The earliest studies of the spatial impact of sales of council houses in Birmingham prior to the Right to Buy were affected by the fact that flats were not included in the properties available for sale but nevertheless showed a very uneven pattern (Forrest & Murie 1976). Subsequent studies in Birmingham and Liverpool confirmed a differential take up of sales with higher sales in more popular and more affluent estates (Forrest & Murie 1990a).

An analysis of changing patterns in the City of Edinburgh between 1981 and 1991 provides another illustration of patterns of change (Murie 1998). In this case the analysis was based upon the population census in two years (1981 and 1991) covering the significant early impact of the first ten years of the Right to Buy. The research also used local authority data on housing satisfaction and dwelling type to categorise council estates within the city as: tower blocks, unpopular estates, popular areas and other. This enabled the additional dimension of popularity to be introduced into the debate. In both 1981 and 1991, tower blocks and the least popular estates had particularly high levels of unemployment and of female lone parent households. The conclusions drawn from the analysis were consistent with earlier analyses of the residualisation of council housing and the patterns of social change associated both with residualisation and privatisation. Not all council estates were affected by these changes to the same extent, although there was a widening gap between the city as a whole and the council estates as a group.

Most importantly this research identified two extreme cases within the council estates. The first was more popular estates which were rapidly being privatised. In these areas the 1991 census showed major tenure change but less dramatic social change. These are relatively stable and affluent areas and social change is likely to be slower and cumulative with market exchanges accounting for an increasing proportion of residential movement, and resulting in some gentrification as a comparatively affluent younger population moves in. The second extreme case was less popular areas and tower blocks which have established profiles more like residual estates. In these areas privatisation had not been so extensive. Patterns of social change relate to demand for council housing and the processes of allocation and transfer within the sector. Different council estates are subject to different processes and have different trajectories. Some areas are being consolidated as relatively affluent, popular and private; others are increasingly excluded with high and increasing concentrations of deprivation. The analysis of data for Edinburgh shows that those council areas that have seen most tenure change are those which were most affluent at the outset (Murie 1998).

Two more recent studies demonstrate the dramatic differences in sales within urban areas. Jones and Murie (1999) show that in Glasgow the proportion of properties sold between 1980 and 1995 varied from 33% in Anniesland, an area of good quality housing (much of it built as family houses in the 1920s), to 4% in the large peripheral estate of Castlemilk. A similar if more extreme story was told for Edinburgh by Pawson *et al.* (2002) for the period up to 2000. In popular areas of Edinburgh such as Saughtonhall or Corstorphine and the suburban areas of Currie or Balerno, sales amounted to 82% of the 1980 stock. In contrast, sales in the large estates of Wester Hailes, Niddrie and Craigmillar were less than 3% of the stock.

Sales in rural areas of Scotland tend to have been more uniform between communities, partly as a reflection of the reduced variation in the quality of the stock. For example in Badenoch and Strathspey, one settlement had sales representing 79% of the 1980 stock and Right to Buy sales in all the major settlements were above 50% (Pawson *et al.* 2002). Rosenburg (2001) reported that all the council stock in some settlements in East Lothian had been sold, a scenario which is undoubtedly not unique to that area and reflects the original low level of council housing in these communities. Figures for South Ayrshire, discussed below, were not so high but of a similar pattern in the sense that the range of sale by percentage in each settlement was narrow.

These same case studies examined the variation in house types and sizes. Although sales in Glasgow were relatively low compared with other areas, the Right to Buy had still had a significant impact on the stock of certain house types by 1996. At one extreme only 1% of the high rise stock had been sold compared with 48% of semi-detached houses at the other extreme. The most common house type sold was four-in-a-block flats – 38% of these had been sold. This was broadly equivalent to the proportion (39%) of terraced houses sold. In terms of dwelling size, the highest proportion sold were in the three-bedroom category where 40% had been sold (Jones & Murie 1999).

In the later study Pawson *et al.* (2002) examined the impact on three different types of areas – rural area, commuter area and a city where there had been high levels of sales. Table 5.5 illustrates that a high proportion of the three or more bedroom housing stock has been sold: well over half in the two rural areas. The sales in Edinburgh of larger homes might have been higher but for the city's large demolition and transfer programme that accounted for a further 23% of the 1980 housing stock of four or more bedrooms. The relatively low sales rate for small dwellings is perhaps partially influenced by the fact that sheltered housing has been exempt from the Right to Buy regime.

Table 5.5 Sales by house type as a percentage of 1980 stock in case study areas.

	No of bedrooms			
	1	2	3	4+
Badenoch and Strathspey	15.6	42.4	62.0	56.1
Edinburgh	16.0	40.0	44.3	37.2
Gordon	4.6	44.6	55.8	63.9

Source: Pawson *et al.* 2002.

The remainder of this chapter considers the relationship between sales and lettings. As discussed above it is often argued that the direct impact of the Right to Buy on lettings does not occur until a resale occurs. This implies that households' decisions about moving are the same as owners after the Right to Buy as they would have been as tenants. In practice this seems unlikely but it is a useful concept by which to assess the Right to Buy. In particular the cumulative number of first resales can be regarded as the number of properties lost to lettings. In the analysis below, taken from Jones and Murie (1999), resales are compared with the number of properties let for a range of sub-areas of Glasgow. These are based on administrative units within the housing department of Glasgow City Council at that time and reflect natural estate boundaries. There are 16 administrative areas and 146 sub-areas, each of which comprises a small number of estates. Glasgow City Council kindly provided data on individual sales from 1982 until the end of 1994. There were 26 457 Right to Buy sales records for this period. For each property record there are details of house type, age, size and location. There are some discrepancies with the timing of sales reported by the Scottish Office, but with official statistics showing just 18 sales in Glasgow in 1981 and none in 1980 the data represents the large majority of sales to the end of 1994.

The council also provided a breakdown of the council housing stock by sub-area for 31 March 1996. While not an exact method, this has enabled us to estimate the 'stock' in 1980 by adding back in Right to Buy sales. This gives a 'purer' estimate than taking the exact 1980 stock because it extracts demolitions and block sales which would lead to an underestimate of the proportion of properties sold under the Right to Buy. Unfortunately it was not possible to acquire from the council either a 1995 stock database or comprehensive data on Right to Buy sales in 1995. The result is that the 1980 stock estimate is a slight underestimate (approximately 2% overall) because of the omission of 15 months of data after 1994, plus sales in 1981.

Table 5.6 Average annual lettings and cumulative resales in sub-areas of the Anniesland area of Glasgow 1981–1994.

Sub-area	Average lettings as % of 1980 housing stock	Cumulative first resales as % of 1980 housing stock
Kelvindale	5	13
Anniesland	6	10
Mid Knightswood	7	9
North Knightswood	5	9
Garscadden	5	8
Peterson Park	3	7
South Knightswood	6	6
Jordanhill	4	5
Garscube/Netherton	5	4
Scotstoun	11	4
Temple	11	2
Yoker	12	1
Whiteinch	10	1

Source: Jones & Murie 1999.

In the city as a whole there is a clear inverse relationship between the number of resales in a sub-area and the number of lettings. Average annual lettings during the mid 1990s in the higher turnover estates were over 20% of the 1980 stock. Three of the sub-areas in Castlemilk fall into this mould, the area of lowest sales. This contrasts with the position in Anniesland, the area of Glasgow where sales were highest in 1996. The area is adjacent to established owner-occupied housing markets. Table 5.6 shows that in the most popular sub-areas where turnover is low, cumulative annual resales (or lost lettings) are equivalent to the order of 10% of the 1980 stock, or approaching twice the number of average annual lettings in the early 1990s. This suggests that while the impact of the Right to Buy has apparently bypassed tenants in high turnover estates, the restrictions on the popular estates many aspire to have increased.

These results indicate that if the cumulative number of first resales can be regarded as the numbers of properties lost to lettings then in parts of the Anniesland area of Glasgow resales by the end of 1996 were equivalent to the loss of at least a year's lettings. There are a number of caveats to this conclusion but this gives a broad indication of the impact the Right to Buy has had on the opportunities to rent in one of the most popular areas of the city. At the same time the Right to Buy has hardly impinged on access to the less popular areas. This picture can probably be generalised across all urban areas. Further, the recent trend of increased turnover of lettings in council housing has not balanced out the number of Right to Buy sales because these lettings are to be found in the least popular estates and so an aggregate view masks the reduction in access to the better quality housing.

It is important to remember that each resale is a permanent loss and resales therefore have a cumulative effect on lettings. As Chapter 6 notes, resales in Glasgow started to become significant at the beginning of the 1990s. This suggests that the impact of the Right to Buy on access to housing began as much as ten years ago, and the cumulative effect of first resales, housing lost to the council stock, continues to grow. Some 16.2% of all Right to Buy sales in Glasgow had been resold by the end of 1996. This is further illustrated by research on East Lothian showing that, by 2000, 28% of the homes sold under the Right to Buy had been traded, with the ownership of another 7% having been transferred free of charge (Rosenburg 2001).

Overall the local evidence of the impact of the Right to Buy on lettings showed that it was initially minimal. The position changed in the 1990s with the cumulative effects becoming significant in the popular estates and likely to be magnified in the future with resales accelerating in these areas (see Chapter 6). This is also likely to be true for larger family accommodation. The empirical evidence presented here for Glasgow is probably an underestimate of other areas which have a higher proportion of owner-occupation or are in areas subject to heavy pressure on housing markets such as the south-east of England. Overall the long term effect has been to significantly reduce the opportunities to rent good quality council housing in urban areas. A wider perspective is that there is a profound funnelling of the households with least choice into a more restricted range of neighbourhoods and properties.

In rural areas the Right to Buy operates in a different context. There is often an insufficient supply of housing. Incomers buying former council housing and other housing for second homes are an important force especially in the tourist areas or areas within commuting reach of large employment centres. However, there is not always a serious affordability problem in the deep rural areas (see Bramley 2003). Satsangi *et al.* (2001) identify land supply for affordable housing (including cheaper owner-occupied) as a constraint in many parts of the highlands and islands of Scotland. Development opportunities in many rural villages are limited to small sites, which are often expensive to develop due to their size and location. Land designated for housing by the planning system often exhibits infrastructural and topographical problems as well as ownership issues. In deep rural communities there are also high development costs associated with site servicing and the transport of labour and materials.

The consequence is that these costs are passed on and land that is developable has a high value. In the highlands of Scotland, for example, speculative house building outside of the wider Inverness area is rare and so most new housing is provided either on a self-build basis or by the public sector.

The precise role of the Right to Buy on access to social housing in a rural area can be gauged by a study of South Ayrshire. Table 5.7 summarises key parameters in net loss of houses through the Right to Buy, waiting time and waiting lists in the villages and small settlements in this rural area. The statistics cited are part of the local authority's case to the Scottish Executive for 'pressured area' status (see Chapter 2). The Right to Buy accounts for the loss of over 50% of their affordable rented stock in five villages with one village having lost all its council stock since 1980. The data on waiting lists contains an element of double counting and so cannot be considered in isolation but the numbers are high relative to the local authority housing stock. At the extreme in Loans there are 366 households on the waiting list for only 22 properties. The high ratio of waiting list to stock is exacerbated by very low turnover; this is actually zero in Crosshill. In many other villages the annual relets are in single figures. The waiting times are as a result long; for those that are successful it is often years. The average waiting time for a two-bedroom house in Kirkmichael is 10.4 years. There are very few larger houses let at all.

Average waiting times have evident difficulties of interpretation. An alternative measure of comparative housing pressure is the 'effective waiting time' calculated by the local authority as the ratio of the number of new waiting and homeless list applicants to the number of relets over a given period. Figure 5.4 shows a calculation of effective waiting time. This means, for example, that in Colmonnell there are 61 applicants for every house let. Whatever the limitations or precision of these housing pressure indicators, the combination of low turnover, high waiting lists and small absolute numbers of council houses is a potent mix. Together they amount to strong pressure on the housing stock. The impact of the Right to Buy is a major causal factor in this recipe.

This evidence from South Ayrshire provides a flavour of the rural Right to Buy problem. In rural settlements where the supply of council housing is more constrained and the quality less variable the impact of the Right to Buy has been to reduce access to social rented housing for low income households. In some settlements there is no social rented housing left. This has compounded a long standing shortage of social rented housing in rural areas.

Table 5.7 Waiting lists, waiting times and relets in rural settlements of South Ayrshire 2002–03.

Village	Population	Council stock	RSL stock current	RSL stock prog'd	Waiting list information (April 02–March 03) Local authority					Relets (April 02–March 03) Local authority					Average waiting time (days) (Local authority) (April 02–March 03)				% reduction through the Right to Buy	Shortfall of amenity housing
					1 bed	2 bed	3 bed	4 bed	Total	1 bed	2 bed	3 bed	4 bed	Total	1 bed	2 bed	3 bed	4 bed		
Annbank	854	107			34	59	16	6	115	3	5	0	0	8	1449	2364	N/A	N/A	55	20
Ballantrae	369	50	8	19	13	23	15	1	52	3	3	0	0	6	191	324	N/A	N/A	28	11
Barr	173	13	8		4	13	7	0	24	0	1	1	0	2	N/A	276	127	N/A	43	4
Barrhill	193	11			1	7	8	0	16	0	0	0	0	0	N/A	N/A	N/A	N/A	31	7
Colmonnell	162	24			5	18	9	0	32	1	0	0	0	1	1113	N/A	N/A	N/A	24	3
Coylton	2409	99			41	76	26	4	147	6	3	1	0	10	469	1455	2901	N/A	45	25
Crosshill	544	31	9		17	34	22	0	73	0	0	0	0	0	N/A	N/A	N/A	N/A	51	10
Dailly	908	122	56		9	22	8	0	39	4	2	1	1	8	135	117	821	1213	29	13
Dundonald	2459	228	85		80	97	31	6	214	11	13	6	0	30	258	1038	976	N/A	26	31
Dunure	470	46			23	38	17	1	79	0	2	2	0	4	N/A	958	179	N/A	47	11
Kirkmichael	473	22	11		15	26	24	0	55	0	1	0	0	1	N/A	3828	N/A	N/A	46	8
Kirkoswald	271	48			13	28	11	1	53	1	4	2	0	7	623	716	310	N/A	26	6
Loans	701	22			106	178	69	13	366	1	1	0	0	2	13	1296	N/A	N/A	51	14
Maidens	463	30			17	41	22	1	81	1	3	0	0	4	2278	1267	N/A	N/A	43	13
Minishant	197	49			17	37	21	1	76	0	0	0	0	1	332	N/A	N/A	N/A	31	7
Monkton	661	57			97	185	75	11	368	0	0	1	0	1	N/A	N/A	1591	N/A	55	16
Mossblown	2038	281			43	65	18	7	133	6	16	10	0	32	522	1188	637	N/A	44	34
Pinmore	4	4			4	8	6	0	18	0	0	0	0	0	N/A	N/A	N/A	N/A	50	NK
Symington	1042	72	4		66	120	44	5	235	2	1	0	0	3	1570	538	N/A	N/A	17	22
Tarbolton	1713	305	30		28	38	14	4	84	3	11	4	0	18	564	498	870	N/A	36	34
					633	1113	463	61		43	66	28	1	138						

Source: South Ayrshire Council, used with permission.

Note: The waiting list information is updated annually to remove inactive applications.

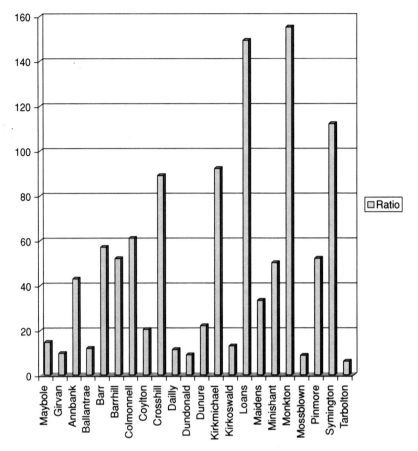

Figure 5.4 Effective waiting time by rural settlement in South Ayrshire, 2002–03.
Source: South Ayrshire Council, used with permission.

Conclusions

The simple arithmetic of an increase of 155 000 new households being formed each year while the net housing stock is currently growing by 120 000 annually means that the housing system is under stress. The cutting edge of this pain is most likely to be experienced by households on low incomes and those who become unemployed or suffer dramatic loss of earnings. Add the fact that for every social housing unit built in the last few years, at least two have been sold under the Right to Buy and the position for these households is likely to be severely affected (ODPM 2003).

These statistics show that the Right to Buy should not be seen in isolation but its cumulative effects have gradually eroded the significance of council housing. The impact of the Right to Buy on lettings did not become substantial until the early 1990s but since then it has had a growing effect on reducing accessibility to council housing. This is seen most strikingly in the growing affordability crisis in the housing system. Local authorities have had to turn to the private sector in large numbers to temporarily rehouse the statutorily homeless, and many of these households spend long periods in inadequate accommodation before social housing becomes available.

Shortages of housing and especially of good quality affordable housing exist in every part of Britain but the influence of the Right to Buy extends beyond simply the reduction in the crude numbers of council lettings. Certainly in rural communities where the supply of council housing is more constrained and the quality less variable the impact of the Right to Buy has primarily been through the reduced access to social rented housing for low income households, but even here the evidence for South Ayrshire shows a differential impact through the lack of large council housing to let.

The effect of the Right to Buy in many towns has been less on households seeking access to council housing but more on those within the sector who anticipated a move to bigger or better housing. In towns, much of the better and larger housing has been lost to those aspiring to move upwards within the sector. If the better housing in urban areas that has been sold is then resold to households who would otherwise have been council tenants this does not negate the loss of opportunity for those who cannot afford to buy and remain in the poorer housing. The consequences are that many people are now living in council housing or temporary housing in the private sector that it is too small for their requirements. There is a mismatch between the type of housing available and demand. In urban areas overcrowding is on the increase.

The Right to Buy has had much less impact on poor quality unpopular estates. The increase in turnover in the sector is partly because these estates now represent a higher proportion of the council housing stock. The corollary is that it is on these estates where the majority of vacancies available to new entrants into the sector are. This housing is no longer subsidised and is not very attractive to households, and not surprisingly those who can choose to buy or rent privately elsewhere.

In Chapter 4 evidence was presented that many council tenants exercise the Right to Buy in order to facilitate movement out of the neighbourhood or their home. In the past households moved from the privately rented sector to a tenure which would provide them with housing for the rest of their lives. Council tenants graduated to a property which they would invest in as their home and where they would form part of a stable community. This is no longer true. The Right to Buy has contributed to a changed, more transient role for the council sector, one much more like that which used to be associated with the private rented sector. This is a role associated with providing housing for people at particular stages of their lives and during periods in which they have limited resources. This role for council housing has risen by default without any conscious policy decision.

This has implications for policies toward council housing. Council housing in 2005 is very different from council housing in 1980. It is no longer the tenure of the working class which itself has changed. Council housing has lost its mantle as a demonstration to the private sector of how to build good quality housing to rent. In this context one of the most crucial debates which has emerged relates to the general position of the council house tenure and council estates. The debate about residualisation of council housing and the increased concentration of lower income households on council estates in the 1970s has been extended from council estates to council housing as a whole. Council housing has become disproportionately the domain of the elderly and the young on low incomes. However, it has some way to go before it becomes welfare housing in the US mould where the public housing sector accounts for 2–3% of the nation's stock and is mainly comprised of flats (Obrinsky & Meron 2002). Social housing ranged from 13% of the housing stock (in 2003) in the south-east of England to 27% in the north-east of England and 28% in Scotland.

Nye Bevan's vision of a socially mixed council housing (see Chapter 2) is now a pipe dream while the sector is also not fully addressing one of its original goals to redress housing shortages, or at least not that of the first decade of the twenty-first century. Shelter (2005) describes the consequences in the report, *Generation Squalor*, that provides testimonies of life for those rationed out by the present housing system. A weakened council housing sector transformed and unbalanced by the cumulative effects of the Right to Buy and other factors has yet to develop a new raison d'etre.

6

Extending the Owner-Occupied Housing Market

The impact of the Right to Buy extends beyond social housing. This chapter examines its impact on the private housing market. The Right to Buy was designed to increase the numbers of home owners but ultimately, for the policy to be sustained and thrive, it is essential that people are able to resell the properties they have acquired. This begs the question of what role former Right to Buy properties play in a housing system with an expanded private housing market and diminished social housing sector. This chapter sets out to make an assessment of the available evidence on the development and sustainability of the markets for former Right to Buy properties. Beyond this narrow perspective it also examines how the private market has changed since the Right to Buy was introduced in 1980.

The chapter begins with a reminder of the tenure structure in the 1970s and the underlying market attitudes to home ownership by council tenants at that time. The next section examines the subsequent growth of home ownership at the regional level and the contribution of sales since 1980. This is followed by a focus on the development of the private market through resales. This includes an examination of the characteristics of the purchasers of these properties and the role of resales within the owner-occupied market. In the final section an overview is drawn of the changed housing market system.

The housing system in the 1970s

To understand the impact of the Right to Buy on the private sector it is useful to consider the housing system of the 1970s, prior to its introduction. The Labour Government's 1977 Green Paper argued that owning one's home was a basic and natural desire, but in 1975 only 55% of the housing stock was owner-occupied in England and Wales, while in Scotland the figure was just a third (DoE 1977a).

At this time home ownership received preferential tax treatment compared with other investments. This primarily took the form of tax relief on the mortgage interest paid by house buyers (phased out in the latter half of the 1990s) and no capital gains tax applicable on a household's main home. Council housing, while offering low rents, began to suffer serious problems as the new council properties built in the 1960s and 1970s were proving unpopular. Many former private tenants had been rehoused through slum clearance programmes into this new housing and entry into council housing in the 1970s was primarily through this route in many urban areas. Private rented housing was in long term decline accelerated by the major urban redevelopment programmes.

The motivations for buying versus renting are complex and are likely to vary by household group. Jones (1982) summarised a number of studies of the attitudes towards home ownership in the 1970s which reflect the relative cost and housing opportunities in the different tenures. A national consumer survey found that 69% of respondents wanted to be owner-occupiers in two years' time, with as many as 40% of council tenants expressing such a preference (NEDO 1977). Other studies put this last figure as high as 60%. Despite these stated preferences only 11% of first time purchasers with a mortgage were former local authority tenants. The largest group of first time purchasers (43%) was newly formed households (DoE 1977b). What these statistics do not reveal is the more indirect transfer process between the tenures by the adult children of council tenants choosing to buy; such households accounted for 36% of first time purchasers during 1976–77 in a study in Glasgow.

As Chapter 2 notes, council house purchase was available on a discretionary basis in individual local authorities before 1980. A study in Leeds in the mid 1970s draws a distinction between the characteristics of council house purchasers and council tenants who move home to buy. It notes the following:

'In summary, the buyers of council houses were comparatively older than those who were moving into owner-occupation. They were council tenants of long standing and their children were older or had grown up and were working. A high proportion of wives tended to be in full time employment and, consequently, household income was only slightly below that of households who made a physical move to become owner-occupiers. Generally, therefore, these households were at a comparatively advanced stage in the family life cycle.' (Jones 1982, p. 126)

In contrast council tenants in the city who moved to buy their home were younger, with more than half the heads of households aged 34 or less, in the first stages of the family cycle, and were predominantly skilled. These households moved primarily to semi-detached and terraced houses.

While only a small number of former council tenants had bought, Jones (1982) suggests that some 30% of council tenants in the mid 1970s probably had a level of current income that was not a barrier to purchase. This is perhaps strange given the apparent high numbers who stated they wanted to buy in surveys as noted above but barriers may have existed such as lack of capital for a deposit or building societies' attitudes toward potential variability in their incomes. These barriers may well have blocked the desire to move house. The evidence from the pre-1979 buyers of council housing in Birmingham is consistent with this (Murie 1975). These purchasers had higher incomes than some households which had bought in the open market. It was not the case that they could not afford to buy per se, but they could not afford to buy such a high quality property as the one they rented so they preferred to continue to rent rather than trade down to buy. However, when given the opportunity to buy the house they rented this was an offer worth accepting.

The growth of the owner-occupied stock

The stock of owner-occupied housing in the UK rose from 12.44 million in 1981 to 18.14 million in 2003. The Right to Buy contributed significantly to this growth in home ownership. But new build for sale outnumbered Right to Buy sales by the order of two to one. The Right to Buy has therefore only played a partial role in a movement toward buying one's own home derived in large part from rising real incomes. Owner-occupation has risen from 58% in 1980 to over 70% in 2005.

The regional perspective, as shown in Table 6.1, is slightly different. In Scotland, the north-east of England and in London the Right to Buy has been more important than new building in promoting home ownership. It has been of least significance in the southern regions of England outside London. The relative contribution of the Right to Buy to the growth of owner-occupation is inversely correlated with the percentage of the stock that is owner-occupied: the lower the level of home ownership the greater

Table 6.1 Components of change in the regional owner-occupation stock between 1981 and 2003.

	New build	Right to Buy sales	Ratio of new build to Right to Buy sales	% of owner-occupation 2003
North-east	131 510	142 857	0.92	66
North-west	354 588	191 592	1.85	71
Yorkshire and Humberside	272 253	184 933	1.47	69
East Midlands	313 333	153 065	2.05	74
West Midlands	300 537	202 436	1.48	71
East	441 887	178 831	2.47	74
London	230 502	270 981	0.85	59
South-east	579 181	198 486	2.92	76
South-west	387 618	135 588	2.86	75
Wales*	166 436	123 609	1.35	74
Scotland	375 171	444 189	0.84	63
Northern Ireland	174 642	108 258	1.61	73

* end of 2003.

Source: ODPM, Scottish Executive, National Assembly of Wales, Northern Ireland Office.

the contribution of the Right to Buy to its growth. This is not surprising because a large public housing sector in a region means a greater potential supply for the Right to Buy.

The transfer of ownership under the Right to Buy simply changes the tenure of a dwelling; it has no impact on the operation of the private housing market. Even if a property is subsequently inherited this has no direct market implications unless it is let out to a household unrelated to the owner. A meaningful market in former Right to Buy properties is essential in the medium to long term otherwise there would be difficulties in the reallocation of the housing stock as household requirements change through demographic change or household break up. Without a resale market, and some commentators initially had doubts about its development, the Right to Buy policy could suffer serious constraints on its success. When properties bought under the Right to Buy become available on the open market, either for resale or letting, then there are also potential ramifications for the existing market in terms of its structure and size. To study the impact of the Right to Buy on the private housing market it is necessary to examine the history of resales and any subsequent private letting (see Chapter 7).

The focus of this chapter is on the owner-occupied market and it is presumed initially that resales are bought for this purpose. The chapter draws particularly on a comprehensive study on the pattern of resales in Glasgow during the first 15 years of the Right to Buy undertaken by Jones and Murie (1999). This case study of Glasgow is the only empirical study to provide a complete analysis of resales within a local area. It provides the central core of the market analysis in this section but it is augmented with other studies to provide a wider perspective. These studies include surveys of households who have purchased former Right to Buy properties and interviews with property professionals.

Resales and the owner-occupied housing market

Some of the early proponents of council house sales argued that by transferring local authority owned housing to the owner-occupied market, a new rung on the housing ladder would be provided and accessibility to owner-occupation would be increased (see the discussion in Forrest & Murie 1990a). This assumed that former council properties would be priced lower than much of the rest of the market. However, the earliest research which addressed this issue cast doubt on this proposition. While the initial stage of transfer from council ownership to individual ownership was carried out at a very low price, this was because of the entitlement to discount linked to length of tenancy. The properties which were involved in Right to Buy sales and in earlier sales under discretionary powers were disproportionately more attractive, better quality and larger houses with gardens (Forrest & Murie 1984a; 1984b; 1990b; Foulis 1985; Kerr 1988). There were fewer sales of flats and acquired properties, of properties in less popular estates and of small dwellings. It was because of this that, at resale, ex-council properties did not fit into the lowest price band but rather entered the market above that level (Forrest & Murie 1990a; Twine & Williams 1993).

It was also suggested that there was a need to distinguish between privatisation, the process of transfer from the public sector to an individual exercising their right to buy a particular dwelling at a discounted price, and commodification which related to the open market sale of such properties (Forrest & Murie 1995). It was suggested that because of the quality of privatised council housing they were commodified at a price above the lowest available in the market. In certain market conditions this resulted in a reduction in the price of alternative properties – flats and smaller pre-1919 terraces, for example. Because these properties were smaller and in poorer condition, less well designed and built, with smaller gardens, and so on, they continued to provide the bottom end of the housing market.

This perspective on the role of former council houses is vividly illustrated by data about who bought former council houses through open market purchase. The only major study providing robust data for England indicated that 51% of council properties were bought by households that were already owner-occupiers (Forrest *et al.* 1995b). In this way rather than providing a first step on the owner-occupier housing ladder they provided opportunities to trade-up in terms of size, space and quality.

Although it caused some argument that there was a continuing discounted price effect which meant that former council houses were priced some 10% lower than other properties of an equivalent size, age and type, it was also true that the market role of former council houses varied. For example, in the north of England where house prices were generally much lower, former council properties were more likely to be accessible to first time buyers and to be bought by households with very similar characteristics to those who had previously sought to rent council houses. Nevertheless, the previous tenure of purchasers of former council homes was still most likely to be owner-occupation and the figures for the three 'broad' regions referred to in the study show that the proportion of former home owners was 48% in the north, 47% in the Midlands/south-west and 58% in the south. In the higher house price areas of the south of England, the size and quality of council housing meant that it was resold at prices that were well beyond the reach of first time buyers, but in the rest of England these properties were still attractive to first time buyers.

The starting point for more recent analysis is the experience of Glasgow, a city with a large public housing sector and owner-occupation accounting for only 25% of the total housing stock in 1981. Some 30 071 council houses were sold to sitting tenants in the city between October 1980 and December 1995. This total represents 16% of the 1980 council stock. Sales rose slowly at first, before accelerating in the late 1980s and peaking in 1990. With new housing concentrated in the private sector there was a significant shift in the tenure structure of the city: owner-occupation rose to 35% in 1991. This represents an increase of 40% in home ownership. Overall, 4277 houses had been resold by the end of the first quarter of 1996, representing 16.2% of all Right to Buy sales. (Market transactions including resales are identified from a land registry database at the University of Paisley.)

Right to Buy sales and resales in Glasgow were lower than in many other places over this period. A study of Scotland (Pawson *et al.* 1997) examined a representative sample of resales up to 1995 in 11 local authorities across Scotland. The average resale rate in Scotland was 19.4%, with resales in urban areas ranging from 16.1% in Glasgow (sample) to 23.4% in Edinburgh and, in rural areas, from 14.8% to 19.4%. Rosenburg (2001) showed that 30% of former East Lothian council houses had been retraded. Forrest *et al.* (1995b) found an average resale rate of 14% in England by 1991 but again with considerable variation, 8–30% over the 35 sample local authority areas. Resale rates were found to be greater in the higher priced areas in the south of England.

In Glasgow the first resales began as early as 1984 but it was not until 1988 that the number rose above 100. During the period up to the end of the first quarter in 1996, with the exception of 1991, resales showed an upward trend with a significant jump in 1992. By 1995 resales had risen tenfold in only seven years. The study of resales in England similarly found that they rose sharply from the mid 1980s to peak in 1988 but then declined consistently each year until 1991 (the end of the study period). Both studies suggest that market conditions have an impact on numbers but undoubtedly the number of resales increased over time reflecting the cumulative impact of sales and the establishment of a resale market for these properties. Pawson *et al.* (2002) also found a steady upward trend in resales throughout the 1990s in four different areas of Scotland. Although resales were gaining momentum in Glasgow during the early half of the 1990s and it appeared houses were capable of changing hands on a regular basis, only 1.5% had been resold twice by the end of 1995.

The growing significance of Right to Buy sales is illustrated by Table 6.2. 'Second hand sales' refers to all second hand transactions and resales which

Table 6.2 Annual numbers and mean prices of second hand sales and resales in Glasgow 1983–95.

Year of resale	Mean annual price of second hand sales	Mean annual price of resales	Annual number of second hand sales	Annual number of resales
1983	22 728	0	6512	0
1984	23 978	23 500	7364	2
1985	26 205	18 499	8137	11
1986	27 539	23 407	9333	35
1987	28 958	26 422	8923	58
1988	30 763	27 017	10 488	183
1989	37 319	30 102	11 113	211
1990	42 079	35 843	11 276	410
1991	44 309	37 434	10 933	157
1992	46 808	40 107	9106	759
1993	47 485	37 495	9425	918
1994	48 775	39 917	8376	948
1995	49 553	40 551	8014	1215

involve former council dwellings. First resales amounted to more than 10% of second hand sales within Glasgow in 1995, and of all resales from 1994. While sales are spread across much of the price spectrum of the city they have had their most significant impact in the lower/middle price deciles. Perhaps because of the increased numbers, (first) resale prices were broadly stationary in the first half of the 1990s while average second hand prices in the city rose by about 20%. A breakdown of these trends by house type reveals that the resale prices of tenement properties fell whereas the prices of semi-detached or terraced houses and four in a block/cottage flats had risen marginally. There are no significant differences in price trends between areas.

The evidence from these studies is that resales began to accelerate in the late 1980s and markets began to be established in the early 1990s. More often than not these properties were priced in a narrow band between the lowest and the average price for all houses. Right to Buy resale properties have traditionally been seen as lower priced than their equivalents but as resale markets have become more established it would be expected that this differential would be reduced. A recent study by Jones (2003) interviewed estate agents on the role and place of resales in the local housing markets of Birmingham, Leeds and three boroughs in London, shedding light on this matter (see Box 6.1).

The results suggest that Right to Buy resales are embedded in the housing market primarily as larger homes for young families to trade up to or as 'starter' homes for new households. These houses are sold at a discount compared to similar non-council built housing although the negative differential varies across regions. In some places resales are 25% cheaper than equivalent mainstream housing nearby but the differential can be much

Box 6.1   The role of resales in Birmingham, Leeds and London.

Birmingham
The study was undertaken in three different postcode areas of Birmingham – Kings Heath, Selly Oak, and Bearwood. The prices of mainstream housing in these areas ranged from below £90 000 to £120 000. Council house resales were generally cheaper, selling in the range £70 000 to £110 000 with a negative price differential of at least 5% and more in Selly Oak (30%). Their key attraction is that they are cheaper compared with equivalent mainstream housing.

Resales have been integrated into the established housing market. The proportion of market sales comprising Right to Buy resales was significant, varying between areas from 10% in Kings Heath to 20% in Selly Oak and 25–30% of the market in Bearwood.

Leeds

The study examined the experience of Morley and Moortown. The prices of Right to Buy resales in Morley are around £50 500 for terraces and £60–80 000 for semi-detached houses, with an average of around £60 500. In comparison three-bedroom semi-detached houses from non-council housing stock are selling for around £100 000.

Former council housing in Moortown is mainly houses although one-fifth is flats. Approximately 70% of the houses are semi-detached and the remainder terraced. The average three-bedroom semi-detached resells for around £70 000 although they can range up to £90 000. In contrast an equivalent three-bedroom semi-detached of non council construction sells for £100 000 plus, with an average of about £120 000.

Resales in both Morley and Moortown are therefore valued at least 25% less than their mainstream equivalent. These sales represent about 5–10% of the market in Morley while in Moortown they are a marginally higher proportion, 10–15%.

London, Havering

Estate agents were interviewed in two different postcode areas – Harold Wood and Gidea Park/Collier Row. Houses are priced in the range £115 000 to £200 000 with former council housing toward the bottom of this price range. A typical former council house would have a value of around £140 000 and a flat around £115 000, although their prices have a wide price range. In the Harold Wood area there is a large council estate, Harold Hill, built by the Greater London Council in the 1950s. This estate is now approximately 85% privately owned and so almost all properties in the Harold Hill area are houses formerly bought under the Right to Buy. In Gidea Park/Collier Row former council housing represents about a third of the market. Ex-council housing stock is generally seen as being of good quality.

London, Camden

Estate agents were interviewed in NW1 and covered the areas Camden Town, Kentish Town, Chalk Farm and part of Primrose Hill. Former council properties in these areas are primarily one or three-bedroom flats. For a one-bedroom flat prices range between £100 000 and £170 000, and for a three-bedroom flat they vary between £170 000 and £250 000 depending on the precise area. In comparison a modern one-bedroom purpose built flat of non council housing origin is selling at £180 000 to £210 000 and for a high specification or a period conversion of the same size the price range is £200 000 to £230 000.

London, Lambeth

The estate agents interviewed all had a focus on former council housing. Waterloo, Vauxhall and Kennington are fairly well regarded as places to live partly because they are accessible to central London. Former council housing in these areas is quite well integrated into the market because of the high demand hence there is little or no discount in price with equivalent properties in these areas. Elsewhere in Lambeth there tends to be a discount and there are pockets of council housing where there is no private market. In these areas former council housing is not stigmatised.

The prices of two-bedroom flats originally sold under the Right to Buy in the central locations noted above range from £210 000 to £260 000 and three-bedroom flats from £250 000 to £280 000. One-bedroom properties are quite rare and sell for between £130 000 and £170 000. Prices are lower elsewhere in Lambeth, for example two-bedroom flats are priced around £140 000 in Brixton.

Source: Jones (2003).

lower, almost disappearing dependent on house types and market pressures. Resales have been integrated into the local housing market in all areas, typically accounting for at least 10% of the market. Former council housing flats in parts of London are readily marketable at prices in excess of £200 000. These profiles are therefore broadly consistent with the experience of the Glasgow market.

Research related to the Belfast metropolitan area provides an additional insight into the role of former council houses (NIHE 2003). This study involved a survey of 200 households in the Belfast metropolitan area living in property that was previously owned by the Northern Ireland Housing Executive (NIHE) which had been disposed of to sitting tenants under the voluntary sales scheme. The sample was drawn from properties purchased on the open market in 1999 or the first half of 2000. The method of selecting the sample means that all of those interviewed were recent movers.

Former NIHE properties purchased on the open market were mainly terraced houses (78%) with some semi-detached houses (19%) but no detached properties. The data suggests that these homes have provided an important addition to the low priced housing stock. Of these properties 69% were purchased for £50 000 or less and 95% were purchased for £65 000 or less. The comparable figures in the Belfast new build study carried out at the same time were 32% at £50 000 or less and 67% at £65 000 or less. The mean price of £47 122 differs little by the previous tenure of respondents though those previously in the private rented sector tend to pay slightly more (mean price paid £48 944).

The previous tenure of households buying former NIHE properties had a very different profile from those buying new build properties. Of those buying former Housing Executive properties 43% previously lived with family and friends (15% of those buying new build properties); 28% had previously had a mortgage or owned a property outright (compared with 62% of those buying a newly built house); 17% of households were previously in the social rented sector; and 13% were previously living independently in the private rental sector. The higher income purchasers mainly came from this private rental sector group whereas the lower income purchasers had a wider spread across the tenure categories. Resale purchasers were younger, less affluent and less likely to be in managerial or professional occupations than mainstream owner-occupiers. Former NIHE properties clearly provided more opportunities for first time buyers than newly built properties. When comparison is made with similar research for England and Scotland, Northern Ireland shows some important differences. A much lower proportion of purchasers of former public sector dwellings were home owners and this holds even if the comparison is with the north of England where the probability of purchasers of former public sector dwellings being home owners was 20 percentage points greater than in Northern Ireland.

Property characteristics of Right to Buy resales

The analysis above suggests that there is a varied experience of resales dependent on house type and location and this is now considered in more detail by reference back to the Glasgow study, introduced in Chapter 5 (Jones & Murie 1999). The research covers 16 administrative areas and 146 sub-areas, each of which is comprised of a small number of estates.

Sales were dominated by two-bedroom (51%) and three-bedroom (39%) housing, accounting for more than 90% of the total. Just over 50% of sales were of inter-war (pre-1948) properties. With 53% of all resales, two-bedroom dwellings were slightly over represented compared with their proportion of overall sales. Three-bedroom housing was marginally under represented in resales. In fact resale rates were highest in the smaller properties, with 21% of one-room and 18% of one-bedroom Right to Buy properties resold compared with 14% of all properties.

A higher proportion of the inter-war Right to Buy properties were resold (17.2%) than post-war properties (14.3%). These differences may partly reflect the timing of the original sales – there was a slower build up for resales of the post-war Right to Buy properties. The rate of resale of tenement flats was just above the city average (Table 6.3), and these sales made up 31% of dwellings resold on the open market. Of the houses the highest rate of resale, 19%, was for semi-detached houses while the lowest, perhaps surprisingly, was for terraced houses. In absolute terms, four-in-a-block (cottage) flats were the most popular property type resold. It is evident that some former council properties, especially high rise (above six storey) flats, can be unsaleable. At the other extreme there are highly desirable properties.

Area resale rates given in Table 6.4 show some correlation between the numbers of properties bought under the Right to Buy and resale rates. Area resale rates varied within Glasgow between 19.8% in Anniesland, which included some of the most popular council housing built in the 1920s in an area located on the edge of the popular middle income west end city housing market, and 7.2% in the peripheral estate of Castlemilk. The

Table 6.3 Frequency of Right to Buy sales and first resales 1980–1995 in Glasgow.

House type	Number of Right to Buy sales	Number of Right to Buy sales as a % of the total	Number of first resales	Number of first resales as a % of the total first resales	Number of first resales as a % of the initial Right to Buy sales
Detached	12	0.1	5	0.1	41.7
Elderly	95	0.4	17	0.4	17.9
Four-in-a-block	8090	30.6	1318	30.8	16.3
Multi-storey/high rise	120	0.5	10	0.2	8.3
Semi-detached	3558	13.5	677	15.8	19.0
Tenement/medium rise	7538	28.5	1235	28.9	16.4
Terraced	7028	26.4	1008	23.6	14.3
Others	16	0.1	7	0.2	43.8
Total	26 457	100	4277	100	

Table 6.4 Area resales rates to 1995.

Area name	Right to Buy sales	First resale	Second resale	Third resale	Fourth resale	First resale rate (%)	Second resale rate (%)	Third resale rate (%)
Anniesland	4951	979	105	6	0	19.8	2.1	0.1
Bailleston	818	106	9	2	0	13.0	1.1	0.2
Cambuslang	1266	144	14	2	0	11.4	1.1	0.2
Carmunnock	20	6	0	0	0	30.0	0.0	0.0
Carntyne/Riddrie	2425	378	36	1	0	15.6	1.5	0.0
Castlemilk	221	16	0	0	0	7.2	0.0	0.0
City Centre North	636	100	10	1	1	15.7	1.6	0.2
Croftfoot	2348	455	40	4	0	19.4	1.7	0.2
Drumchapel	669	115	8	0	0	17.2	1.2	0.0
Easterhouse	680	117	8	1	0	17.2	1.2	0.2
Maryhill	913	161	10	1	0	17.6	1.1	0.1
Mosspark	3544	648	64	9	0	18.3	1.8	0.3
Parkhead	1306	190	15	1	0	14.6	1.2	0.1
Pollok	1521	227	22	3	0	14.9	1.5	0.2
Pollokshields/Govanhill	627	106	10	1	1	16.9	1.6	0.2
Possilpark/Milton	1347	162	12	0	0	12.0	0.9	0.0
Rutherglen	1620	202	22	2	0	12.5	1.4	0.1
Springburn	1540	165	12	0	0	10.7	0.8	0.0
Toryglen	5	0	0	0	0	0.0	0.0	0.0

village of Carmunnock on the city's boundaries had the highest overall rate at 30%.

The breakdown of resales at the sub-area level for the two extremes, Anniesland and Castlemilk, is given in Table 6.5. A rate of 27% was reached in one sub-area of Anniesland where generally this figure was in the teens.

Table 6.5 Frequency of sales and first resales by 1995 in sub-areas of Anniesland and Castlemilk.

Sub-area	Number of Right to Buy sales	Number of first resales	Resale rate (%)
Anniesland			
Scotstoun	463	84	18
Kelvindale	78	21	27
Anniesland	313	53	17
Garscube/Netherton	109	22	20
Whiteinch	52	3	6
South Knightswood	829	138	17
Garscadden	179	37	21
Yoker	87	8	9
Peterson Park	247	41	17
Jordanhill	94	19	20
North Knightswood	947	203	21
Mid Knightswood	1507	343	23
Temple	44	7	16
Castlemilk			
Croftfoot	85	3	4
Machrie Barlia	45	7	16
Glenwood	2	1	50
Valley	69	5	7
Holmbyre	2	0	0
Dougrie	12	0	0
Windlaw	3	0	0
Tormusk	3	0	0
Pinewood	32	6	19

Within Castlemilk resale rates ranged from zero to 16.3%, but the overall picture is one of low sales and resale rates. This again suggests some correlation between levels of sales and resales. Resales in Anniesland began in 1985 and since 1992 have averaged 200 per year, but in some sub-areas of the city, such as Castlemilk, no resale market has developed. Subsequent resales are again biased toward areas where there were large numbers of initial sales.

The findings from the Glasgow study demonstrate that a range of house types can prove attractive to house buyers on the open market. In other studies the characteristics of properties resold has been derived from sample household surveys. Forrest *et al.* (1995) found that 95% of resales in England were semi-detached and detached houses. The flats resold (4%) were predominantly in buildings of three storeys or less. This pattern of resales broadly reflects the characteristics of the total properties bought under the Right to Buy, although terraced houses are over-represented and flats under-represented in resales. However, as noted earlier, Jones (2003) reported that flats in areas of inner London are easily marketable.

The evidence suggests that the properties and areas that are attractive to purchase under the Right to Buy are the same ones that are popular when available on the open market. There is undoubtedly an interaction here as would-be Right to Buy purchasers are likely to consider their home as a potential investment (see Chapter 9). The most popular properties resold are smaller while there is effectively no market for multi-storey flats and certain estates. The lack of investment potential of these latter properties is an effective constraint on the operation of the Right to Buy.

Characteristics of Right to Buy resale purchasers

Studies over a number of years in a range of different locations show a fairly consistent demographic profile of resale purchasers. Forrest *et al.* (1995b) found that a typical purchasing household in England was a young couple with or without children with at least one full time earner in skilled manual, professional or managerial employment. Overall, households were concentrated in the 25–34 age group, almost 40% were in some form of white collar employment and over a third had more than one earner in the household.

They found some regional and local variation in socioeconomic characteristics reflecting individual market structures. Purchasers in the south of England were more likely to be childless, dual income professional workers and the majority were owner-occupiers already. Purchasers in the north of England had a more varied profile with more families and households on low incomes and with more movers from rented property. Similarly Pawson *et al.* (1997) found that resale purchasers in Scotland were likely to be young family households or childless couples, with almost three-fifths aged between 25 and 39 years.

Pawson *et al.* (2002) in a further study of four Scottish areas comprising Edinburgh, Dumfries, Gordon and Badenoch and Strathspey (Aviemore) found a similar common theme of households in the early stages of the family cycle. The most common household type in these surveys of resale purchasers was a working couple with no children (38%). A further 21% were single buyers and 28% were couples with children under 16 (Table 6.6). More than half of the purchasers were couples who were both working and half were in social group A, B or C1. Pensioners made up another 10% (Table 6.7). The Edinburgh sample included rather more single buyers

Table 6.6 Resale purchasers by household type.

Household type	Edinburgh (%)	Badenoch and Strathspey (%)	Gordon (%)	Dumfries (%)	All areas (%)
Single, no children	32	11	6	22	21
Single, child(ren) under 16	3	0	6	0	2
Couple, no children	20	51	50	42	38
Couple, child(ren) under 16	32	23	29	24	28
Single pensioner	8	9	6	7	7
Pensioner couple	5	6	3	5	5
Number of respondents	65	35	34	55	189

Source: Pawson *et al.* 2002.

Table 6.7 Resale purchasers by employment status and social class distribution.

Working status	Edinburgh (%)	Badenoch and Strathspey (%)	Gordon (%)	Dumfries (%)	All areas (%)
Single, not working	3	0	0	5	3
Single, working	34	14	12	16	21
Couple, working	40	66	71	58	56
Couple, one working	12	9	9	9	10
Couple, neither working	0	0	0	0	0
Pensioner(s)	11	11	9	12	10
Respondents in social classes A, B or C1	59	46	56	38	50
Number of respondents	65	35	34	55	189

Source: Pawson *et al.* 2002.

than the other areas. This probably reflects the fact that a greater proportion of resales in Edinburgh will involve (smaller) flats rather than (larger) houses. The proportion of pensioners was small but significant.

It must be noted that all these studies were based on interviews with households occupying former Right to Buy properties who may or may not have been recent movers. As such the sociodemographic characteristics may not be a close reflection of when they actually bought. On the other hand there is a general consistent picture of such buyers at the beginning of the family cycle.

Forrest *et al.* (1995b) found that purchasers of Right to Buy resales in England were almost equally split between previous owner-occupiers and first time purchasers. Of the half who were buying for the first time, some 35% were newly formed households. The remainder were established households moving from (mainly private) rented accommodation. Almost identical results for Scotland were reported by Twine and Williams (1993) and Pawson *et al.* (1997). In the most recent study by Pawson *et al.* (2002), only two-fifths of purchasers were previously home owners. However, all the studies show the balance between continuing owners and first time purchasers varies by the position or role of former Right to Buy property sales within local markets.

The study by Forrest *et al.* (1995b) notes that the local profile of purchasers of formerly state owned dwellings and the price relationships between such dwellings and other properties on the market is related to affordability problems which were particularly evident in the booming English housing market in the late 1980s. For example in the Mole Valley area in Kent, incorporating Dorking and Leatherhead, many resales are bought by first time purchasers migrating from South London. More generally in areas of high housing demand, particularly the core region of Britain's economy (the south-east of England including Greater London), a much higher proportion of buyers of former council dwellings were households with heads in professional or managerial employment and were existing home owners.

In the Mole Valley area on the periphery of Greater London, more than half of the buyers were in high status employment categories and 73% were existing home owners. In lower demand areas, however, in northern England the pattern was very different with higher proportions of purchasers in manual work and fewer existing home owners. For example, in Knowsley, near Liverpool, only a quarter of purchasers were existing home owners. Forrest *et al.* (1995b) argue these lower demand areas typically had disproportionately high levels of council housing, above average levels of unemployment and deprivation, lower levels of privatisation and lower than average house prices. Similar high proportions of first time purchasers were found in the rural area of Badenoch and Strathspey (Aviemore) and in the large town of Dumfries where the local market conditions were different again (see Table 6.8).

The proportion of Right to Buy resale purchasers originating from the public housing sector is also dependent on local tenure structures. The average figure for England, derived by Forrest *et al.* (1995b), was 15%, which included households who were either local authority tenants in their own right or children of tenants. In Glasgow, Jones and Murie (1999) found that 49% of resale purchasers had formerly lived in publicly funded housing. Interestingly, about one in five of the previous owner-occupiers of the Pawson *et al.* resale purchasers survey (2002) were living in former council housing and the majority of them had acquired their homes via the Right to Buy.

Table 6.8 Previous tenure of resale purchasers.

Previous tenure	Edinburgh (%)	Badenoch and Strathspey (%)	Gordon (%)	Dumfries (%)	All areas (%)
Owner-occupier	51	26	53	31	41
Rent privately	11	29	18	22	19
Rent from social landlord	3	11	15	16	11
Institutional accommodation	0	0	0	2	1
Tied housing	2	6	12	2	4
Parents'/in-laws' home	31	17	3	25	22
(All first time buyers)	(49)	(74)	(47)	(69)	(59)
Number of respondents	65	35	34	55	189

Source: Pawson *et al.* 2002.

These studies collectively demonstrate that households which purchase former Right to Buy properties are generally small and at least half are first time purchasers seeking starter homes. These households tend to be at the beginning of the family cycle although they do include pensioners. The socioeconomic characteristics of these buyers, particularly of second time buyers, vary depending on local housing market pressures. Where afford-ability problems are greatest dual income professional families are more often the purchasers of Right to Buy resales. The characteristics of these resale purchasers mean that the original Right to Buy purchasers of the 1980s are being replaced by much younger households, many of whom intend to move on in the foreseeable future as their families expand.

The transformed housing market

In the mid 1970s, 69% of households wanted to be owner-occupiers. By 2005 this percentage had been achieved and the housing system was very different. The typical housing career of council tenants has changed significantly. Prior to the Right to Buy most council tenants who wished to buy a property had to purchase on the open market whereas since 1980 exercising the Right to Buy has been for many the first step toward buy-ing a home. The Right to Buy has removed some of the hurdles to owner-occupation that existed in the 1970s but these have also been moderated by easier access to mortgage lending and other developments. Households which have used the Right to Buy as a first rung on the housing ladder have also effectively pulled it up behind them. The supply of social housing through relets has been reduced while the availability of owner-occupation has increased through resales.

The big question is whether households with reduced access to council housing because of the cumulative impact of the Right to Buy are in a position to afford the housing opportunities provided by resales. In other words, while low income council tenants have a route into home owner- ship directly via the Right to Buy, can resales offer an avenue for low income non-council tenants to owner-occupation? In a wider perspective, if former Right to Buy properties are sold to local people (not necessarily on low incomes) then these resales will contribute to meeting housing need in an area and thereby reduce any pressure on opportunities for low income households caused by high levels of Right to Buy sales.

The evidence of this chapter is that resales are cheaper than equivalent housing not built by the public sector and that households who purchase these properties are generally small and tend to be at the beginning of the family cycle. However, with only approximately half of these house- holds being first time purchasers there is not necessarily a direct link. Furthermore where local affordability problems are greatest, dual income professional households are often the purchasers of Right to Buy resales, suggesting that for these areas at least the resales cannot be a panacea for lost relets.

The issue remains contentious, especially in rural areas, and has become a major policy issue in Scotland where it forms part of the basis for the establishment of pressured area status and hence the suspension of sales. Pawson *et al.* (2002) were commissioned by the Scottish Executive with developing a research framework for local authorities to assess the exist- ence of this phenomenon. The analysis proved far from straightforward and the following paragraphs which outline their underlying theory with regard to the role of migration, local house price trends and holding periods are illustrative of the difficulties involved.

In this study, buyers of former Right to Buy properties from outside the local area emerged as an important influence, whether they were buying a principal residence or a second home. Migration patterns in a local area are therefore potentially important indicators of the alleviation of hous- ing pressure caused by high Right to Buy sales. In particular the micro- dynamics of a local housing market are such that if it becomes generally more pressured households may increasingly view resales as better value compared with close substitutes in the non-council built sector. If a significant proportion of Right to Buy resale purchasers originate from outside a neighbourhood, whether from the wider local housing market or further afield, this is a demonstration of increased pressure on local residents to find homes to buy nearby.

Price increases of former Right to Buy housing are relative to both the local housing market and the market as a whole. Turnover rates or the average property holding period may also be seen as an additional indicator of local market pressures. Resales as starter homes turn over more quickly than mainstream housing market properties and are therefore more susceptible to short term market trends. Demand from a wider (external) group of households wishing to buy these properties will increase prices and turnover when the market is pressured. This results in a relative rise in prices in the lower deciles of the market.

However, it is also possible that if market pressure stems from higher income groups pushing up prices at the top end of the market then the logic turns the market experience on its head. In these circumstances market pressures are such that households occupying houses in the lower deciles are unable to trade up and constrained to their existing home, in other words house prices would not rise in the resale market but the opportunities for potential purchasers in the lower price deciles would be reduced.

Pressure can therefore originate from different sectors of the market and manifest itself differently in turnover rates of former Right to Buy properties. Pressure from below, perhaps from low income households unable to access social housing, may well increase turnover and reduce the holding period of former Right to Buy properties but raise prices at the bottom end of the market. In contrast, pressure from above could restrict turnover of resales, increase the holding period before sale, and reduce opportunities to purchase at the bottom end of the market. This variation means that conclusions about average holding periods of properties must be made in conjunction with other indicators.

Based on these theoretical underpinnings the Pawson *et al.* study (2002) analysed the four case study areas identified earlier. The empirical analysis proved even more complex and was ultimately limited by spatial disaggregation and micro-data that was insufficient for statistical techniques. The evidence from Edinburgh suggested that relatively high resale prices and reduced turnover in this stock was caused by market pressures at the top end of the market. At the other extreme in Dumfries there was a high proportion of locally based purchasers of Right to Buy resales, stable prices generally, possibly falling resale prices and slow sales movement of these properties. The other two case studies gave a mixed message.

The results of this study demonstrate that there is not a clear cut answer to whether resales provide affordable housing to buy for households who would have traditionally been housed in council housing. They reinforce the conclusion of Forrest *et al.* (1995b) that resales are bought by different groups dependent on local market conditions. In many areas resales are providing 'affordable' housing to buy but it is important to remember that for many households owner-occupation is still not affordable. For these households the fundamental availability relationship is not determined by local pressures in the owner-occupied market but by the balance between the demand for and supply of private and social rented housing.

Conclusions

This chapter set out to assess the influence of the Right to Buy on the owner-occupied market. To achieve this aim the analysis looked beyond the simple numbers of home owners created to the specific impact on the owner-occupied market. At the time of the introduction of the Right to Buy there were doubts about the ability of purchasers to subsequently sell their properties which in turn would limit the success of the policy.

Beginning in the late 1980s there was a gradual acceptance of former council houses as marketable investments. Resale markets have matured and resales have been integrated into the local housing market in all areas, typically accounting for at least 10% of the market. These houses are sold at a discount compared to equivalent housing not built by the public sector, although the negative differential varies between areas. In some places resales are 25% cheaper than equivalent mainstream housing nearby but the differential can be much lower, almost disappearing depending on house types and market pressures. The picture is very different from that imagined by some critics at the outset of the Right to Buy.

The same properties and areas that are attractive to purchase under the Right to Buy are also the ones that are popular when available on the open market. There is an interaction between the resale market and the take-up of the Right to Buy – as local resale markets mature and tenants realise the investment potential of their homes there is in effect a second wave of Right to Buy sales. Where resale markets are not established the reverse effect is experienced. The most popular properties resold are smaller properties while at the other extreme the practice of lenders may mean that there is effectively no market for multi-storey flats and properties on certain estates. This lack of investment potential has affected the operation of the Right to Buy.

Households which purchase former Right to Buy housing are generally small and at least half are first time purchasers seeking starter homes. The socioeconomic characteristics of these buyers, particularly of second time buyers, vary depending on local housing market pressures. Where affordability problems are greatest dual income professional families are often the purchasers of Right to Buy resales. The characteristics of these resale purchasers mean that the original Right to Buy purchasers of the 1980s are being replaced by much younger households, many of whom intend to move on in the foreseeable future as their families expand. The consequences for life on former council estates are discussed in Chapter 8.

The Right to Buy has transformed the owner-occupied market extending home ownership down the income scale. The process of tenure transfer has changed since the 1970s with the Right to Buy becoming a staging post for many tenants on the way to buying on the open market. Many households who prior to the Right to Buy would have been housed in council housing are able to purchase a former council home. Yet there remain affordability problems in the housing market as many households who wish to be owner-occupiers are excluded and there are record numbers of homeless households seeking rented accommodation. The reasons for the housing shortage in parts of the UK lie partly in the operation of the planning system and its impact on the supply of land for housing but also on the cessation of house building by local authorities (Barker 2004). However, the impact of the Right to Buy on the housing system cannot be ignored – it has had a real redistributive influence, changing the pattern of opportunity for different types of household in the housing market.

7

Promoting the Private Rented Sector

The planned consequence of the Right to Buy was an extension of owner-occupation but the cumulative impact of the policy has inevitably been to change the structure and dynamics of the wider housing system. The growth of council housing through much of the twentieth century had contributed to the dramatic decline of the private rented sector. A substantial reduction in the supply of public rented housing therefore leads naturally to the question of whether there will be a return of private rental provision for low income households. Prior to the Right to Buy private housing for rent had already been in decline. This chapter considers to what extent the Right to Buy has contributed to reversing that trend and promoted the private rented sector.

The starting point for the chapter is a review of recent developments in the private rental sector. The analysis then considers to what extent resales have been harnessed as part of the 'buy to let' phenomenon. The next section examines the role of private letting companies in purchasing former council housing. Following this broadly qualitative analysis is a more quantitative assessment of the supply of former Right to Buy properties as private rented investments. Finally, the chapter assesses the characteristics of the 'new tenants' and discusses the implications of these findings for public policy.

Developments in the private rented sector

For much of the twentieth century the private rented sector was in decline; rent control and regulation of the sector, as well as the favourable tax and subsidy treatment of other tenures, were contributing factors. The 1988 Housing Act deregulated the sector and relaxed security of tenure. These actions and a range of subsequent government initiatives had an impact in encouraging investment in the sector but by the end of the century private rented property still represented only 10% of the UK housing stock. There is only one major specialist residential property management company quoted on the stock exchange and the sector remains dominated by small landlords.

There is, however, growing interest in this sector across the whole spectrum of the market from housing associations, small landlords, public property companies and a number of residential investment funds established since 1998. Small landlords have increased their proportion of the market as part of the buy to let phenomenon. This was facilitated through a joint venture by letting agents and mortgage lenders which enabled private individuals to invest in property to let without being penalised by high mortgage surcharges. The scheme was initiated in September 1996 by the Association of Residential Letting Agents (ARLA) and four lenders. At the end of 2003 there were 408 300 outstanding 'buy to let' mortgages representing over £39 billion, although some were remortgages of earlier loans, and the Council of Mortgage Lenders reported that more than 6% of all new mortgage lending was supporting buy to let. In 2003 there were 188 000 new mortgages for this purpose, a four-fold increase on 1999.

The success of the scheme has arisen as a consequence of the market dynamics of this period. Excess demand for housing combined with falling interest rates led to a boom in house prices. The role of house prices is important in influencing both the demand for and supply of rented accommodation. The rise in house prices in recent years has resulted in young people delaying entry to home ownership and this encouraged greater renting. At the same time rising housing market prices stimulate investment returns for private landlords via potential capital gains and increasing rents. The stimulus to the demand for housing in the private rented sector has also been aggravated by the shortage of housing in the social rented sector as illustrated by record statutory homeless statistics. This in turn has been driven by the cumulative effect of the Right to Buy on relets and the lack of replacement building. Some local authorities, especially in London, have turned to the private sector to lease temporary housing to meet their statutory obligations to the homeless.

Resales and 'buy to let'

A logical source of properties for 'buy to let' is former Right to Buy properties because the price differentials discussed earlier usually mean they are good value. Research by Jones (2003) introduced in Chapter 6 examined the extent of this occurrence in the inner London boroughs of Camden and Lambeth, the outer London borough of Havering and the cities of Birmingham and Leeds. The study was based on interviews conducted in 2002 with estate agents, property management companies and mortgage lenders in the private sector and housing managers in the public sector. The analysis in Box 7.1 is a distillation of their views.

Box 7.1   Commentaries on Right to Buy resales and relets in Birmingham, Leeds and London.

Birmingham
The picture on reletting varies by location. In King Heath, 15–20% of resales are bought to let out. A similar proportion in Bearwood are bought to let out and 10% in Selly Oak. It is mainly semi-detached and terraced properties that are bought to let. There are mixed views from estate agents in Kings Heath. One agent reports that about a quarter of resales are bought to let by individuals but the market for them is reaching saturation point. The more prevalent view is that sale for rent is minimal, the exception rather than the rule, because Right to Buy properties tend not to be in strong letting areas.

In Kings Heath and Selly Oak there is general agreement that it is only individuals who are buying to let. There are no companies operating in these areas of the letting market. However, in Bearwood one third of buy to let properties are bought by investment companies and the remainder by individuals typically looking for a long term investment to supplement their pension. One estate agent had a client based in London that has a contract to house asylum seekers. Companies usually buy up resales that cannot be sold to first time purchasers because they are in poor condition.

The average rents of former council housing are £350–£400 per month for a two or three-bedroom house. This is cheaper than a typical terraced property outside the public sector, which costs £500–£550 per month. Approximately 10% of properties to let are former Right to Buy properties and these are focused in convenient locations. About 90% of these properties are owned by individuals, although it is difficult to distinguish between individuals and small scale businesses. Tenants tend to be young couples and groups of friends.

Leeds
Virtually all resales are sold for owner-occupation. There is very little evidence of companies or individuals buying these properties to let in Morley, because rents are probably not high enough to make letting viable. One agent in Moortown notes a few have been let out, perhaps 10% maximum, but only by individuals. One agent in Morley is advertising a three-bedroom terraced former council house owned by an individual at £395 per calendar month; significantly more than a council tenant might pay. Other advertisements in the local Leeds press suggest rents of £400–500 per month for properties equivalent to those let by the council for £160 per month. Landlords are normally individuals and there is no evidence of companies active in the market. In some cases properties that are unmarketable through normal channels or repossessions are sold for as little as £3000 at auction.

London, Havering
There is a strong local private letting market and a shortage of rented property in the area has encouraged a high incidence of buy to let by individuals. One estate agent reports that a typical scenario is of the elderly purchasing their home under the Right to Buy, moving in with other family members and then letting their former home out, but this view is not supported elsewhere.

Private rents for former council housing start at £500 per month and are no different to typical rents in the 'never council owned' sector. A two-bedroom brick-built flat/maisonette in Harold Hill lets for around £550 per month and a three-bedroom house for £600. There is one high rise block on the estate that is unattractive to standard high street lenders and landlords have been buying these flats for around £60 000 and letting them out at £500 per month.

London, Camden
One estate agent with 15% of its sales accounted for by former council housing took the view that most of the purchasers of Right to Buy resales are first time buyers, with a minority of individuals buying to let. Another stated that until recently between 40 and 60% of council housing resales were sold for letting although the lettings market peaked around the beginning of 2002. During the boom in buy to let most of the properties for this purpose were bought by individuals but as many as 70% may have been bought by companies subsequently. These property investment companies tend to be small organisations.

These different views may reflect different sectors of the market as the first agent deals primarily with one-bedroom flats. Investors prefer larger flats as higher pro-rata rents can be achieved on these properties.

One letting agent states that most of the properties they deal with are former council houses. The rents charged range from £765–810 per month for a two-bedroom flat to £990–1015 per month for a three-bedroom flat. They manage 100 lettings per year and sell about 40–50 pre-let flats as investments each year.

Some of the individuals letting their property are people who bought under the Right to Buy. Most of these people wait two or three years and then let out. The firm has not been asked to act as a letting agent by recent Right to Buy buyers, except when the household was leaving the area and wanted to let the property from a distance.

Perhaps one in ten of the former council houses in the West Hampstead area, primarily flats, are let out. Many of the properties in Gospel Oak are let to students. In both areas this privately rented housing is mainly owned by individuals and managed by a letting agent. There is very little incidence of property companies owning these properties and letting them out. Private rents for ex-council housing in West Hampstead are around £1700 per month for a two-bedroom flat. It is quite common for a tenant to exercise their Right to Buy and then take on a second mortgage to buy another property. Right to Buy purchasers find that the rent they receive when they let out their property more than covers their mortgage so there is a surplus that contributes to the mortgage of another home, which they actually live in.

London, Lambeth
Companies are attracted to former council housing because of the potential returns. An agent noted, '£200 000 will buy you a period property which will generate a rent of about £250 per week or a 6–8% return in total. The same money will buy a three-bedroom former council flat which will generate a higher return. The main worry is that a downturn will hit the former council sector of the market first. So higher risk and higher return.'

Source: Jones 2003.

The qualitative evidence presented in Jones' study (2003) is sometimes contradictory but a number of conclusions can be drawn. In the areas of Leeds considered there are virtually no resales that are relet except in areas or properties of no interest to home owners. There is greater incidence of reletting in Birmingham but this may reflect the choice of study areas, for example close to a university.

There is a clear gulf between the provincial cities and London. The London housing market experienced much higher house price inflation earlier and had a relatively greater demand for rented properties than the provincial cities at this time. The buy to let market has been much stronger there and Right to Buy resales have been a major source of properties bought to let. Market conditions have been such that some Right to Buy purchasers in London have been able, after three years, to remortgage and acquire an additional property to live in while retaining their original home to let out. There are no constraints on households buying under the Right to Buy subsequently leasing out their property.

Rents of £750–1000 are regularly being charged for former council housing in inner London. Equivalent rents in the provincial cities are broadly half of this level but still above those in the public sector. Most of the former council properties that have been let out are owned by individuals.

The buy to let market in London stalled in the last six months of 2002 because there was an over-supply of rented properties. At that time, as sale prices had not fallen, most people were selling rather than letting out. Since then there has been some modest net disinvestment by these landlords (ARLA 2005a) but there continue to be new investors in the sector (see earlier). Income returns have fallen only modestly from their peak because there continues to be strong demand to rent (ARLA 2004). The continuing interest in this phenomenon reflects a long term belief in housing as an investment and the supply shortages in the owner-occupied and social housing sectors.

The Right to Buy and private companies

In Chapter 6 it is demonstrated how in certain areas (and particular house types) Right to Buy resales have been weak or non-existent and resale markets have not been established. The primary reason is lack of demand but the availability of mortgage finance is also a factor. For example some mortgage providers will not lend on 1960s concrete built housing, because there can be problems with reinforcement, or on any property above the fifth floor of a building, ruling out many high rise properties. Would-be vendors of these types of properties and housing in unpopular areas have difficulty selling to owner-occupiers and this inevitably deflates prices. Many are eventually sold at auction for knock down prices to landlords.

Specialist 'hands on' landlords have emerged in recent years holding portfolios of properties in neighbourhoods with weak owner-occupation markets, including those in inner city areas and Right to Buy resales. These landlords are often small private companies and besides difficult to sell Right to Buy resales their portfolios include reposessions.

For households living in council housing with weak resale opportunities and hence poor investment prospects there is a serious deterrent to their exercising the Right to Buy. The apparently unresolvable problem for these households is how to benefit from the Right to Buy if they wish to move. Into this vacuum came private property companies who operated schemes in central London to accumulate a portfolio of poor quality former council housing from Right to Buy purchasers. The scheme is a forward sale and lease arrangement with council tenants who are eligible to exercise their Right to Buy. This means that the tenant buys their property under the Right to Buy and simultaneously exchanges contracts to sell the property with completion in three years' time to the property company. At the same time the Right to Buy purchaser leases the property to the same company for twenty years. The Right to Buy purchaser immediately walks away from his/her home with a cash sum. Thus the company funds the initial Right to Buy purchase in return for an arrangement whereby it effectively has control and long term ownership of the home. It is immediately able to offer the property to rent. Jones (2003) undertook in-depth research into these schemes including interviews with two of these firms and the next section is based on his findings.

There are perhaps as many as 20 companies who have been active in using such a scheme to purchase council housing in London. These companies were set up in the late 1990s and the scheme operated almost exclusively in inner London for a number of reasons. First, the scale of demand in the area was such that private tenants were prepared to accept relatively poor quality former council housing provided it was in accessible locations. They were therefore especially interested in council housing in inner areas around the river and close to underground stations for ease of public transport. Second, maximum discounts were higher in London than elsewhere in the UK.

The cash lump sum available to tenants who took up the scheme was negotiated between the parties. Companies advertised a range of amounts up to £26 000. With a maximum discount at that time of £38 000 in London and an average discount of £36 451, the advertised range of capital sums available as an incentive to take up the scheme were low. This was backed up by evidence from the National Association of Citizens Advice

Bureaux which, although limited, suggests the sum was £7000–7500. Thus the tenant stood to receive only a quarter or less of the likely discount and the company the rest. From the companies' point of view it was a very cheap way of acquiring a portfolio of properties to rent. In particular the scheme was cheaper than buying via auctions.

According to the companies, the major component of demand for the scheme was the desire to use the lump sum incentive to contribute to a deposit to buy a home. One company reported that about a quarter of people who took up the scheme subsequently moved abroad and some 35% bought a home outside London. Those who moved abroad tended to go to Ireland or Africa. The 30–40% who didn't buy property included up to a quarter moving in with partners, the elderly moving in with relatives (5%) and a small number of young people moving back in with their parents. These figures suggest that at least seven out of ten of these moves would have occurred anyway.

The companies stated that the properties were let at amongst the cheapest rents in central London reflecting the nature of the properties and therefore the scheme fills a hole in the rental market. In 2002, one company was offering one-bedroom flats at a typical rent of £150 per week and two-bedroom flats for £180. Another company noted that its cheapest flat was £145 per week. Most were occupied by young (often foreign) professionals, key workers and students (usually sharing). Some are leased for a minimum of three years to housing associations, local authorities (not necessarily the local authority in which the property lies) and government agencies dealing with asylum seekers.

The precise scale of the activity of these firms is difficult to ascertain. Market trends have moved against the economics of the scheme, the reduction in the maximum discount would have severely curtailed it and the English legislation in 2004 may have effected a fatal blow. Jones (2003) suggests that the number of properties bought to rent by these companies was in the order of low thousands over the peak four year period of its existence, amounting to approximately 6% of the total Right to Buy sales per year in inner London.

Tenure change in former council housing

So far the chapter has demonstrated the potential interaction between the Right to Buy and the activities of private landlords based primarily on interviews with property professionals. A more quantitative assessment of the impact of the attractiveness of Right to Buy properties as private rented investments is shown by a survey of households living in former council houses sold three years earlier (Jones 2003). The survey found that 12% of homes in the case study areas (noted earlier) that had been bought under the Right to Buy were subsequently let out to tenants, either by individuals or companies. In addition, just over 2% of the housing bought under the Right to Buy had been sold on to new owner-occupiers.

In inner London only 74% of households living in former council housing after three years were still the original owner-occupiers. Very few of these houses have been sold on to new owner-occupiers so around 25% of former Right to Buy properties were privately rented. In Lambeth and Camden specifically, of properties bought under the Right to Buy three years earlier, 21% and 31% respectively were no longer owner occupied at the time of the survey. This figure was much lower outside inner London with only 7% in Birmingham, 6% in Havering and 3% in Leeds. These statistics undoubtedly underestimate how many Right to Buy properties are subsequently let out as they relate only to changes within three years but the spatial pattern is consistent with the views of professionals outlined earlier. Of the former Right to Buy properties in inner London 3% were let out by companies and 23% by individuals. Outside London there was no evidence of companies operating in this market with all properties let out by individuals.

The implications of the return of former council homes to renting depend on the characteristics of the new tenants. To examine this issue the analysis here focuses on the 92 households in the Jones survey (2003) who were new tenants. These tenants, as noted above, predominantly had individuals as their landlords, and it is probable that at least 70% of these properties let by individuals were owned by the original Right to Buy purchasers.

More than two-thirds of these tenant households (68%) were comprised of three persons or less, and there were no households with more than five people. All households of more than three people were located in inner London. Across all areas these households were composed primarily of young people with 77% aged less than 34, although the whole spectrum of ages was represented (Table 7.1). Adult only households accounted for three-fifths of the sample, all aged under 60 years (Table 7.2). The overall demographic profile of these tenants demonstrated by this array of statistics is one of small, young, non-family households.

The socioeconomic background of these tenants was quite diverse. They belonged to a range of social classes, most commonly E (unskilled workers)

Table 7.1   Age of private tenants by area.

	Area					Total
	Camden	Lambeth	Havering	Birmingham	Leeds	
18–24	25	23	17	43	100	27
25–34	47	58	50	43		50
35–44	17	8		14		11
45–54	3	10				5
55–64			17			1
65–74		3				1
75+			17			1
Not stated	8					3
Total	36	40	6	7	3	92

Note: Numbers are percentages of the respective column total.

Source: Jones 2003.

Table 7.2   Household types of private tenants by area.

	Area					Total
	Camden	Lambeth	Havering	Birmingham	Leeds	
One adult aged under 60	10	10		57	33	13
One adult aged 60 or over		3	33			3
Two adults, both under 60	36	10	17		67	22
Two adults, at least one aged 60 or over		5				2
Three or more adults aged 16 or over	42	23				26
Single parent family, with at least one child under 16		10	33	43		10
Two parent family, with at least one child under 16	14	33	17			21
Other		8				3
Total	36	40	6	7	3	92

Note: Numbers are percentages of the respective column total.

Source: Jones 2003.

and C1 (skilled, non-manual workers), although the latter group was concentrated in inner London (Table 7.3). There was a similar variation in the total gross income of these households although almost three-quarters (73%) were living on gross incomes below £16 000. Part of the variation reflected regional differences, for example, none of the tenants living in Leeds were earning more than £7279. High income tenants were generally confined to London. Ethnically, almost two-thirds (64%) were white,

Table 7.3 Social class of private tenants by area.

	Area					Total
	Camden	Lambeth	Havering	Birmingham	Leeds	
B	10	13				8
C1	44	20	17	14	33	29
C2	11	8	17		33	10
D	6	15	17		33	11
E	31	45	50	86		41
Total	36	40	6	7	3	92

Note: Numbers are percentages of the respective column total. See Table 4.12 for definitions.

Source: Jones 2003.

Table 7.4 House types of private tenants by area.

	Area					Total
	Camden	Lambeth	Havering	Birmingham	Leeds	
Detached house/bungalow	6					2
Semi-detached house/bungalow	3		17	14	66	5
Terraced house/bungalow	3	10	33	71		13
Purpose-built flat/maisonette	86	83	50	14	33	75
Converted flat/maisonette	3	5				3
Other		3				1
Total	36	40	6	7	3	92

Note: Numbers are percentages of the respective column total.

Source: Jones 2003.

while black Afro-Caribbeans accounted for a further 15%, with the rest a diverse collection of ethnic groups.

Much of the accommodation was small and of low quality. Three-quarters were purpose built flats or maisonettes and 13% terraced houses (Table 7.4). All but one of these terraced houses were located outside inner London whilst 88% of those living in inner London occupied some form of flat or maisonette. All the properties owned by companies were flats or maisonettes. Almost seven in ten tenants (68%) lived in three rooms or less, with only 8% having accommodation containing five or six rooms.

The recorded previous home of more than half these tenants was in the private rented sector. A further 14% had been living with relatives or friends, 6% had been council tenants and only a small minority, 5%, had owned their own home. Almost four in five (77%) had lived in three rooms or less before moving, and three-fifths regarded themselves as better off as a result of the move. Almost a fifth, 17%, had been statutorily homeless prior to moving to their current home.

The results of this survey reinforce the views of the property professionals earlier that the private renting sector is expanding into what was the public sector through the opportunities provided by the Right to Buy. In particular, market conditions at the turn of the twenty-first century led to an unexpected but significant transformation in the tenure of housing bought under the Right to Buy in inner London. Many people who had bought under the Right to Buy in this area were letting out their former home. While this phenomenon was more limited in the provincial cities it was happening, even in Leeds where only 3% of the former council properties in the study areas were privately rented three years after being bought via the Right to Buy. These numbers are likely to rise over time as properties are resold.

The process of tenure transfer is increasing the supply of housing for rent for young people. There appear to be two rental sub-markets of former Right to Buy properties: those with rents below £500 per month and those with rents between £800 and £1000 per month (see also Chapter 9). The latter sub-market only exists in London. The culmination of this process is a change in the occupation of this housing stock – the new tenants have very different characteristics from the Right to Buy purchasers, being primarily younger and non-family households.

The Right to Buy, homelessness and the private sector

In Chapter 5 it was reported that local authorities cannot meet their statutory obligations to house homeless people using their own housing stock. A major contributory factor is lost relets caused by the Right to Buy. To recap, 70% of homeless households in 2004 were rehoused in bed and breakfast hotels, hostels, women's refuges or private sector leased accommodation. The Government, including devolved administrations, has implemented policies to reduce and ultimately abolish the number of homeless families staying in bed and breakfasts. As a result this number fell by 54% in England from the last quarter of 2001 to the end of 2004. However, with the number of homeless households in temporary accommodation rising, privately leased accommodation has had to be utilised to a greater degree.

Homeless households in privately leased housing in England amounted to 55 590 at the end of 2004, a rise of almost 400% on 1997. Some 55%

of homeless households are now accommodated in this way compared with a third in 1997. Four out of five of these households in accommodation that is privately leased or rented directly by a private landlord live in London. The Government states in its homelessness strategy that it is examining options for making greater use of the private rented sector as a source of settled solutions for homeless households (ODPM 2005a). Already some local authorities have developed initiatives in this direction through the provision of rent deposits or guarantees and by offering approved lettings with accredited landlords. As part of its homelessness strategy for England the Government is now considering ways of encouraging the private sector to offer more secure tenancies. This is only one element of the strategy but it is being developed despite the use of private rented accommodation that is currently far from ideal (as discussed in Chapter 5).

Conclusions

The private rented sector suffered a dramatic decline through the twentieth century and council housing replaced it as the housing norm for low income families. The reforms of the 1988 Housing Act did not initially stimulate the sector and it was not until the late 1990s that new investment began to have a substantive effect. This was primarily via the buy to let phenomenon that was encouraged by the housing boom raging at that time in London and the south-east of England. A further ingredient was the shortage of housing to rent in this area brought about by the increase of immigrants, the long term demise of the private sector and the limited supply of social housing. The cumulative impact of the Right to Buy on relets is an important factor influencing this position. Local authorities faced with record numbers of homeless households had to turn to private sector leasing to resolve their housing deficit.

The irony of these market trends is that while the Right to Buy has contributed to the supply shortages pushing up rents that have promoted the private sector, it is also contributing to the sector by being a source of new housing supply. This is via former Right to Buy properties that are either unattractive or otherwise difficult to sell for owner-occupation because of weak resale markets or are general resales that represent good value for money to residential landlords. In inner London many recent Right to Buy purchasers rent the property out and this has brought significant tenure change to the relevant council estates. While the halcyon days of the buy to let market, fuelled by the latest house price boom, appeared to be over by 2005, there remains a strong demand for rented housing. Right to Buy resales will continue to provide new private housing for rent as the original purchasers move on.

The new tenants living in the former council housing are predominantly young households comprising three people or less. Outside London they are generally on low incomes. The tenure changes are increasing the supply of housing for rent for young people but the rents they are being charged are above those applicable for equivalent council housing. In some cases rents are up to £1000 per month in inner London. When these new tenants are receiving housing benefit the state is subsidising higher rents in the private sector having already paid a subsidy through the discount under the Right to Buy. In some cases the new landlord and former council tenant may be the same person.

There must be doubts whether the private rented sector can supersede the public sector in the wider provision of social housing to low income families rather than just young adults who are presently the primary source of demand. The typical buy to let tenant stays an average of only fifteen months and new tenants move after less than a year (ARLA 2005b). The consequences of the return to renting after the Right to Buy is a reduction in the supply of either affordable housing to buy or affordable social housing to let and increases in the cost of housing to the state.

8

Creating Sustainable Communities

In the period since the introduction of the Right to Buy the debate about Britain's social geography has changed considerably. There is a growing concern about increasing social inequality and the concentration of deprivation. These fears are particularly focused upon council estates. It is widely accepted that problems on Britain's mass council housing estates require energetic action and new policy approaches. The Government in 2005 was committed to a large scale improvement programme of council homes as part of its Sustainable Communities Plan. In rural areas there is a continuing debate about the lack of supply of affordable housing. If younger and lower paid local workers are unable to find housing in these areas there are implications for the demographic and social structure and also for the provision of services and viability of some local activities. There are long term consequences for the economic and social viability of these communities.

With over two million sales to date the Right to Buy has had a cumulative and fundamental influence in shaping the composition of former public sector and rural communities. When Right to Buy properties are resold on the open market subsequent purchasers change the socioeconomic and demographic profiles of the community. In areas where the Right to Buy is popular the development of resale markets has meant that homes in these neighbourhoods are predominantly allocated by the market. Meanwhile in areas with low demand for the Right to Buy, housing continues to be allocated on the basis of housing need. It is important therefore to assess more closely how the Right to Buy has influenced the underlying structure and dynamic of communities.

The chapter begins by examining the Government's concept of sustainable communities and the role that the promotion of home ownership and the Right to Buy is perceived to play in their plan for development. It then reviews the dynamics of council housing in rural areas and the implications for sustainable communities. The following sections consider the empirical evidence of the impact the Right to Buy has had on the opportunities for local people to purchase affordable housing, the stability within communities, the changed social mix and the relations between owners and tenants. In the final section the interactions of these different strands are assessed.

Sustainable communities and home ownership

The concept of sustainable communities is at the centre of Government housing policy and has been defined as follows:

> 'Sustainable communities meet the diverse needs of existing and future residents, their children and other users, contribute to a high quality of life and provide opportunity and choice. They achieve this in many ways that make effective use of natural resources, enhance the environment, promote social cohesion and inclusion and strengthen economic prosperity.' (ODPM 2004)

The Government views sustainable communities as embodying the principles of balance, integrating the social, economic and environmental components of their community and meeting the needs of existing and future generations.

The promotion of home ownership is seen by the current UK Government as realising people's aspirations, giving people a bigger stake in their community and promoting self-reliance. It also seeks to encourage local authority tenants to move into home ownership where they can afford to do so, while minimising unnecessary loss of social housing. To achieve this balance, Right to Buy discounts have been lowered and restrictions lifted on the Cash Incentive Scheme so that local authorities are freer to assist their tenants to move out of rented accommodation and buy their own home, freeing up a council home (Chapter 3). The Government is committed to maintaining the Right to Buy as a means of promoting mixed communities (ODPM 2005b).

Like the Conservatives before them, the current Labour Government continues to view the promotion of home ownership as an essential feature of any urban regeneration initiative. This is part of a wider received wisdom that sees the Right to Buy and the development of owner-occupation as increasing stability on estates and reducing the problems of economic and social inequality. The Right to Buy is arguably an ideal policy in this respect because it offers the opportunities to have a fully integrated structure rather than a segmented pattern related to different types or phases of development (Page & Broughton 1997). This perception in turn is set within a broader policy context that views low cost home ownership as a means of tackling social exclusion (Cowans 1999). Introducing new owner-occupiers into an area has also been suggested as providing potential local economic benefits through the boost to local services associated with greater spending power and a different pattern of spending (MacLennan *et al.* 1987).

These ideas came to the forefront of public policy in the 1980s with the promotion of low cost home ownership that encompassed shared ownership and improvement for sale. In particular the encouragement of owner-occupation was extended to the improvement for sale of redundant public sector stock, invariably walk up flats (those without lifts). The policy was introduced in all the major cities in the early 1980s and was subsequently extended to building houses for sale adjacent to council housing, especially in peripheral estates. Through this approach it was envisaged that socially mixed communities would be created.

An early ambitious example of this approach was witnessed in Cantril Farm, on the edge of Liverpool where the Stockbridge Village Trust was set up in 1982 (launched April 1983). The trust, a public/private partnership, took over the estate and pursued a programme of selective demolition, estate redesign, improvement of the existing housing stock, new build for sale on adjacent land and upgrading of local facilities including a shopping centre. It was envisaged that tenants would be encouraged by these developments and seek to buy their homes, leading to an equal tenure split between renting and owning after five years. The forecasts for sales both through new build and to sitting tenants proved over-optimistic, creating financial difficulties for the initiative. Even so, the trust can be seen as the forerunner of what has become a mainstream approach (Jones & Brown 2002).

In Scotland the four Urban Partnerships set up following the 1988 Scottish White Paper, *New Life for Urban Scotland*, all incorporated the common goal of improving tenure choice. Through a combination of new building, improvement for sale, tenants exercising their Right to Buy, and the rent to mortgage scheme, the aim was to increase local home ownership to 20–30% (Scottish Office 1993). The establishment of the City Challenge initiative in England and Wales from 1992–97 identified tenure diversity as central to the creation of community stability, social diversity and the reduction of social exclusion (see Williams 1996). It was also an important criterion in the selection process for funding received under the Government's Estate Action initiative designed to renew and revitalise selected council estates. However, there is little actual research on these questions and the efficacy of these policies (but see for example Pinto 1993; DoE 1996; Atkinson & Kintrea 1998; 2000).

Perspectives on social change in council estates

The discussions in the academic and policy literature about social change on council estates and about what makes council estates work are confused. There has been a long-established discussion in terms of social mix, especially in relation to new towns and estates. Increased attention has been given in recent years to the process of residualisation which has increased the proportion of those living on council estates who are not in employment or have low incomes and have little choice in housing. Some commentators have referred to other aspects of the social mix, including child density (Page 1993; Power & Tunstall 1995) and social balance within estates. Some policy interventions have begun to equate tenure mix or tenure diversification with social mix or social balance. In many cases however these terms are not used with any precision. What is meant by social mix or by social balance and when and under what circumstances are high child densities a problem?

The context for this discussion is one of concern about the downward spiral affecting council estates. Commentators have identified a process through which the differential migration to council housing and particularly less popular council estates forms part of a spiral of decline which affects the life chances of those living on estates (Power & Tunstall 1995; Taylor 1995). The notion of a downward spiral is a helpful one but focuses attention on what dynamics previously operated within council housing. The academic literature makes it very clear that council housing was not always the sector of last resort, especially when high quality, newly built traditional houses were much superior to most of what was available in the private rented sector and even to much that was available in the owner-occupied sector. Nor was council housing an option attractive to those with low incomes: rents in the council sector were relatively high and rebates and housing benefit were not always available. Lower priced housing was available in the private rented sector and even in the owner-occupied market.

From this it could be argued that what made council housing work was its desirability and this fits with the literature, which emphasises the importance of choice. However, other aspects of council estates proved crucial. Significantly, in a period of full employment (such as the one from 1946 to the 1970s), the role of council housing was often to house relatively well paid sectors of the working class, and this might create strong local workplace associations among people living on estates. These well functioning council estates were not necessarily marked by social mix in terms of key social categories. They may have been estates that predominantly housed people from similar educational and social backgrounds with similar occupations, incomes or position in the housing market at the stage in their lives when they first became tenants. However, there was a mix in terms of family sizes, ages, more recent employment history, precise income levels, seniority in work, strength of family and kinship networks locally, political attitudes and how people used their leisure and financial resources. It may be argued that this relates more to activity mix than to social mix.

There was a relative homogeneity of the population but a variation in how people behaved (see for example Harloe 1995; Murie 1997). There were few cases where there was ever any substantial social mix in terms of neighbourhoods that housed a cross section of the population in income or class terms. Where this did exist it most probably related to special schemes such as those operating in new towns and those targeted at key workers and executives. While council housing did accommodate white collar and professional groups as well as skilled manual workers this very rarely produced a representative social mix.

The concept of social balance at a basic level suggests estates or neighbourhoods which have a social mix comparable to that in the population as a whole. Very few neighbourhoods have ever operated in this way and the notion of balance implies a single point at which social mix works. There is no evidence that this is the case. The notion of social balance is idealistic, historical, theological and artificial. It is more useful to pursue the concept of social mix with two things in mind. First, social mix does not represent social balance and there is no one correct mix. Second, it does not imply a mix comparable with that in the population as a whole; rather it implies some variation within communities and neighbourhoods. However there is a weakness even here with a term which emphasises the characteristics of a population rather than the activities within neighbourhoods.

Rather than talking about a degree of mix within the population of a neighbourhood, it is more appropriate to talk about activities and social relationships. The alternative imagery to the spiral of decline is more about functioning communities where social sanctions and community processes make neighbourhoods work for the people living within them. Initially, the sources of cohesion relate to work and work place: when those living on estates worked in a relatively small number of local places of employment, met at work, were members of the same trade unions and so on, this provided the glue which affected how communities functioned. Where households were exposed to similar regimes of work, albeit perhaps in different work places, and were members of similar organisations the common experience and constraints would provide solidarity and cohesion. Households whose opportunities and choices were worked out through similar employment regimes, who used local schools, transport facilities and other public services had some common sense of what was reasonable and in the interest of the community as a whole.

This perspective on the role of work indicates how fragmentation of employment and unemployment has damaged the solidarity and functioning of council neighbourhoods. The rise of unemployment that began in the 1970s weakened the glue that held communities together and the base for agreement over what behaviours were acceptable and what sanctions on behaviour were reasonable. It fundamentally changed the nature of council estates. With the end of the period of full employment and the increased concentration of those without employment in council housing, sources of solidarity and cohesion have been weakened.

The implication of this is that neighbourhoods functioned not because of social mix but because of solidarity and common experiences related to employment and economic circumstances. The lowest income groups were not so prominent in council housing. Those with the lowest incomes who did get into council housing were likely to be living in less desirable estates where the language of decline was evident even in the 1950s and 1960s. Dump estates have always existed. Indeed it may be that it was some of the ingredients of the social mix or prosperity on other estates that created the problems for those living on these estates.

In discussing solidarity and social cohesion, however, it would be wrong to focus purely upon common levels and experience of employment. What is being discussed includes family and kinship bonds and those links which are built up through reciprocal exchanges over a long period. These include situations where children attend the same school and where parents and families interact in helping, watching and supporting their families.

There is no reason why those without employment might not develop strong community and neighbour links. However it is more difficult if there are less opportunities for contact and building links of this type takes time. Newcomers to estates where they have no existing family or friendship links and do not have links through work are likely to start from a situation of social isolation and it will be some time before networks of association develop. High turnover of population within estates makes it difficult to build community.

This discussion suggests that we should be less preoccupied with the characteristics of populations or some idealised notion of social balance and more concerned with activities and relationships on estates. It is not so much the lack of social mix which threatens the functioning of neighbourhoods as isolation and the lack of employment. A homogenous working class community with similar incomes and employment regimes may not represent social mix but did appear to produce functioning ordered communities. An equally homogeneous community but where the characteristics of that community are not associated with work involves a lack of social mix which presents problems.

Marginalisation and economic and labour market inequalities affect neighbourhoods. If the housing system functions in a way which leads to a concentration of those who are most marginal to the functioning of the economy, then there will be problems associated with concentrations of such people who are disadvantaged by exclusion from the opportunities and activities which people living elsewhere take for granted (Atkinson & Kintrea 1998).

The debate does not stop here. The enormous differences in how different estates function cannot be explained just by factors such as unemployment and incomes. It is essential to work with a model in which social and economic attributes and social interaction are brought together. Changes in employment and economic and social structure may weaken the sanctions and unwritten rules which have created order within neighbourhoods. At certain critical points and where circumstances do not change or revert back to what was the norm, these sanctions and rules may be severely weakened. In this context it is particularly valuable to use the term 'order' in the context widely used by criminologists: order which is socially maintained within communities themselves (Ormerod 1997). This is as opposed to external rules and management. Communities and households which are living in a continuing state of emergency are more exposed to disorder and decline. In this context the shift from ordered to disordered communities relates to the pressures and tensions placed on communities, as well as their internal operation and their responses to these pressures.

How does this all relate to the discussion about council estates? The implication is that it is insufficient to be preoccupied with the socioeconomic composition of estates but that the increasingly marginalised position of these estates and the communities living on them is a relevant consideration. Areas which are more uniformly deprived and marginalised are under greater pressure. Existing social sanctions and community solidarity will not collapse instantly but rather will affect the pace and extent of decline or the resilience of the community under pressure.

It is reasonable to suggest that a variety of factors are likely to reduce the resilience of communities and this includes stability. This does not refer to local economic changes because these have already been taken into account in increased marginalisation. There are other things which affect the stability of neighbourhoods and two key elements can be distinguished. First, there is the quality of the built environment and the resources, management and maintenance of the estate as well as housing by a range of agencies, in particular public sector agencies (see Groves *et al.* 2003). These deal with schools, transport, shops, leisure facilities and the social and economic infrastructure. For instance they may make it easier for people to work outside the area of residence or otherwise enable people to succeed and achieve.

The second element is related to family and kinship networks, friendship and reciprocity. The argument is that some of the order, glue and cohesion within council neighbourhoods has derived from family links within estates and the ability of families to support themselves between and across generations and, similarly, supportive and reciprocal relationships between people who have been born and brought up in the same neighbourhoods, attended the same schools and perhaps were employed in similar parts of the economy. These relationships are likely to be more resilient and to enable communities to cope with pressure more effectively than where reciprocity is weak. The stability of population on estates is likely to be a measure of the extent to which these family and friendship resources are evident. Areas with a high turnover or transient population or little commitment and investment in the area are more likely to be disordered and ineffective for those living in them. Social isolation is more likely to be common in such communities.

The analysis above has been expounded implicitly in terms of urban areas but similar arguments apply to rural areas. In the sustainability of rural communities more emphasis is placed on family and kinship networks but the same basic issues apply. In urban and rural areas the key element of sustainable communities related to council housing and the functioning of council housing neighbourhoods is not social mix or social balance in isolation but is social interaction (Ormerod 1997). There is also a dimension of concern with economic marginalisation brought about by the instability of local populations through lack of opportunities or high turnover.

The Right to Buy and sustainable communities

It has been argued that the key to sustainable communities is a stable population and housing opportunities that meet the needs of existing and future generations. The potential role of the Right to Buy in supporting this process is by meeting the increasing aspirations of households to buy a home in their local communities either immediately or subsequently through resales. However, there are counter concerns that the impact of sales may destabilise areas via the introduction of new households from outside of the area and the operation of market forces. In addition the differential sales within urban areas may have implications for the dynamics of communities even where Right to Buy sales have been minimal through its wider impact on social housing allocation policies.

The implications of differential sales can be worked through by simplifying into two kinds of estate, the desirable and undesirable. The less desirable have lower rates of sale and as a result these areas may become even more exposed to the high turnover of lettings and the process of residualisation identified in Chapter 5. Reduced stability could increase the spiral of decline. The desirable estates with high levels of sales are to some extent insulated from this potential spiral of decline and instability. However, the introduction of market forces leads to a different set of issues. The market segment within these neighbourhoods may provide a stable, long term housing resource through the development of sustainable resale markets, but these market segments could become increasingly transitional because of their role within the wider local housing market. For example, an area becomes a locus for low income owner-occupiers and the once stable desirable council estate becomes a neighbourhood suffering from high levels of mortgage foreclosure, high sales turnover and an increase in private tenancy.

It is these questions which are considered by reference to a number of case studies. First, the analysis examines the opportunities proffered by resales to local residents. Second, the impact of the Right to Buy on the stability of estates is considered. The following section examines the social mix implications for the new communities created by the Right to Buy.

Housing opportunities to local people

As noted above a potential positive role of resales in achieving sustainable communities is as providers of affordable houses to buy for local households. This would enable people brought up in an area to continue to live in the same neighbourhood or community as owner-occupiers. The goal can be seen in the context of a local housing estate or rural village. In this way local community links could be continued, even strengthened, by enabling people who wish to buy to stay locally. Thus generations are able to live close to each other.

Some evidence on this is given by the household survey of resale purchasers by Pawson *et al.* (2002) in four areas of Scotland (see Chapter 6 for details). About seven in ten of the resale purchasers interviewed moved into their current home as 'existing households' and only two-fifths of purchasers were previously home owners. Some 90% of these households had previously lived in the same region of the country as their current home, but only about six in ten were previously living in the same settlement, neighbourhood or area. These findings are consistent with other studies of resale purchasers that have found the majority of moves were over short distances (for example Pawson *et al.* 1997).

In the rural area of Badenoch and Strathspey, including the town of Aviemore, over half the purchases had been made by people moving within the same settlement so sales were dominated by indigenous demand (Table 8.1). The results for Edinburgh were similar with almost three-quarters of resale purchasers moving within the city. Estate agents reported that many purchasers of former Right to Buy stock were local or had local connections, perhaps having been brought up on the council estates. Many were second time buyers moving from small flats in the inner part of the city.

Table 8.1   Location of previous home of resale purchasers.

Location of last home	Edinburgh (%)	Badenoch and Strathspey (%)	Gordon (%)	Dumfries (%)	All areas (%)
Same settlement/neighbourhood	29	51	6	18	26
Elsewhere in same area	42	17	24	36	32
Elsewhere in same region	23	11	46	31	29
Elsewhere in Scotland	6	15	15	11	9
Outside Scotland	0	6	9	4	4
Number of respondents	65	35	34	55	189

Source: Pawson *et al.* 2002.

Former Right to Buy properties in the other two study areas had more open markets. Only about one in five resale purchasers in Dumfries moved within the same settlement but this may be misleading as these households moved on average around five or six miles. In Gordon the position was more extreme: only 30% had lived in the same area, reflecting its proximity to Aberdeen and the dormitory suburb of Westhill. Estate agents saw purchasers of former Right to Buy properties in this suburb as predominantly either first time purchasers or existing buyers on a tight budget, many moving out from Aberdeen.

In terms of the original hypothesis that resales support sustainable communities by providing opportunities for people to purchase affordable homes in the areas where they were brought up, what can be interpreted from this research? The analytical problem is that most house buyers move only short distances within their existing settlements or within local submarkets (Jones 2002; Jones *et al.* 2004). Certainly it would seem that resales do offer such opportunities but because of the open nature of housing markets they also afford opportunities to other households. Even in relatively 'closed' deep rural housing markets, resales are often purchased by 'incomers'. Resales are not the cheapest housing available, as the Edinburgh example illustrates, but offer good value within the context of a local housing market. As such, resales inevitably attract buyers from beyond the immediate community and there is no guarantee that these buyers will not outbid local demand. This is highlighted most in tourist areas where resales may become second homes or retirement homes.

Stability on council estates

The impact of the Right to Buy on the stability on council estates is now assessed. As a precursor to this analysis it is worth recalling that Chapter 5 draws a picture of a high proportion of tenants on the more popular, and historically stable, estates exercising the Right to Buy whereas sales are minimal in the poor quality unpopular estates where there is a high turnover of tenancies. Chapter 4 also notes that Right to Buy purchasers are most likely to be a two parent family with children at school who have the express intention of moving away from the estate they are living on within a few years. At the same time Chapter 6 finds that households who purchase former Right to Buy housing are generally small and at least half are first time purchasers seeking starter homes. These households tend to be at the beginning of the family cycle although they do include pensioners.

One study of the impact of the Right to Buy on the large Wester Hailes estate on the edge of the city of Edinburgh illustrated these patterns through interviews with Right to Buy purchasers who had moved and resale purchasers (Murie 1994). Wester Hailes is identified in Chapter 5 as a low sales estate. A most revealing response in the survey of Right to Buy purchasers was that 61% (higher than figures from studies referred to in Chapter 4) had expected that when they bought their property it would help them to move out of the area and they did not expect to stay for a long time. Only 22% indicated that they had expected to continue living indefinitely in Wester Hailes at the time of purchase. Over half (55%) of resale purchasers expected to move in the next five years suggesting the creation of a relatively unstable owner-occupied sector.

A study by Jones and Murie (1999) took a wider perspective by examining stability across the whole spectrum of estates in Birmingham and Glasgow. Before turning to the results it is important to note that there are problems with analysing some of this data. Definitions of estates for management purposes may not accord completely with those which would be ideal for research. Administrative data also partly reflects policy and practice and for example data on refusals of offers cannot be taken as an indication of differential demand because it will reflect the offer practices within a local authority. Properties which are regarded by allocators as being in low demand may only be offered to those with little or no choice and hence refusal rates may not be particularly high in these areas. For smaller estates the number of lettings is inevitably low and a small number of lettings may give a false impression of the rate of turnover. On small estates, annual fluctuations will also be much more marked. At the same time the number of lettings itself may indicate a number of different factors and not just popularity, for instance, the age profile of the population or the proportion of elderly persons dwellings.

With these provisos some indicative data is now presented to illustrate the links between evidence on the Right to Buy and turnover in the remaining council housing stock and the privatised stock in the two cities. For Birmingham the study examined the relationships between sales and turnover and a range of other linked letting indicators within the local authority rental stock at estate level. In order to present the results in a manageable form the study presented data only for the 25 estates with the highest level of sales and the 25 with the lowest level of sales in each city. In Birmingham the study analysed the relationship between the proportion of the council stock which was sold between 1979 and 1995 and lettings indicators. The contrasts between these two groups of estates, the highest and lowest sellers, presented in Table 8.2, were consistent with

Table 8.2 Letting indicators of council estates in Birmingham with high and low levels of sales.

	Top 25 sellers	Lowest 25 sellers
% sales (range)	34–68	2–14
Median	39	10
Size of estate (range)	50–4935	77–3256
Median	332	756
% houses (range)	31–92	0–85
Median	74	20
Allocations 1994–7 as % stock 1995 (range)	15–42	19–72
Median	20	45
Average points level (range)	31–196	6–181
Median	96	73
% lettings to homeless (range)	5–50	3–66
Median	24	41
% lettings to transfers (range)	4–57	0–30
Median	15	10

Source: Jones & Murie 1999.

the broad pattern indicated by the whole data set. There are not exclusive distinctions between indicators relating to these estates but rather a marked pattern of probabilities.

Both the high and low selling estates included a great variation of sizes of estate, although the high selling estates were more likely to be smaller. A more dramatic contrast related to dwelling type. The high selling estates had between 31% and 92% of their properties as houses. The lowest selling estates had between zero and 85% of their properties as houses. However, the median was 74% amongst high sellers and only 20% amongst low sellers. The overlap between these two groups of estates in terms of dwelling types was considerable but they clustered at different ends of the distribution. The same pattern applied in relation to allocations. The range of turnover in the stock overlapped enormously. Allocations made between 1994 and 1997 represented between 15% and 42% of the stock amongst the high selling estates. In contrast allocations were between 19% and 72% amongst the low selling estates but the median figures indicate what their relative positions were in the distribution. The median position for the high sellers was 20% and for the low sellers 46%.

Council housing in the city is allocated to households based on a points system reflecting a household's housing requirements and the urgency of their housing need. The average number of points which households had when they were allocated to properties on the estates showed a similar pattern. There was a wide variation in point levels but the median points level was significantly higher amongst the high selling estates than the low selling estates. Finally, the likelihood of households being allocated from the homelessness route or being transferred from other council housing showed a consistent pattern. The high selling estates were less likely to have a high proportion of lettings to homeless people (median 24%) than the low selling estates (41%) and the high selling estates were more likely to be recipients of transfer lettings (15%) than the low selling estates (10%). This data indicates that estates with lower turnover in the rented stock were also the high selling estates, thereby confirming the arguments presented in Chapter 5.

The research in Glasgow was able to go further because the Sasines land register provided data on the sale of properties and the city council provided data on the turnover of local authority stock. Hence it was possible to directly compare the turnover of properties sold under the Right to Buy and the rates of turnover in the market. For Glasgow the following indicators were estimated:

(1) Average turnover in public sector sub-areas as % of 1996 stock.
(2) Annual turnover of resales in 1995 as % of Right to Buy sales sold in each sub-area.
(3) Absolute numbers of turnover in public sector added to resales in 1995 and expressed as % of 1980 stock.

The calculation of these three indicators is shown in Table 8.3 for the estates where the highest and lowest sales rates occurred. Turnover in the private sector was higher in only two sub-areas, one of which, Carmunnock, is a small village on the Glasgow boundary. For most sub-areas Right to Buy resales turnover was significantly less than lettings turnover in 1996, and in the estates with the lowest sales the Right to

Table 8.3 Turnover in council estates in Glasgow with high and low levels of sales in 1995.

Indicator	Top 25 sellers			Lowest 25 sellers		
	Range	Median	Mean	Range	Median	Mean
Turnover of lets as % of 1996 stock	7–23	12	10	4–26	19	21
Resales as % of total Right to Buy sales	5–25	7	6	0	0	0
Lets and resales as % of 1980 stock	6–22	11	9	4–26	18	20

Source: Jones & Murie 1999.

Buy had had no effect whatsoever on turnover of the housing stock. In estates where the Right to Buy had been most popular overall turnover was approximately half that of the least popular estates. In the most popular estates it seems that, at least up until the mid 1990s, the Right to Buy reduced local turnover.

Although caution should be exercised about the precise detail of this kind of data, the above shows that sales and resales are linked inversely to turnover in council estates. High sales occurred in what were traditionally stable council estates. The analysis suggests the likely causal relationship is that low turnover estates lead to high sales. Right to Buy resales appear to have had no direct effect on the stability of the estates with the highest turnover but they seem to have reduced turnover in the already low turnover desirable estates in the short to medium term. Fears of the former stable public sector communities spiralling into transient areas as a result of the Right to Buy do not seem to have materialised. However, the expansion of resales as these markets mature and the attraction of this housing as starter homes will have seen turnover rise since the study. Overall turnover appears to have increased in all communities and the Right to Buy has not changed the pecking order of the stability of communities although it has altered their social composition.

Social mix and stability

The role of the Right to Buy in shaping communities extends beyond simply the levels of turnover in individual estates. Chapter 5 discusses the causal link between the Right to Buy and declining housing opportunities in the sector. In effect the exclusion of properties from the rental stock had a slow cumulative effect in closing off the neighbourhoods with the most popular housing to new applicants, as well as to those tenants seeking transfers. At the same time the Right to Buy has encouraged council tenants with access to the financial resources to purchase their homes. Today, as Chapter 5 notes, council tenants are predominantly economically inactive, many are unemployed and benefit dependent and their number includes a considerable proportion of lone parents. In addition there has been a change in the characteristics of households seeking entry to the council housing sector with a high proportion of statutorily homeless households and young people. The implications for communities can be seen by considering the most and least desirable estates.

Households constrained by low incomes and minimal choice had been concentrated in the less desirable dwellings and estates before the Right to Buy (English 1979). There are a range of commentaries which have suggested that the high turnover on these estates is largely a function of housing management and allocation policies (Young & Lemos 1997; Power & Tunstall 1995). It is important to review management policies in this context. For example where households are allocated to low demand dwellings in high turnover estates unconnected with their existing social networks and where people are out at work, the likelihood of social isolation is considerable. The problems experienced by households are a mix of those related to work, to income, to housing and to isolation. Unless these properties are removed from the dwelling stock the problems are experienced by whoever moves into them and the management tasks relate to managing a low demand stock. However, the process which leads to a concentration of those with least choice and bargaining power in the labour market in these estates is not simply about allocation policies and changes in these will not be sufficient to change the role and social profile of the most residualised estates.

It is unlikely that these are the fundamental factors operating in the most residualised estates. In these areas the driving influences relate to demographic change and demand, the local economy, the position of the estate in the housing market and the preferences associated with dwelling types, locations and the range of services and opportunities afforded by an area. These three factors are inter-related. The concentration of the sections of the community with fewest skills and least opportunities in employment on certain estates is all to do with lack of bargaining power and the pattern of offers and refusals within council housing and cannot simply be attributed to allocation policies. There is a need to review more widely the factors which lead to a concentration of people in estates which offer few opportunities. Certainly the effect of the Right to Buy has been to reduce the alternatives for tenants and for managers and to increase the likelihood of concentrations which will affect opportunities.

By 2005 avenues out of these estates were even more constrained and the proportion of economically inactive much greater. Households are unlikely to become rooted and attached to these neighbourhoods because their circumstances are themselves less stable. The concentration of instability deriving from economic and demographic factors is focused upon the least popular part of the council housing stock which has dwellings available to rent. The hypothesis must be that the combination of factors affecting these neighbourhoods further destabilises them and makes them less attractive to live in. It inhibits the development of ordered relations within the neighbourhoods. The higher turnover of population prevents the formation of strong reciprocal relationships and the environment of constrained public expenditure and greater economic inequality puts more pressure on households than existed before. This is a recipe for the creation of disordered, unstable neighbourhoods to a much greater extent than in the past.

The social glue of these neighbourhoods is potentially further undermined by the introduction of private tenants. In Chapter 7 it was demonstrated how in these undesirable areas Right to Buy resale markets are weak and many of the resales have been bought up by landlords. This brings with it more instability as private tenants tend to be very mobile; as noted earlier a typical private tenant stays an average of only 15 months in their home and new tenants tend to move after less than a year (ARLA 2005b). Overall the Right to Buy has magnified the destabilisation forces in the less desirable estates.

In the more desirable estates where the Right to Buy achieved much higher levels of sales the picture is very different. Prior to the Right to Buy these neighbourhoods were seen as stable with concentrations of older tenants and little or no turnover. As discussed earlier many of these tenants had a very similar socioeconomic background. At first the Right to Buy probably had little influence on these areas as the initial group of purchasers did not generally buy with a speculative intent but intended to stay in their home for the rest of their lives. However, as Chapters 5 and 6 show, this changed in the 1990s as resales began. In the subsequent decade resales became established as properties offering good value for money and in particular took on a role in the wider local housing market as starter homes or homes for households at the beginning of the family cycle.

As homes for households in the pre-child and child bearing stages of the family cycle it is likely that these estates are subject to a regular turnover of sales. It would be wrong to argue that this will be true in all cases. Large properties in rural areas and small towns, often forming small estates in good locations, may immediately be attractive and achieve a market role that means there is relatively little turnover. However, in many of the larger estates in cities, former council properties will often be seen as family homes for a short period, rather than for the rest of peoples' lives. Turnover is therefore higher than in the pre-Right to Buy era but may not be as high as the in the remaining council owned stock (Table 8.3).

The social composition of these estates since the Right to Buy was introduced has undergone a significant transformation compared with the less dramatic and reinforcing changes on the less desirable estates. The residents are on the whole younger but there is an economic chasm between the owners and the tenants. As Chapter 6 indicates resale purchasers are often in white collar occupations with more than a third having more than one earner. Most of these households are car owners. This contrasts with council tenants predominantly on state benefits and with only a third owning a car. This has major implications for social relations on these estates.

Some perspective on this can be derived from the research of Atkinson and Kintrea (1998; 2000) who looked at the impact of new houses built for sale on or adjacent to three council estates in Scotland. Based on an empirical study of diaries of occupiers they found that the new owner-occupiers and tenants had distinct lifestyles. They found that many tenants lived lives that were confined to relatively small areas and that they came into speaking contact with relatively few outsiders. Much of the tenants' lives were centred around the local neighbourhood including friends, relatives, local shops and leisure facilities. Patterns of social life were undoubtedly similar to life on council estates 50 years ago. Many owner-occupiers only used the estate as a home base and they seldom or never used their local shops or visited friends locally. If they had family members living on the estate they visited them more infrequently than local tenants. The one focal point for both owners and tenants was the local primary school.

Atkinson and Kintrea (1998) developed a typology of residents set out in Table 8.4 that distinguished between 'metropolitan owner', the 'would-be local' owner, tenants who were the 'stalwart of the community' and the 'disconnected local'. Metropolitan owners had purchased in the area because the housing was affordable. Their contacts with other residents were very limited and they were likely to move elsewhere relatively quickly. Would-be locals had bought in the area because they had some local connection such as relatives nearby or they were brought up in the area. These households would like to move eventually to larger accommodation in the area.

The research by Atkinson and Kintrea was about newly built houses for sale in public sector communities but the results are applicable here because undoubtedly the elements of the demand for this housing overlap with the demand for resales. Similarly the tenants' profiles are applicable to residents on any council estate. The evidence suggests that the successful introduction of tenure mix into a community, via high sales in the most desirable areas, does not necessarily change the relationships and dynamic of the population of council tenants. Part of the reason lies in the home-centred lives that now dominate society. The long term key to truly mixed communities lies in persuading young families to stay in an

Table 8.4 Typology of owner and tenant residents.

	The 'metropolitan owner'	The 'would-be-local'	The 'stalwart of the community'	The 'disconnected local'
Family status	Single or couple	Young family	Couple with older/grown up children	Older single person/single parent
Job(s)	Full time	Full time	Part-time/voluntary	None
Balance of activities off/on estate (%)	90/10	65/35	50/50	20/80
Local social contacts – relatives	No relatives	Some relatives on one side of the family	Some relatives on both sides of the family	Majority of relatives live locally
Local social contacts – others	Hates tenants' kids; knows a few fellow owners.	Knows neighbours who are owners; knows some renters through school	Knows everybody, even some of the owners	Knows neighbours; thinks owners are snobby
Use of local facilities	Never except shops if desperate for milk/cigarettes, etc.	Moderate; does a little local shopping; uses schools	Extensive; however, does weekly shopping off estate at superstore	All the time; rarely goes elsewhere
Feels part of community	What community?	Sometimes but 'keep themselves to themselves'	Definitely	Not much
Typical leisure	Visiting friends Eating out Drinking at home	Her: focused on children; Him: plays sport/goes to gym	Something at the Community Centre; walking dog; coaching boys' football team	Baby-sitting for aunt/niece; watching TV
Transport	Access to car	Owns a car	Bus/gets lifts/bicycle	Walk/bus
Aspirations	Move to a better area or to a better job in another town	Move to a bigger house	Stay in area; campaign for better facilities; exercise Right to Buy	None
Sum up	Outsider	The foot soldiers for social inclusion	Estate focused but not excluded	Socially excluded

Source: Atkinson & Kintrea 1998.

area and the development of activities from interaction centred on the primary schools in the first instance.

The analysis above suggests that the Right to Buy at least in the short term is not creating a mixed or even a stable community, rather the outcome is the creation of parallel communities. The Right to Buy is not impinging strongly on the life of council tenants except in reducing their housing opportunities. It also seems unlikely that opening access to council housing neighbourhoods for affluent households will have the effect of connecting council tenants in these neighbourhoods back into the world of work and affluence. It is possible that the increase in white collar workers resident via resales in a particular area may reduce stigmatisation in the labour market for remaining tenants. However, the less desirable estates that suffer from this problem are where Right to Buy sales are lowest.

Conclusions

Community life in rural and urban areas today is on the whole very different from that of 1980. Many of these changes have been brought about by the changing structure of the economy, social trends and attitudes, and the demographic composition of the population. These changes have been reflected differentially in the lives of tenants and owner-occupiers. The Right to Buy has been a significant contributory factor as part of the processes influencing the housing market. However, the scale of change has been such that it is difficult to assess the counterfactual question about what would have been the position had Right to Buy sales not occurred.

The received wisdom in Government is that expanding owner-occupation into public sector communities encourages sustainability by ensuring greater social mix and social cohesion, promotes inclusion and strengthens economic prosperity, and helps to meet the needs and aspirations of existing and future generations. The Right to Buy is seen as one element in this wider strategy that ensures opportunities for affordable homes to purchase in areas where people were brought up and improves social mix. However, the traditional uniformity of social structure on council estates and argues that the essential dynamics of sustainable communities related to council housing and the functioning of council housing neighbourhoods is not about social mix or social balance in isolation but is about activities and relationships on estates.

In terms of its role as providing affordable housing for local people to buy the Right to Buy is restricted by market forces that necessarily ensure openness. Right to Buy resales offer value for money and so attract a range of households, not all with local connections, especially in urban areas and rural areas within commuting reach of large employment centres. As the empirical analysis demonstrates even in relatively 'closed' deep rural housing markets resales are purchased by outsiders, some of whom are retiring or buying a second home. Thus resales on their own are not sufficient to ensure the long term social cohesion and viability of rural areas or balance the loss of social housing supply lost through the Right to Buy.

In urban areas the coincidence of Right to Buy sales and a period of widening social inequality has exacerbated the funnelling of poorer sections of the community or marginalised groups into the least desirable estates. Obtaining a house in these neighbourhoods, whatever condition and quality, demonstrates some elements of social disadvantage by tenants. At the same the changes in the characteristics of the council tenant population, encouraged by the Right to Buy siphoning off those with financial resources, has meant that the council housing stock is subject to higher turnover. The Right to Buy has therefore destabilised the remaining council housing stock and the least desirable estates in particular. This has inevitably increased social exclusion and economic marginalisation and reduced the sustainability of communities in these areas through the instability of local populations. The precise scale of this problem depends on much wider questions about the development of cities and regions and their economies.

In contrast the high sale estates in high demand areas retain relatively stable populations if less stable than in 1980. Initially sitting tenant purchasers, who in the main intended to spend the rest of their lives in their homes, formed the backbone of stability on these estates. The Right to Buy did not increase stability but nor did it reduce it. However, as resales have become prevalent, Right to Buy purchasers have bought with the intention of moving and, as resale purchasers have tended to be in the early stages of the family cycle, the Right to Buy has instigated higher turnover. Former council properties are proving attractive to many households as starter homes and as a result in the longer term this housing will come more regularly onto the market. However, in the mid-1990s turnover in the market sector of these estates was still lower than in the rented sector.

Differentiation between council estates now includes differentiation in terms of the level of home ownership on those estates. The introduction of the market into once very successful and stable public sector communities creates the risk of neighbourhood decline through for example housing abandonment. The evidence from Glasgow and Birmingham is, judging by the stability measures, that this has not occurred and the previous social standings of neighbourhoods remain broadly stationary. The most desirable areas continue to have the lowest level of turnover in their rented sectors and attract the highest level of sales and resales.

In the desirable estates an important policy issue is the potential social inclusive spillover effects that arise from the introduction of relatively affluent owners into these areas through resales. However, the evidence from new house buyers in public sector communities suggests that the Right to Buy, at least in the short term, is not promoting links between owners and tenants. Owners tend to have at least one member in full time employment while tenants are predominantly economically inactive. Life for many council tenants is very localised and little different from that in the 1950s whereas many owners are car owners and have much more spatially open life styles. There are different communities living alongside each other but leading very different lives. Owners, with the exception of the local primary school, use very few of the local facilities. At least in the short term the Right to Buy appears to have had a minimal effect on reducing unemployment prospects of the tenants in these areas.

The arguments in favour of the Right to Buy based on social mix are misplaced. The Right to Buy is not impinging strongly on the life of council tenants except in reducing their housing opportunities. Increased residualisation caused by the Right to Buy means for the poorest sections of the population a more unequal society, greater instability and social exclusion. Right to Buy resales have also not stabilised the more desirable neighbourhoods, especially where resales act as starter homes and form the part of the segment of the housing market with the highest turnover. The implications of this are that both council estates with higher levels of home ownership and those with lower levels of home ownership are likely to be characterised by higher turnover now than in the past and that in the future this higher turnover may increase further. It is unrealistic to believe that but for the Right to Buy the council sector would comprise stable working class communities, such a phenomenon was never all pervasive. Nonetheless there is reason to believe that the Right to Buy has destabilised some council estate neighbourhoods and, in some cases, has changed the way that these areas function as communities.

9

Housing Management and Housing Quality

Much of the discussion of the Right to Buy has focused on the extension of home ownership and access to housing but there are a number of other potential consequences for the management and the quality of the housing stock. The sale of flats in particular raises immediate issues about management. In the early years of the Right to Buy the sale of flats did not feature prominently but now there are over 200 000 leaseholders in former local authority flats in England and Wales. Similarly the increasing number of low income owner-occupiers inevitably leads to questions concerning their ability to maintain and upgrade their homes. The emergence of mixed tenure estates also represents a new challenge for estate management. At first these issues were not perceived as problematic but they have grown in significance with the cumulative number of sales under the Right to Buy.

A crucial consequence of the Right to Buy has been that housing management is not a simple matter of managing the council housing stock but also involves dealing with common maintenance, repair and improvement issues with purchasers. All flats and maisonettes in England and Wales sold under the Right to Buy are sold on a leasehold basis. The local authority (or housing association) is normally the freeholder and this responsibility remains for the duration of the lease. The way that local authorities and housing associations fulfil their responsibilities operates within a framework of housing and landlord and tenant law which sets out the rights of leaseholders and tenants as well as the responsibilities of landlords. Purchasers of flats are advised that they will be charged for services that they receive, including the costs associated with maintaining and repairing the buildings and common areas (but not the interior of individual flats) and providing common services (such as lifts, lighting and cleaning common areas, door entry schemes, insurance). The lease-holders and other tenants paying variable service charges in this context have a number of rights that may be exercised and which the landlord is required to comply with.

In England and Wales the rights of leaseholders and other tenants paying variable service charges were improved by the Commonhold and Leasehold Reform Act 2002. The new terms included:

- the right to be consulted about long term agreements to be entered into by the landlord, where the agreement is for more than 12 months *and* the amount payable by any leaseholder/tenant in any of the account-ing periods relevant to the agreement amounts to more than £100;
- the right to be consulted about works which are to be undertaken, either separately or as part of a long term agreement, where the amount payable by any tenant is more than £250;
- the right to seek a determination from a leasehold valuation tribunal on certain matters.

There is also legislative provision to enable leaseholders to exercise choices in relation to the management of a property but this requires a number of conditions to be fulfilled and the agreement of the majority of residents in a block.

This chapter begins by examining housing management and the issues that arise from the sale of flats. For ease of exposition specific references are largely to the management of leasehold flats in England. However, the majority of the same issues apply to Scotland (see Jones & Murie 1999). The establishment of the Right to Buy in effect initiated the management of private properties by local authorities and subsequently housing asso-ciations. Prior to 1980 the management of such properties was not a significant feature. Most properties sold under discretionary policies were conventional houses and, consequently, prior to the Right to Buy there was no significant issue about leasehold management (Murie 1975; Forrest & Murie 1990b).

Management and maintenance costs

Previous chapters have looked at the differential impact of the Right to Buy in terms of house types sold and the variations between areas. Selling good quality houses to affluent tenants is relatively unproblematic from a management perspective. It is a very different proposition when less desirable properties are sold to less affluent tenants. Private ownership, as Chapter 7 demonstrates, has also increasingly led to former council property now being let out privately, adding to the tenure mix. Within one block of flats, therefore, there may be students renting from an absentee private landlord, ageing owners and a group of low income, state dependent families. The management of blocks of flats in mixed ownership in particular creates problems, problems which are exacerbated when owners are on low incomes. This section considers the nature of the issues that may arise, drawing on Jones and Murie (1999) and more recent research by the authors.

The fact that public sector tenants living in flats (and particularly high rise flats) tend to have lower incomes than those living in family houses is essential for understanding some of the difficulties which have arisen. Not all flats in the public rental stock are problematic in terms of maintenance or repair (for example, cottage or four-in-a-block flats), but such problems do exist in high rise tower blocks in inner city locations or on peripheral estates. Maintenance is much less of an issue in high quality houses with gardens and these, once sold, are no longer the council's responsibility.

Some difficulties arise because of the basic design of the dwellings and their production and management histories in the public sector. Blocks of flats built by local authorities were designed to be managed on a collective basis. When a single property is sold to a tenant, complex and often imprecise calculations are required to apportion responsibility and financial liability for management, repairs and maintenance. The apportionment of costs has to cover a proportion of the general management costs for the overall building: routine maintenance and repair, cleaning and maintenance of common areas such as hallways and open spaces, lift maintenance and replacement, capital works associated with roofs and windows, charges for communal heating systems, and so forth. All of these charges are open to challenge from individual leaseholders. All require detailed justification by the authority and, fundamentally, some justifiable charges have proved unaffordable for the new owners.

For most of the 1980s the growing portfolio of leasehold properties managed by local authorities was almost wholly occupied by Right to Buy purchasers. Very few properties at this stage had changed hands through open market transactions. The initial purchasers had been sitting tenants of local authorities and often had a considerable number of years of tenancy with the local authority. They had been familiar with local authority management, although it is apparent from the research carried out subsequently that most of these purchasers had not really anticipated the continuing nature of the relationship with the local authority and the obligation to make service charge payments in the way that subsequently emerged. Some of the tensions between leaseholders and their 'landlords' (the local council) were attributable to the lack of clarity of understanding about the responsibilities of each party.

The early 1990s began to see a change in the debate about leaseholders and leasehold management. Initially the problems that were drawn to the attention of Members of Parliament and others were the emerging concerns of leaseholders regarding the scale and fluctuation of service charges. These concerns exposed a number of underlying issues. Neither Right to Buy purchasers nor the increasing number of subsequent open market purchasers had been well advised about the likely level of service charges or the factors that affected them (for example, maintenance costs).

In parallel with the Right to Buy scheme and policies to encourage sitting tenant purchase, Government encouraged local authorities to cost their various functions more precisely and to recover costs as fully as possible. Many local authorities had initially made nominal charges (for example, for management). As their leasehold portfolio grew they inevitably looked at the adequacy of these charges and sought to base them on a fairer, proper figure. This inevitably involved an increase over the previous nominal rates charged (Forrest *et al.* 1995b).

There was a coincidence between the revision of charging regimes following the growth in number of leasehold properties, the increasing number of leaseholders who had bought on the open market rather than through the Right to Buy and therefore appear to have been inclined to ask different questions, and the downturn in the housing market in the early 1990s. This downturn appears to have had a particular impact on accommodation in flats in some parts of the country. Some open market purchasers were probably exposed to negative equity. Some owners of leasehold properties wishing to sell and move on found it very difficult to do so (Forrest *et al.* 1995b). The impact of this on the ability to sell and on resale prices was significant and in some cases it contributed to the introduction of sub-lessees and absentee leaseholders.

Most importantly the balance between open market purchased leasehold properties and Right to Buy properties shifted at this time, and indeed continues to do so. It appears likely that the rate of resale is higher among flats than other former council properties. This is no doubt associated with the property type and the households who originally bought them. As service charges rose landlords were increasingly concerned with problems of arrears, arrears recovery and hardship and they were aware of some lease-holders' concerns over resale. The main reasons for arrears were an un-expected period of unemployment for a household member and higher than expected living costs. Perhaps surprisingly, households who experi-enced difficulty over paying service charges on leasehold properties were more likely to have bought the property on the open market.

Those who had bought public sector flats were progressively exposed to a new regime where local authority service charges were increasing and where the justification for such charges was more transparent. Formerly maintenance costs were pooled across the entire local council housing stock with probably no provision for life cycle costing of components at the block or even estate level. In contrast blocks of flats which were built for and have always been in the private sector usually have arrangements for routine and major maintenance (including sinking funds) built in from the outset.

There are other important differences between privately built flats and privatised public sector flats. Where large bills arise, owner-occupiers/ leaseholders in the traditional private sector are generally able to cope with such bills through their income, savings or ability to raise a loan on a valuable asset. Right to Buy flat purchasers and their successors tend to be on lower incomes and are likely to face higher maintenance and repair costs as prefabricated dwellings often have design faults. In addition state built properties tend to be of lower value because they are more difficult to sell and this reduces the incentive to invest in the property's main-tenance to a high level.

Mixed tenure blocks are a recipe for conflicts of interest between councils, private landlords and residents. There is often tension between tenants who may seek a higher level of service and owners/leaseholders who may want to minimise services and extend maintenance periods to reduce costs. At the same time, councils are encouraged by central gov-ernment to provide a responsive and high quality service to their tenants which inevitably produces higher costs and service charges for those who have moved out of tenancy into home ownership.

Improvements are often an even greater source of bitterness and conflict and hence create substantial administrative headaches and delays. There have been well publicised situations where purchasers of flats have on occasion been presented with bills for capital works which exceeded the current value of their properties. Low income purchasers may simply not have sufficient funds although tenants on social security in some circumstances may be entitled to subsidies for these major works bills.

Beyond these resource issues there are often problems of community participation in improvement schemes where households are driven by different agendas. Conflicting views about quality and cost are not easily resolved. The general attitude of leaseholders is to minimise costs. This may become more pronounced if they expect to only stay for a relatively short time in the property. The council's interest in maintaining the asset in the interests of their tenants means adopting more expensive, longer life approaches. While some leaseholders may resent a solution which involves high costs, others do respond to arguments about advantages in investment terms that relate to minimising disruption; the comparison is with poorer quality work that would require more repeat attention. However, for this and other reasons leaseholders can be demanding in their expectations about quality and seeing the bills and other evidence for costs.

Where owner-occupiers find difficulty funding their share of community renewal schemes councils may be able to help with an improvement grant or a loan. On occasion endowment loan schemes have been arranged whereby payment is made on death and sale of property. Sometimes there is the reverse problem, namely home owners are seeking improvements but the local authority has constraints on its capital budget. Even when the plans have been drawn up it may not be clear how many owners wish to participate at the point when a contract is being tendered for.

The Right to Buy can also create additional costs and delays to major comprehensive redevelopment programmes incorporating demolition. Details are reported by Jones (2003) and the Association of London Government (2003). The essential problem is that the announcement of an initiative can stimulate Right to Buy applications and then these households have to be compensated at full market value despite purchasing at a discount. In England this phenomenon has manifested itself mainly in London. Jones and Murie (1999) also make reference to its occurrence in Scotland. Legislation has now been introduced to resolve this issue.

Besides the management of maintenance, repairs and improvement, every day living frictions between owner-occupiers and tenants can also be delicate matters that the local authority is expected to resolve. Access and ownership rights can be a major problem. For example, in Glasgow access changes for a disabled tenant were refused by an owner-occupier in a four-in-a-block (cottage) flat. Sometimes owner-occupiers' rights under their deeds differ from the rights that they had when they were tenants. Rules about the division of land around flats can be awkward and not follow previous practice or custom. Neighbour disputes for example about the cleaning of common areas, noise, or the siting of satellite dishes are not always the province of local authority housing management departments but are often addressed on a goodwill basis for the benefit of the community.

Leasehold management

Today leasehold management is primarily the management of properties which have been purchased on the open market rather than those which have been purchased under the Right to Buy. Data on assignment of leases and turnover is incomplete. However, case studies completed in 2002 (Murie 2002) indicate a high rate of turnover and it is likely that open market sales now considerably outnumber Right to Buy sales in many areas. Some properties sold on the open market have changed hands a number of times since their original Right to Buy sale. This means that leasehold management is considerably different to when it largely involved the management of former tenants.

In Westminster in 2002 62% of leaseholders were not former council tenants as these properties had been sold on the open market. Of leasehold flats, 15% were registered as sub-let and a further 8% could have been sub-let as there was an alternative address provided for notices. These figures suggest both a high rate of turnover of properties in the sector and a high rate of sub-letting. Both of these factors are likely to become increasingly apparent in the future. The data related to assignment of leases (i.e. sales of leasehold properties) provided by the London Borough of Westminster suggests an increasing number of assignments between 1998/99 and 2002. Assignments ran at over 7% of new leasehold properties each year, or at about 12% of all leasehold properties which were not currently occupied by former council tenants. Assuming that the former council tenants were less likely to move, especially if they had not already done so, then the long term rate of turnover is likely to lie somewhere between these two figures.

Research carried out in this area suggests that the characteristics of open market purchasers of leasehold property are considerably different from those of Right to Buy purchasers. This builds on the evidence from previous research. In London especially, and in the high priced parts of the London market, there are affluent purchasers who own other properties which may be regarded as their principal or family home. The attitudes of these owners may be very different from those of Right to Buy purchasers. The existence of absentee landlords and sub-leases raises another set of issues about the attitudes of owners. Acquisitions of properties by housing associations in inner London would appear to have added to the demand for these properties and the rate of sub-leasing. These issues may be more important in high price markets and may be very different in lower priced markets in the Midlands and the north of England where owners will let at much lower rents to different households and their business plans may be based purely upon the income stream deriving from rent with no assumptions about appreciation in property value. This is part of a more general debate about the development of the private rented sector in different parts of the country.

The importance of leasehold ownership varies substantially between districts. In Westminster, for example, leasehold properties comprised 38% of the properties within the local authority's management in 2002. They formed a major part of the housing function for the local authority and the effective collection of costs was critical to the circumstances of tenants and the management of the housing stock in general. This situation applies in varying degrees to other London boroughs, but outside London the importance of leasehold properties to the council treasury is rarely so critical, except in parts of Scotland.

The management issues in different market environments are likely to be significantly different. For example, in London, flats which are subleased in Westminster commonly achieved a rent in excess of £1000 per month in 2002 and sometimes as high as £5000 per month. Rents on street properties tended to be higher. The rate of outright sales in Westminster (at 220–230 per year) was running well below the rate of assignment of leases at over 500 a year. The rate of appreciation and value and returns on investment was very high in central London. In contrast both values and rents can be very low in the Midlands and the north and assets may have declined in value rather than appreciating in some low demand areas.

A number of important issues have arisen in relation to leasehold property. Leaseholders are not well informed or advised at the point of purchase about the nature and extent of their obligations, the responsibilities of the local authority and the types of charges which they will be liable for. They appear to rarely be given advice about the level of service charges which have applied in the past and the kind of service charges which will apply in the future in relation to major repairs and maintenance. In spite of improved billing and charging procedures, arrears remain an important issue for all landlords. The London Borough of Westminster estimates that referrals to solicitors in 2001–2002 related to 9% of properties and some £1.5 million.

There is now an effective body of practice involving procedures for consultation with leaseholders in general. It is common for leaseholders to be members of residents' associations and communication through these associations and through literature and newsletters directed at leaseholders alone shows a considerable improvement on past practice. Leaseholders are most likely to be animated by matters that affect them individually rather than participating in the generality of debates about the development of estates; consequently, councils or housing associations managing the lease have some difficulty in maintaining continuity of participation.

Where blocks of properties have become predominantly leasehold it may be appropriate for the council/housing association to sell the freehold or to set up an alternative management arrangement, effectively subcontracting to a resident-managed process. This may also apply where there are limited numbers of local authority tenancies still within a block that is predominantly leasehold. The effect of this would be to reduce the management costs associated with leasehold properties which can otherwise be exaggerated by issues such as leaseholders practising continuing complaint.

This response could however generate problems of its own. In some cases leaseholder purchase of a block could make it more difficult for the council as landlord of the remaining rented properties to improve these or to achieve the standards required by the Decent Homes Standard (a UK Government strategy). This issue may be most problematic in blocks where leaseholders are not resident and there is significant sub-letting. New legislation requires 50% of leaseholders to support enfranchisement and there is no residency requirement.

House condition issues

A concern at the beginning of the Right to Buy was that affordability problems of purchasers would be reflected in poor maintenance and in long term deterioration of the condition of the housing stock. Such a perspective is a simplification as it ignores the factor of resale but as Chapter 6 indicates new purchasers are either also families on low incomes or first time purchasers buying a starter home with a view to moving on in a few years. In either case there must also be doubts about whether these repurchasers will be concerned or able to address long term maintenance. These issues have already been highlighted in the management issues discussed above and are important reasons to examine more closely what has happened to the maintenance and repair of former council houses.

It is evident from a wide range of data that there is a problem of maintenance and repair within the owner-occupied sector of former council housing in Britain. This particularly applies to older properties but is generally associated with the resources of households. As owner-occupation has expanded down the income scale, so there are an increasing number of owners who do not have sufficient resources to maintain properties in good condition. This is particularly so in periods of economic recession and among elderly owner-occupiers with permanently low incomes. It may be argued that the Right to Buy and the discount formula adopted for it will have particularly encouraged lower or variable income households to purchase properties. At the time of purchase these properties would have been well maintained but ten years on, an accumulation of repair requirements may have emerged.

The general picture is that purchasers embark upon significant investments and modifications immediately after purchase, i.e. early in their career as a home owner (Forrest & Murie 1990b; Jones & Murie 1999). Some of these are cosmetic and do not materially improve the condition of the property. The question marks over the long term condition of the housing stock have been considered in a range of studies. Forrest and Murie (1990) undertook a small house condition survey of council houses in 1989 which had been sold under discretionary policies in the period 1968–74. This study involved an external survey only and a comparison with neighbouring equivalent properties still in council ownership. The resulting picture was striking. Some 15 years after privatisation former council dwellings fell into two clear groups. A majority had very limited repair costs required and a minority showed considerable signs of dilapidation. This minority requiring high repair costs included both pre-war and post-war dwellings, terraced and semi-detached properties. The report of this study commented as follows:

'Fifteen or more years after sale, the house condition and housing repairs profile of former council homes differs from that of existing council homes in the same city. These differences do not seem likely to reflect differences which existed at the time of initial sale. At that stage it is likely that the sold houses were of better than average condition. More than 15 years later they were also generally in better condition.

However, there is a clear indication that former council homes exhibit a wider variation of condition than council homes do. In this they reflect the fact that decisions on repairs and maintenance in the private sector will reflect individual resources and inclination. In contrast council house repairs and maintenance decisions are bureaucratically determined following planned maintenance or refurbishment programmes, as well as responding to demand. The market produces both higher standards of repair and a greater likelihood of neglect of repair.' (Forrest & Murie 1990b, p. 79)

Jones and Murie (1999) undertook a more detailed, but still limited, house condition survey of 200 former Right to Buy properties in Birmingham. All of these dwellings had been sold in 1983, 14 years before the survey was carried out. Flats were not included because decisions about maintenance of these properties involved different processes and actors, including the local authority and its relationship to its leaseholders. The surveyors completed a house condition survey form which classified the principal external and internal elements of the dwelling as excellent, reasonable or unsatisfactory. Where the condition was regarded as unsatisfactory, some further detail was provided. Any extensions, including porches, kitchen/bathroom and conservatory, were identified. The occupier was also asked his or her views on problems of disrepair.

Table 9.1 presents the results of this assessment. A considerable variation in condition emerges. An assessment as unsatisfactory was unusual for new extensions and additions to the property, to bathrooms, external doors and to floors. The highest levels of unsatisfactory condition related to external decoration and heating. With respect to heating, such dwellings had not been upgraded to include central heating. Unsatisfactory external decoration was a significant factor, although this did not necessarily indicate a serious problem unless it was not remedied quickly. The more important indicators of condition were more basic, such as windows, rainwater goods, roofs, chimneys, electric/wiring and dampness, and between 8% and 15% of properties appeared to be unsatisfactory in respect of these.

There was no clear pattern between different dwelling types in terms of house condition. The small kitchens and bathrooms of pre-war properties affected the extent to which they could be modernised but there was no particular pattern in terms of condition related to the age of property. Some prefabricated properties had been upgraded under the Housing Defects Act and, where properties had been improved with the addition of plastic windows, in general this had been done to a good standard. Some porches and do-it-yourself amendments were not of a high standard and

Table 9.1   The condition of sold council dwellings in Birmingham.

	Excellent (%)	Unsatisfactory (%)
External decoration	18	28
Heating	20	25
Windows	58	15
Rainwater goods	20	11
Fences/boundaries	34	11
Roof	13	10
Chimney	7	10
Electrics/wiring	8	8
External walls	17	8
Dampness	77	8
Kitchen	41	5
Conservatory	5	6
External doors	49	4
Porch	23	4
Floors	48	3
Bathroom	36	2
Kitchen/bathroom extension	3	2

Source: Jones & Murie 1999.

rot was appearing in some porches. However, the more serious problems appeared to relate to problems with flat roofs and a lack of awareness of chimneys, roofs and rainwater goods (guttering and downpipes). It is also apparent that central heating was not serviced as often as was the case under the council. Elderly owners often completed major refurbishment of the property immediately after purchase and did not consider there to be any need for subsequent work. The implication of this is that properties will gradually deteriorate. Where unsatisfactory conditions exist, the response of occupiers relates to their ability to afford to have work carried out or a lack of awareness of work being needed – often because the house had previously been refurbished by the present owner.

Further analysis of the House Condition Survey in Birmingham revealed 127 out of the 200 respondents had identified at least one element of their home as unsatisfactory. For 50 households (25% of the total sample), only one element was coded in this way. Thirty-one households had two elements identified as unsatisfactory. At the extreme, one dwelling was coded as having nine unsatisfactory elements, three as having seven, four as having six and another four as having five.

Two other observations should be made relating to issues of house condition in this stock. First of all where estate action or other major refurbishment programmes had been carried out which bypassed purchased properties, the condition of owner-occupied properties within estates (or of properties which were bought prior to the estate action or other initiative) was visibly worse than that of neighbouring properties. This affects the value of the property. Second, it is important to have some perspective on the level of disrepair and poor condition indicated in this survey. A figure of around 10% is high by national standards (Jones & Murie 1999).

The condition of former council properties has been the subject of other studies of house condition in Scotland and Northern Ireland. In both cases the conclusions were somewhat tentative. Leather and Anderson (1999) made use of the 1996 Scottish House Condition Survey to examine the condition of properties sold via the Right to Buy in Scotland. They concluded that the condition of the former council stock was generally better than that of other unoccupied stock or of dwellings remaining in the social rented sector. Average visible repair costs for the former Right to Buy stock were about 60% of those of the dwelling stock as a whole. A small proportion of former Right to Buy dwellings (19%) were in poorer repair than the stock in general. These ratios were true for all sizes, ages and types of dwelling. In Scotland, a high proportion of the former Right to Buy stock is in flats, but the cost of repairs to common parts formed only a small proportion of outstanding repair costs, partly no doubt because the maintenance of common parts was still influenced by previous ownership and less determined by the individual characteristics of the resale purchaser.

Leather and Anderson (1999) commented that the current condition of former council properties was misleading and that real problems could emerge in future. They commented on the evidence that resold Right to Buy dwellings appeared to be in poorer condition than those which were still occupied by their original purchaser. They also commented that the problems of identifying these properties mean that this conclusion has to be tentative. The Scottish House Condition Survey data confirmed the evidence that the profile of Right to Buy owners, compared with other owner-occupiers, is skewed towards older people on relatively low incomes with limited savings. There was a particular concentration of Right to Buy owners in the age group 45–74. It was also evident that poorer and older people spend less on repairs and find it more difficult to organise work, or to carry out work themselves.

The study concluded that the relatively good performance to date may be explained by the high incidence of middle aged and early retirement period owners, by the inheritance of relatively well maintained dwellings from the social rented sector and by the burst of spending on improvements that accompanies many Right to Buy sales. In the coming decades, many currently middle aged owners will retire, older owners will become too frail to carry out the work, and the impact of past maintenance will weaken. Unless there is substantial turnover in the stock, some deterioration is therefore inevitable. Where there is turnover, tentative evidence from this study suggests that conditions also deteriorate.

This pessimistic scenario was not borne out by a more recent study of the influence of the Right to Buy undertaken as part of the 2002 Scottish House Condition Survey (Communities Scotland 2005). It compared the level of disrepair of dwellings bought under the Right to Buy with other owner-occupied properties and those owned by local authorities and housing associations. 'Urgent disrepair' is found to be equally likely to exist in all tenures although the incidence of 'any disrepair' was higher for Right to Buy properties and social housing than other owner-occupied. Generally the incidence of elements of disrepair was not as high as in the Birmingham study above. There is some evidence to suggest that Right to Buy purchasers had spent less on the outside of their homes than other owner-occupiers, but still more than social housing landlords. Overall the study concludes that the results indicate that dwellings bought under the Right to Buy are no more likely to be in disrepair than other owner-occupied dwellings or social housing. Right to Buy owners and non-Right to Buy owners are very similar in the amount and type of work that they report having undertaken to their homes. Further, both groups report having done far more work to their dwellings than local authorities or housing associations.

A similar study based on the 1996 Northern Ireland House Condition Survey was undertaken by Murie and Leather (2000). Before considering the results of the Northern Ireland study, it is important to bear in mind some features of the public sector housing stock and its sales. The stock sold by the Northern Ireland Housing Executive tended to be more modern than the owner-occupied stock in general and there was an over-representation of detached houses and a virtual absence of flats. The expectation was that former public sector properties would be in good condition, disrepair would be small at the time of purchase and the property types are ones that are easy to repair. This expectation was borne out by the analysis. The study concluded that there was an uneven pattern in relation to former council and housing association owned properties. Those properties that were in good condition before purchase were generally in good condition afterwards.

Right to Buy purchasers in Northern Ireland were no different from other home owners in having varying knowledge, resources and activity in relation to maintenance and repair, but this meant that, some years after purchase, there was a great variation in housing conditions, rather than a common pattern of higher or lower disrepair. While no clear relationship between repair costs and time elapsed since date of purchase emerged, there was a general increase in average repair costs on resale.

With the exception of the Birmingham analysis these studies do not differentiate by house type or area. This is of significance because the state of social housing is particularly variable. It has been argued in previous chapters how the Right to Buy has exacerbated the concentration of poor people in undesirable and difficult to let housing estates. Often these estates were badly built and poorly designed. The standard of repair in these estates tends to be low. A whole gamut of national initiatives have been implemented to arrest physical decline and wider social issues in these areas, stretching from 'Priority Estates' through to 'New Deal for Communities' and the 'National Strategy for Neighbourhood Renewal', although the latter two are not exclusively public sector focused. Wholehearted success in these initiatives has proved elusive not least because of the continual inflow into these areas of households in extreme social need (Kintrea & Morgan 2005).

Overall these studies leave some uncertainty about the impact of the Right to Buy on house condition. The simple relationship posited between date of sale and property condition has not been sustained and these analyses do not in general point to a massive problem of disrepair. They also remain cautious about longer term trends, and there is speculation that as the population of original purchasers ages, house condition problems will become more apparent. At the time that these studies were carried out, it may be argued that the full impact of the ageing of the early Right to Buy purchasers would not have shown through. While the situation is obviously more complex than these studies have been able to capture there is some limited evidence that a minority of owners are unable in the long term to maintain their properties and that these properties become significantly dilapidated. Some sold properties are now visible because of external dilapidation whereas in the early 1980s they were evident because of the pristine new porches, extensions and windows which were added immediately after purchase.

Conclusions

This chapter has reviewed the aspects of housing management affected by the Right to Buy sector after 25 years. Management of council housing has been transformed during this period. Selling flats has created severe management problems and management has generally become more complex and more expensive. Public sector improvement programmes can be disrupted and modified by owner-occupiers who are reluctant or unable to invest (sometimes roles can be reversed). In the early years of the Right to Buy these issues were less problematic. The management of an estate with only a small number of owners is very different from management of an estate where the majority of the estate is privately owned. As the estates have been colonised by owners, unit management costs have not fallen proportionately, quite the reverse. The allocation of lettings and other fixed central management costs are averaged over less housing stock and in high demand areas the administration of statutory homeless rights have increased. Overall the consequences are higher real public sector housing management costs to be paid out of the rents from the remaining rump of tenants.

The low and variable incomes of purchasers (or their successors) have led to doubts about the maintenance and long-term condition of housing sold under the Right to Buy. The limited evidence to date only partially supports these concerns. In flats this also has consequences for the remaining public sector stock.

10

The Financial Equation

The finances of the Right to Buy have been and continue to be the subject of much debate. When the policy was introduced it was dubbed the sale of the century with many critics arguing that the sell off of the public housing stock was at give-away prices. Much time and energy was addressed to resolving this matter, partially stimulated by research for a report on the subject by the Environment Select Committee of the House of Commons (House of Commons 1981). Other critics argued at that time that the Right to Buy could lead to large numbers of purchasers over-stretching themselves financially in the medium to long term and potentially losing their homes. On the positive side the Right to Buy was seen as a means of redistributing wealth. In 2005 financial concerns have changed and the contentious issues relate to the impact of the Right to Buy on the cost of housing the homeless and the maintenance of the remaining housing stock.

This chapter begins by reviewing the fundamentals of the financial economics from the perspective of the state. This review encompasses the profitability of the Right to Buy and the use of capital receipts from sales. The next section looks at the consequences of the Right to Buy for management of the remaining council housing stock. This is followed by an analysis of the benefits of the Right to Buy from the tenants' perspective and addresses the issues of affordability and wealth redistribution. Finally the chapter summarises the financial impact of the Right to Buy.

Public sector perspectives

From the start of the Right to Buy the underlying finances were questioned with the Conservative Government arguing it was a good deal for both tenants and councils. The framework to assess this is a financial appraisal that summarises revenue and expenditure flows in each year and assesses them in present value terms. As £1 today is worth more than £1 next year the value of future financial flows is reduced by a discount factor or rate per year. This discount rate is linked to the prevailing and expected future interest rates. This framework is known as discounted cash flow analysis.

At its simplest the financial analysis of a council house sale compares the rent foregone with the mortgage repayments received and the lack of subsequent management/maintenance costs and subsidy by the state over time. This assumes that the state would provide the mortgage to the purchaser, but even if the mortgage is provided by a building society or a bank the analysis is not different because mortgage repayments are replaced by interest payments on the capital sum received. The essentials of the financial appraisal remain unchanged.

Unfortunately the simplicity of the task is only superficial as there are a whole range of issues beneath the surface of the trade-offs. First, there is the question of whether modernisation costs should be included besides maintenance costs but this will depend on the age and condition of individual properties. The timing of any modernisation for identical properties will also vary by local authority, reflecting potentially differing priorities and resources. Second, what discount to capital value, or selling price, should be applied? This will vary with the length of the tenancy of the household purchasing. Third, should the financial appraisal include the cost of replacing the housing unit and at what point in the future? Fourth, what personal subsidies should be included – households purchasing under the Right to Buy may not be claiming rent rebates at the time but might have eventually done so in retirement. Households purchasing with a mortgage would receive tax relief on the interest paid (abolished in 2000) and on any further loan to renovate the property, as would any future purchasers with a mortgage on resale. This too should be accounted for.

In addition to these specific issues linked to the house there is another set of variables that require assumptions. What is going to happen to the real value of council house rents in the future? The answer to this question has a local dimension but it is likely to be primarily determined by central government policy toward subsidy. Similarly, are maintenance costs likely to rise in line with inflation? To an extent this is also influenced by policy decisions. Finally, what discount rate should be applied to future financial flows? The answer depends on the expected state of the economy, notably the level of inflation and interest rates.

When the House of Commons Environment Select Committee considered the financial consequences in 1980, the precise assumptions were a matter of conjecture and debate because of the lack of past experience of a national sales scheme. At the centre of this debate were two financial appraisals undertaken by the civil servants at the Department of the Environment (DoE), one completed for the Labour Government in 1978 and a revision for the Conservatives in January 1980. A further appraisal was completed by the Comptroller and Auditor General in May of that year (published in 1981) based on the latter DoE effort.

The starting point for the DoE discounted cash flow analysis was a selling price of £8400 estimated by taking the average market value at the time and deducting a discount of 40%. The analysis set out four long term potential macroeconomic scenarios:

- 4% inflation, 1% increase in real earnings, 1% real interest rate;
- 4% inflation, 2% increase in real earnings, 3% real interest rate;
- 9% inflation, 1% increase in real earnings, 1% real interest rate;
- 9% inflation, 2% increase in real earnings, 3% real interest rate.

Building on these scenarios a range of assumptions were considered for the variables listed above. It is not worthwhile considering the detail of all these assumptions but a number are of interest in the light of subsequent experience (see Kilroy 1982 for a critique).

The appraisal by the Comptroller and Auditor General (1981) demonstrated that the single assumption with the greatest effect was the future pattern of rents. Under the assumptions considered, rents rising in line with earnings over the long term, combined with a low level of renovation, led to a net loss to the public purse. On the other hand if rents rose only 75% as fast as prices (as in the period 1974–79) and renovation costs were high then sales would be profitable.

The DoE's financial calculations made no allowance for replacement of any houses sold because they argued that:

'nearly all sitting tenant purchasers would otherwise have remained tenants until their death, when the widow would take over the tenancy. Not until she ceases to live as a tenant is there any effect on the number of new tenants that can be accommodated.' (DoE 1980, Annex, para 17)

In another part of its assessment it also states:

'. . . some 30–40 years would typically elapse before there is an effect on number of houses vacant and available for letting to new tenants.' (DoE 1980, para 50)

Webster (1981) pointed out the limitation of this argument, namely that in the absence of the Right to Buy some households would have moved out of the tenure, buying on the open market or renting privately. Combined with emigration, remarriage, death and household dissolution he estimated the immediate loss of relets at that time as lying between 2.5 and 4.5%. In other words for every 100 houses sold under the Right to Buy scheme approximately three or four houses should be built each year.

Webster undertook a systematic scrutiny of all the assumptions made by the DoE and repeated the financial analysis with differing 'realistic' assumptions including allowing for some replacement as set out above. This study concluded:

'. . . that the sale of council houses on the terms provided by the Housing Act 1980 is overwhelmingly likely to result in long term financial losses in excess of £12 500 per dwelling sold.' (Webster 1981, para 149)

The figure quoted is broadly linked to what Webster saw as the most likely scenario for future rents, with rises at the average rate as occurred between 1959 and 1979.

In retrospect this debate about the underlying variables influencing the financial probity of the Right to Buy at one level seems arcane. Rent levels of council houses rose much faster than inflation and faster than earnings over the next two decades (see Chapter 5). Very few council houses were built in the subsequent 25 years and so there has been limited direct replacement of houses lost to Right to Buy sales, as postulated in the original DoE appraisal. However, the picture is clouded by the expansion of housing associations. The scale of social house building in comparison to the flow of lost relets is difficult to ascertain precisely but the level of Right to Buy resales since the beginning of the 1990s and the historically low social house building suggests that replacement building has not kept pace by a long way. Furthermore, as Chapter 4 shows, there has been much greater subsequent mobility of Right to Buy purchasers in the last decade exacerbating this position.

Local authorities in 1980 were predominantly of the view that replacement building would be necessary to discharge their social housing duties, especially with regard to housing suitable for the elderly, but even then many authorities recognised that shortages of land or finances would make this difficult. This was accepted even though it was recognised that the availability of additional dwellings in the owner-occupied properties through resales of Right to Buy properties would not reduce housing need and the demand for council housing.

Today the picture is more complicated. It is accepted that shortages and the need for replacement depend on locality. After a quarter of a century of the Right to Buy and the subsequent changes in the housing market some policy makers believe that the gulf between tenures has narrowed in certain areas. For example, one of the tests for pressured area status in Scotland is to what extent resales provide affordable housing, i.e. substitutes for social rented housing (see Chapters 3 and 7). This means that it is not possible to establish a national perspective on the finances of the Right to Buy (if it ever was).

This spatial variation was reflected in a recent illustrative discounted cash flow analysis by Hargreaves (2002). Variations in circumstances mean a greater emphasis was put on the role of replacement in the analysis where it is necessary. A further distinction from the original appraisals published in 1980 was the realisation that management costs are not simply proportional to the number of properties owned by a council but include an element of fixed costs.

Hargreaves' financial evaluation comparing the difference between selling and letting was undertaken for a 30 year period. The discount rate applied was the social discount rate of 3.5% set by the Treasury for all public projects. The sale price of the council house was taken to be £88 000 and this figure was also used as its replacement value and its terminal value after 30 years if it continues to be rented. The analysis was conducted in real terms and rents, management costs, etc. were assumed to be constant in real terms, hence the income and expenditure position was assumed to be unchanged over the appraisal period, and 10% of management costs were fixed. Four dates of replacement were considered – 0, 10, 20 and 30 years – and two levels of discount – 20% and 40%.

The results are summarised in Figure 10.1 for an area where there is an active housing market and a shortage of social housing. It shows how the break even point for the Right to Buy from a business point of view is linked to when replacement is necessary. When the discount is 20% then the Right to Buy is profitable if replacement is not necessary until after seven years or more. On the other hand if the discount is 40% then the sale is not profitable unless replacement is delayed for more than 15 years.

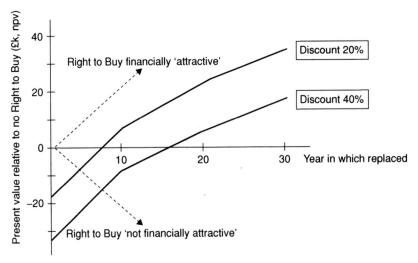

Figure 10.1   The effect of replacement and the Right to Buy discount on financial viability.

Source: Hargreaves 2002.

These figures demonstrate that with many households now moving on quickly after house purchase the Right to Buy does not make financial sense in areas where there is excess demand for social housing (and new housing is built). In fact, from a business perspective, a higher discount rate is arguably applicable and replication of the analysis using a 6% real discount rate reduces the viability point from seven to five years for purchasers with a 20% discount. On the other hand Hargreaves (2002) argued that where there is a surplus of council housing, for example in some northern cities, not only will replacement not be necessary but any income from a sale will be beneficial. While in strictly financial terms this may be true the argument ignores the differential quality of the social housing stock and distribution effects. As shown in Chapter 5 even when there is a social housing surplus the sale of the better stock reduces the opportunities for tenants living in the poorer quality stock to move.

An alternative recent analysis of the financial implications was undertaken by the Association of London Government (2003) for London. This appraisal of a 'normal' Right to Buy sale in London did not fully spell out its assumptions. As it is a high demand area the analysis added in the cost of housing homeless households in temporary accommodation rather than in relets lost via the Right to Buy. Hence its focus was not on replacement but the cost of lack of replacement. It presumed that properties sold under the Right to Buy would otherwise have generated relets just below the average prevailing relet rate in London of 4.5% and that the cost of temporary accommodation was about £16 000. While this cost is met by central government via housing benefit the appraisal argued that it should be included. The conclusion was that, despite a conservative view on the loss of relets, the high costs associated with temporary accommodation (ignored by Hargreaves) rendered the Right to Buy in London a substantial financial burden on the state.

Munro *et al.* (2005) reported on an unpublished recent ODPM (Office of the Deputy Prime Minister) appraisal that estimated the average cost to the Government of a Right to Buy sale as being in the range of £11 100–£23 300. While not all the assumptions of the analysis were spelt out in this text it did note that costs are greater where the housing unit is replaced more quickly and for higher cost areas of London and the south-east of England. This study estimated that a Right to Buy sale in London costs £40 100 or £17 700 depending on whether a dwelling is replaced in five or ten years respectively. In comparison a Right to Buy sale costs £12 300 in the south-east and £10 700 in Yorkshire and Humberside assuming a replacement in year ten.

To summarise, financial appraisal of the Right to Buy is crucially dependent on the assumptions and inputs to the analysis. These inputs can be and have been the subject of energetic debate. Looking at the appraisals undertaken at the outset of the Right to Buy with hindsight there are limitations to their forecasts, but the conclusions by independent analysts that the Right to Buy was a financial loss to the public purse (even removing the requirement for any replacement) seem watertight. Rents in particular, as the key variable, rose much faster than anticipated thereby increasing probable losses above the levels initially forecast. Twenty-five years on the financial position is more diverse. In areas where there are strong demand pressures on social housing the issue of replacement is now of much greater significance. Accounting either for replacement or the lack of replacement means that the Right to Buy in areas of high demand still appears to remain untenable in purely financial terms to the Exchequer.

As the previous section notes a key policy issue is the replacement of the lost stock. The funds generated could be recycled to fund replacement social housing. However, this has not happened partly because central government has constrained the sums retained by local authorities. The precise arrangements have varied by region and over time. Local authorities receive a proportion of the capital receipts but this sum is not necessarily available for new building. Local authorities' house building is constrained by a system of 'capital allocations' whereby central government limits the amount of borrowing and Right to Buy receipts eligible for capital expenditure on

Table 10.1   Capital receipts from the sale of council houses in Great Britain 1980–2003 (£ million cash).

Year	Receipts from sales
1980/81	692
1981/82	1394
1982/83	1981
1983/84	1499
1984/85	1269
1985/86	1209
1986/87	1408
1987/88	1922
1988/89	3020
1989/90	3153
1990/91	1945
1991/92	1379
1992/93	1135
1993/94	1305
1994/95	1239
1995/96	896
1996/97	964
1997/98	1200
1998/99	1175
1999/00	1687
2000/01	1752
2001/02	1886
2002/03	2705

Source: Wilcox (various).

social housing. Where funds are not used for new building or refurbishment then the receipts reduce the local authority's debt repayments on its housing revenue account.

Sales of public sector dwellings under the Right to Buy in Great Britain had generated £36.8 billion by the end of the financial year 2002/03 and over the first 25 years will probably amount to £40 billion (Table 10.1). The large capital receipts accruing to local authorities were not used to replace dwellings or boost housing investment as capital spending shifted from building to renovation and improvement. In the 1980s the Conservative Government used the capital allocations facility to drive down public expenditure and borrowing as part of its macroeconomic policy. Receipts from the sales yielded short term benefits, substantially financing spending on public sector housing and enabling Government to cut net expenditure (gross expenditure less capital receipts).

A further variable affecting both the public viability and the scale of capital receipts from sales is the level of discounts. Average discount levels reflect partly the administrative rules on eligibility. As indicated in Chapter 3, the levels of discount available under the Right to Buy were initially significantly higher than those available under previous discretionary schemes, including a higher differential rate of discount applying for flats. However, since 1999 the maximum level of discount has been reduced. The average rate of discount on sales of properties under discretionary schemes in 1979 was 27%. Under the Right to Buy it rose to 42% (1981–84) before the legislation of 1984 contributed to an increase to 46% in 1985 to 1987. The 1986 legislation no doubt contributed to the further increase notable after this year. In 1993–95 the average level of discount was 50% and in 1999/2000 it was still 49%. Since then the average discount has fallen relatively quickly to 44% in the second quarter of 2002.

This decline in the discount level is not wholly attributable to the introduction of the maximum discount rule. It is also partially explained by a declining proportion of flats amongst the properties sold and by a change in the characteristics of households buying under the Right to Buy. As indicated in Chapter 4, the Right to Buy in its early years was particularly attractive to households in the middle of the family cycle. By the late 1990s the proportion of tenants who were in this category had declined significantly and social survey evidence indicates that there was a higher proportion of younger purchasers with fewer years of tenancy. Time series data from Birmingham confirms that purchasers with shorter periods of tenancy are more prominent among those taking advantage of the Right to Buy. This can be seen in Figure 10.2 as a decrease in the average tenancy length from the early 1990s and particularly the sharper decrease that took place from 1999 to 2002.

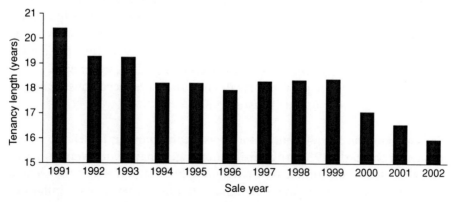

Figure 10.2 Mean tenancy length of Right to Buy purchasers in Birmingham, 1991–2002.

One of the key questions relating to the Right to Buy is the extent to which the level of discount has influenced the take up of sales and hence receipts. Certainly at the inception of the Right to Buy the higher discount levels, compared with previous discretionary schemes, and then the increased discount for flats in the mid 1980s, stimulated demand. However, the sale numbers, as discussed in Chapter 4, are also closely linked to the performance of the housing market. In this respect it is interesting to note that Right to Buy sales rose in the housing boom at the end of the 1990s, despite the fall in discount levels. In 2003/04 total sales were the highest for a decade. This phenomenon suggests that levels of discount have been greater than those necessary to achieve the policy objective and as a consequence capital receipts lower than they needed to be. A caveat to this conclusion must be that the nature of the decision by a tenant to exercise the Right to Buy has changed over time (see below). Nevertheless the prominence of purchasers with shorter tenancies, along with the introduction of a lower maximum discount rule, means that the financial cost to the public sector has been reduced. A higher number of sales is now being achieved with a lower average level of discount and this makes more sense in terms of value for money.

Tenants' perspectives

One of the original arguments in favour of the Right to Buy was a redistribution of wealth in favour of tenants; to be precise a redistribution from the state to its tenants. This redistribution in theory takes the form of the discount to market value. Housing in 1980 was already the major asset held by individual households accounting for 40% of the wealth of the adult population. The growth of home ownership in the previous 20 years had had a significant equalising effect on the distribution of personal wealth. By implementing the Right to Buy this equalisation process would be continued. However, there were concerns that it would be only the better off tenants who would take advantage of the opportunity so that the equity benefits would be uneven. Furthermore some argued these benefits would be at the expense of the poor, principally in terms of reduced housing opportunities (see Chapter 5 and Webster 1981).

Notwithstanding the discounts for most people buying under the Right to Buy, in the early 1980s the initial mortgage repayments were going to be higher than their former rent payments. In common with other house buyers, their mortgage repayments tend to fall in real terms with inflation, even though interest rates rise accordingly, because repayments are linked to the original fixed purchase price. The scale of this effect is greater with higher rates of inflation, while mortgage repayments decline in real terms the alternative rent payments will rise with inflation. Although some tenants may perceive the Right to Buy choice in these stark terms the decision to exercise the Right to Buy is more than this simple financial comparison of rents and mortgage repayments over time. On the 'cost' side there should also be added maintenance costs, insurance and, in the case of flats, service charges, balanced on the 'benefits' side of the equation by the acquisition of an 'appreciating asset'.

There is no doubt that tenants have found this an attractive proposition as shown by the more than two million who have exercised their right. Yet, within this financial framework the nature of the decision has been subtly changing, for example the significance of the appreciating asset. As noted in Chapter 4 initial purchasers were very much of a view that they intended to spend the rest of their lives in their home. In these circumstances the purchase decision may not be an overt investment decision and the home may be seen more as a consumption good. The investment element would then be seen in terms of providing a long term inheritance, a future home for their offspring. Such an approach is entirely logical as there was no widespread evidence of a resale market at that time except in new towns (Jones 1982). No-one could be sure that there would not be problems of reselling.

The lack of a resale market also meant that valuations of Right to Buy properties were very low at the outset of the policy. There was no comparable sales evidence of directly equivalent properties in terms of location or, often, of house type on which to base valuations. The result was that properties were initially valued at a much lower price than broadly comparable housing in the existing private market. The development of a resale market (Chapter 6) has had two effects. First, it has become much easier to assess market value and, second, it has increased prices and Right to Buy valuations have risen much faster than the market as a whole.

One of the curious consequences of the rise in values is the benefit to the initial purchasers (or their heirs) who tended to express little interest in the investment dimension of buying. If they still own their property they have been the greatest financial winners from the policy. Subsequent Right to Buy purchasers have received a lesser financial deal in the sense that valuations are now higher and therefore so are purchase prices, but there is now less investment risk. The Right to Buy purchase is generally a safe investment provided it is in an area where there are already sales. The safety of the investment was also assured by building in potential lags to the process whereby a valuation, once made, could apply for up to two years while the tenant decided whether to exercise the option or not. Although this facility was not widely used and was withdrawn, the time taken to complete sales generally meant, in a rising market, an immediate (notional) capital gain on purchase and when there was a housing boom, as for example in the south-east of England at the end of the 1990s, this was substantial.

There is another key variable in a tenant's financial equation that has changed. As noted earlier council house rents have risen substantially in real terms. This has been part of a policy whereby traditional 'bricks and mortar' subsidies linked to specific housing have been replaced by housing benefit, a subsidy linked to individual households' incomes. For households in work the higher cost of remaining a tenant has been a major push factor toward exercising their Right to Buy.

Tenants who have not exercised the Right to Buy of course do not receive the equity share provided by the discount. As noted in Chapter 4 these tend to be tenants either living in properties comprising non-standard house types or in unpopular estates or on very low incomes, for example long term unemployed or the elderly living on state benefits which effectively pay their rent. There is some overlap between these groups because the tenants living in unpopular housing are often there because they do not have the financial ability to move. Thus it tends to be low income council tenants who have been 'excluded' from the wealth redistribution from the state.

The Right to Buy purchaser ultimately has the opportunity to buy another home by using the equity in the property provided by the discount (and any subsequent capital gain) as a deposit on a house on the open market. For some households this discount is in effect the gateway not only to home purchase but in a relatively short time period to a move 'upmarket' that otherwise would not have been possible. It is difficult to assess this phenomenon but Jones (2003) illustrates that many people move on relatively quickly. In fact studies of resales have found that the decision to resell had been made before they bought under the Right to Buy (for example Pawson *et al.* 1997).

Where the information is available all studies report strong capital gains on resale. Forrest *et al.* (1995b) also noted that many ex-council tenants make large capital gains which they do not necessarily reinvest in housing. For example the capital gains estimated by Jones and Murie (1999) on resales in Glasgow up to 1996 were significant, even allowing for the improvements undertaken by the new owners. The gains depended partly on the length of period before sale but the mean gross capital gain was not less than £27 000 for resales between 1990 and 1996. These capital gains were over £30 000 for houses. In percentage terms these capital gains were generally over 275% of the original price with the most profitable being four-in-a-block/cottage flats (340% plus).

The acquisition of equity, provided by the state, is clearly a necessary condition for this trading-up process but it is not in itself sufficient. Buying a more expensive property requires a greater mortgage commitment, and the increased borrowing capacity is crucially dependent on income. Not surprisingly, therefore, the evidence on Right to Buy households who resell is that they tend to be younger, more affluent, and more likely to be in professional or managerial occupations than other households who remain in their Right to Buy home (Forrest *et al.* 1995b). The most comprehensive Scottish study (Pawson *et al.* 1997) similarly found that resellers tend to be young, but with a small number in the junior non-manual and skilled socioeconomic groups. The upwardly mobile Right to Buy purchaser has not become able to trade-up simply because of the Right to Buy but also because of occupational and income circumstances which enable a wider choice in the housing market. Even so the Right to Buy can provide a financial helping hand up the housing ladder, an advantage unavailable to non-council tenants.

For those who do not have the income and capacity to expand their borrowings substantially the opportunities to move afforded by the Right to Buy are more limited. In common with the rest of the private sector, Right to Buy purchase does proffer the potential to subsequently adjust housing circumstances with changing needs associated with the family cycle. This includes, for example, empty nesters approaching retirement, adjusting their housing requirements after their children had left home. It may give them the option if they have bought in a high price area to move to a larger home in a lower price area (see Jones 2003).

Some initial critics of the Right to Buy were concerned about the long term affordability of home ownership for some purchasers. In fact, taking up the Right to Buy for most tenants, as discussed above, is a very safe financial decision as long as they live in popular estates. The discounts (combined with a resale market) minimise risk to both purchasers and providers of mortgage finance and mean that it is possible to get 100% mortgages. Banks and building societies have proved very willing to finance council house sales and any initial nervousness associated with a lack of tradition of lending on these kinds of properties was eliminated at an early stage. In fact many purchasers are able to borrow more than

100% of the purchase price to undertake improvements (Jones 2003; Jones & Murie 1999).

A view of underlying household finances was given by the Jones and Murie surveys (1999) of Right to Buy purchasers in Birmingham and Croydon. These households were not wholly an affluent group, with 15% of them having been in arrears with their rent at some stage in the past five years. Perhaps surprisingly those who had been in arrears were more likely to include households which were younger and which currently had two or more earners. This suggests households had experienced a considerable change in their circumstances. As many as 35% had been in receipt of housing benefit at some point during the past five years. This was most common amongst those with no full time earners and those on low incomes.

Most households in the study felt that they would be paying more if they were still renting. The proportion of households with mortgage arrears was very low. However, a small number of households were finding it difficult to afford their mortgage. This was generally the result of changed circumstances such as the loss of a job, reduced earnings, retirement, relationship breakdown or the payment of other debts.

The picture drawn of Right to Buy purchasers is of a group of households with relatively low variable incomes who have nevertheless taken the opportunity to buy. Like the rest of the population they are subject to financial stresses and strains brought about by relationship breakdown or changed employment prospects. The age and stage in the family cycle of many sitting tenant purchasers means that they are not in the group most prone to problems of relationship breakdown. However, they may be particularly exposed to loss of overtime payments and unemployment.

There are however a range of other factors associated with the particular circumstances of their house purchase which would make it likely that Right to Buy purchasers are under-represented amongst those with arrears and repossessions. The key element in this relates to the levels of discount available to sitting tenant purchasers. This means that sitting tenant purchasers have generally borrowed less and have not borrowed to the maximum potential of their income. If they are extended through borrowing it is as a result of subsequent loans associated with house improvement or other credit, rather than the initial purchase of the house. Moreover, because they have a substantial equity in the property (usually around 50%), their ability to negotiate with lenders if they do experience problems is much greater than amongst other first time buyers who have borrowed 100% of the purchase price. It can also be argued that Right to Buy purchasers, as established households, have not usually faced the associated expenses of house purchase such as new furniture, carpets and curtains.

All in all, sitting tenant purchasers are much less likely than other house buyers to be exposed through excessive borrowing and much more likely to be able to ride out the contingencies that arise in the early years when people are often most vulnerable in relation to their mortgage. Even in a period of falling property values these advantages are significant. The problems of negative equity and the difficulties this presents in terms of mobility or of selling properties if there are difficulties of other kinds are much less likely to be experienced by Right to Buy purchasers – again because of the substantial insulation provided by the discount and the equity it represents. Even where properties have fallen in value by 30%, sitting tenant purchasers will not have moved into negative equity, unless they borrowed on the security of the dwelling after the initial purchase. Jones (2003) reported that between 1993 and 1997 there were 250 requests to the local authority by former tenants in Leeds to repurchase their home, although there is no obligation on the council to do so (see also DETR 1998b). Many of these were not because of mortgage problems but because of difficulties reselling, and the number was relatively low compared with at least 6000 properties sold under the Right to Buy in Leeds over the equivalent period.

Jones (2003) also examined the incidence of statutory homelessness amongst Right to Buy purchasers in Birmingham, Leeds and London. The number of home owners who later applied to the council as homeless was a very small percentage: for example in Birmingham only 1.6% of applicants had become homeless because they were unable to pay their mortgage. Councils do not keep records on whether these households were formerly Right to Buy purchasers but clearly the numbers are small. Where such instances occur affordability is not necessarily the problem. Leeds and Havering Councils noted instances of a small number of cases of the elderly presenting themselves as homeless having some years ago bought their home with the help of their children. They had generally entered into an agreement on the understanding that they would be able to stay in their home while they were alive, only to find their position changed some years on.

While affordability is not an insurmountable problem for Right to Buy purchasers it is evident that affordability problems have become much more prominent in debates about housing over the last two decades. Such problems have been particularly important in the periods of housing market booms of the late 1980s and the early 2000s. It is evident not only through historically high house prices relative to incomes but also through the average age of first time purchasers rising. The expansion of the buy to let market has not resolved this problem because much of it does not cater for medium or large sized families. Inevitably the cumulative loss of good quality council housing through the Right to Buy has exacerbated the problem. The Right to Buy has contributed to the general affordability problem in the housing market of the early 2000s and the rise in house prices but it also made the incentives to sitting tenant purchase more attractive.

Conclusions

The Right to Buy has always been controversial in terms of the scale of discounts and its impact on public finances. The capital receipts generated ostensibly represent a very substantial contribution to public finances but this is very much a short term perspective. A fuller discounted cash flow analysis over the long term taking into account lost rents shows that in the early 1980s the policy produced a net loss to the Government. The precise scale of the deficit depends on the assumptions applied regarding future trends. Repetition of the discounted cash flow analysis in today's radically different circumstances must also be tempered by the assumptions caveat but it seems that in areas of high demand for social housing the Right to Buy remains a financial drain on the Government. A key issue in these financial calculations throughout the life of the Right to Buy has been the inclusion (incorporating scale and timing) of replacement of the 'lost' housing stock. Despite these arguments in practice very few of the more than two million houses sold can be said to have been replaced.

The essential arrangements of the Right to Buy have remained broadly unchanged throughout its existence. The major exception has been the variability in the discount. Yet there are fundamental changes that have occurred as a result of the cumulative impact of the Right to Buy and other housing policies. The economics and management of council housing are now very different as a consequence. Increased council housing management costs can be directly attributed to the Right to Buy. The choice facing council tenants involves the same financial variables but the emphasis has moved very much away from their home as a consumable good to that of an investment.

At the outset of the Right to Buy critics argued that only a small proportion of households would be able to afford to take it up. These views proved to be considerably wide of the mark. The high take up of the Right to Buy has meant that another initial criticism that the redistribution effect would only benefit high income tenants was ultimately unfounded. However, one could argue that it is the higher income groups who have been best able to unlock this equity by trading-up. There is also still a not inconsiderable proportion of households, the poorest, who have been excluded from this wealth share out by the state.

11

Policy Transfer: international perspectives on housing privatisation

Privatisation of state built housing has become a strong theme internationally. There is no doubt that there was international interest in the outcome of the Right to Buy in the United Kingdom. However we should not conclude from this that the UK was the pioneer in privatisation, or that its approach was imitated elsewhere. This chapter considers examples of the privatisation of state housing as pursued in a number of countries. It is important to acknowledge that this is only one aspect of a privatisation strategy. As has been argued elsewhere and, as was true in the UK, other approaches to privatisation have been pursued.

This chapter draws on and develops the picture of different types of experience of privatisation of state housing especially in central and eastern Europe but also refers to such policies elsewhere in Europe and in Asia and America. Five types of privatisation are covered:

(1) The first type, discussed fully elsewhere in this book, is most clearly represented by the UK. This involves active policies, backed by financial incentives, to reduce the size of the public housing sector as part of a wider housing policy to support home ownership. The situation in Ireland has been most like that in the UK. An extremely generous sales programme has been seen as an end in itself and there has been no serious attempt to recycle the income generated back into the housing programme or into the public sector.
(2) The second type of privatisation relates to the disposal of state housing in eastern and central Europe as part of the process of changing economic and political regimes in the late 1980s. These privatisations were strongly influenced by the burden that ownership of properties with high maintenance and repair costs would place on new systems

of local government. In these types of privatisation Right to Buy was a common phenomenon but often existed for a relatively short time before being replaced. In some cases privatisation was accompanied by restitution under which land and property seized by earlier regimes could be reclaimed.

(3) The third type of privatisation refers to policies adopted in south and east Asia where the promotion of home ownership has been an integral part of economic strategies and a distinctive welfare state. Policies in China, which are referred to more fully below, were strongly influenced by Singapore and the financial arrangements to support the development of individual property ownership are of particular interest.

(4) The fourth approach to privatisation is the more cautious approach adopted by most of the northern and western European countries with large public or not-for-profit sectors. These countries have largely avoided the rush for sales associated with Ireland and the UK but they have, to different extents, adopted selective sales schemes.

(5) A fifth type, illustrated by the USA, involves privatisation of a small state housing sector as part of an explicit welfare approach to housing.

Central and eastern Europe

In contrast to the UK, the formerly Communist central and eastern European countries generally adopted the privatisation of state housing in the early 1990s following fundamental changes to their political systems (Tosics 2001). The policies adopted often provided a Right to Buy style scheme but often only for a short time, after which it was replaced by locally variable schemes. For example, unified national schemes operated for two years in Hungary and Slovenia and this limited period of opportunity, as well as high levels of discount, accounted for a high number of sales over a short period.

It is important to recognise that there was great variation in the detail of approaches adopted by countries in this group and that some of them had already taken steps to expand home ownership and to privatise state housing prior to the change of political regime. Bulgaria had adopted a discounted sales policy and transferred the bulk of its public sector stock to sitting tenants prior to the fall of the Communist regime. State sponsored home ownership in Bulgaria was designed to give people a stake in the system rather than being about achieving housing policy goals, but there was an added element associated with low rents and the build up of a maintenance and repair backlog within the public sector housing stock. This latter issue was more important in the central and eastern European privatisations than in Britain where the problems of raising rents were not insurmountable and the public sector housing stock was largely houses with gardens. The costs of repair and maintenance for poorly constructed high rise dwellings were relatively unimportant compared with the situation in central and eastern European countries.

Privatisation of housing has been a major feature of the transformation of eastern European economies. It has generally been characterised as a 'shock absorber' rather than an agency of change, and as having an influence beyond the sector (Struyck 1996). In a similar way Clapham and Kintrea (1996) referred to the sale of state housing, saying that ownership of a house may be seen as offering a degree of security to people at a time of considerable instability and uncertainty, and may also be seen as an important symbol of the advantages of a market economy when other material gains may be slow to materialise.

Other commentators have emphasised the extent to which it is important to see these and other privatisations as path dependent. In Putnam's terms (see Harloe 1999), 'Where you get to depends on where you are coming from.' In this context, it is important to note two things in relation to central and eastern Europe: first, individuals did have property rights under state socialist systems. Privatisation does not involve simply the transfer of rights of ownership from the state to private individuals and enterprises, rather the privatisation process involves repartitioning of rights (see Harloe 1999); second, it is important to recognise that eastern European countries came from very different starting positions. Hegedüs *et al.* (1996b) state that eastern Europeans cities averaged only 28% privately owned dwellings in 1990, compared with 62% among comparators and 65% among western European cities, but this comparison obscures enormous variation within central and eastern Europe. Before the reforms of the 1990s, some of this group of countries had already dismantled the large public sector housing schemes, while others had higher rates of public sector rental. For example, in Russia 67% of housing was still rented from the state in 1990 and the Baltic republics had a similarly large public rental sector. This figure was only 9% in Bulgaria and 20% in Hungary (Baross & Struyk 1993). The Czech Republic, Hungary, Poland, Slovakia, Bulgaria, Croatia and Romania all had rates of public rented housing below 30%, with Slovenia at 32% and Albania at 35% the highest rates outside Russia and the Baltic states (Hegedüs *et al.* 1996b). These are not high levels of public rented housing and the dominant tenures were not quasi public housing but were forms of owner-occupation.

Against this background, the 'shock absorber' involved in relation to housing was likely to have an uneven impact and the approach adopted varied between countries. In some cases there was an active restitution policy. This was significant in the Czech Republic and in Russia. In every country where privatisation was undertaken, sitting tenants were offered extremely generous terms at the outset of the process, although in Poland and Bulgaria these terms were not maintained (Baross & Struyk 1993).

A further important feature of the privatisation of state housing in central and eastern Europe has been the early decentralisation of the ownership of state housing to local governments. This was a response to the over-centralisation endemic under previous regimes: 'However, with ownership local governments also acquired new responsibilities. Often the shift in responsibilities was motivated as much by the wish to remove a difficult issue from [the] national parliament agenda as by the desire to make government more responsive to the people. Typically, national funding for construction of further housing was cut dramatically and local governments were left on their own to find funds with which to maintain already existing housing projects.' (Baross & Struyk 1993).

Privatisation of the state housing stock can be seen as the single most distinguishing feature of the transition from the old political and economic system to the new one, but both the approaches to the funding of privatisation and the progress in achieving it were variable. Among the motivations were a desire for local government to remove ongoing subsidies and the real political gains associated with selling units to sitting tenants at very low prices. Baross and Struyk argue that in the Russian federation another motivation was at work because of the very high rate of state ownership of its housing stock: 'Without an aggressive campaign to shift a significant share of housing to private ownership, there would be no housing market.' However, as experience has shown, the development of housing markets requires more than the privatisation of housing units. The willingness of banks to lend on property is fundamental and, in many cases, the emerging privatised housing market does not have a high level of transactions, except at the upper end of the market. This problem is further complicated by the lack of clear management arrangements especially where ineffective condominium laws were adopted.

Baross and Struyk, referring to the early years of privatisation in central and eastern Europe, said that the share of state units transferred to sitting tenants was highly variable, with only Hungary, Slovenia and Bulgaria transferring 20% or more of the inventory. In some cases, for example Russia, this was because the programmes for privatisation started later. Hegedüs *et al.* (1996b) reported much higher levels of sales – the rate of owner-occupation in the 12 countries they referred to had grown from 58% to 68% between 1990 and 1994.

Kingsley *et al.* (1993) referred to the privatisation programme of the Czech and Slovak Federative Republic (CSFR) in the early 1990s. In 1991, the parliaments of both republics approved new housing policy statements but called for a movement toward a market-oriented housing system. Restitution rules in 1990 and 1991 provided powers to transfer back to the original owners or their heirs buildings that had been confiscated by the state after the Communists assumed power. All claims had to be submitted by the end of September 1991. By 1992, ownership of 30% of the residential buildings owned by the state in certain districts of Prague had been transferred under this law. Restituted buildings were still occupied by tenants who had tenancy rights, rents were still controlled and the new legal owners were obliged to maintain the buildings.

The next step for the CSFR (in May 1991) was to transfer ownership of all communal housing not yet restituted from the state to local governments. This was an interim step towards privatisation. The fear of large operating deficits and uncertainty about the willingness of national governments to continue to subsidise housing meant that local governments tended to be strong supporters of privatisation.

Restitution was not adopted in all countries. In Russia, privatisation involved a rapid and practically cash free transfer to private ownership for sitting tenants, in order to create a private housing market. There were early steps towards privatisation in 1988, with apartments and housing cooperatives turned over to tenants, and an initial programme of sales to tenants of state and public housing, but the pace of privatisation speeded up after the legislation of June 1991 established a new procedure for transferring the state and municipal housing stock to the ownership of tenants. The key element in this was the issue of a voucher, the value of which was calculated on the value of a single square metre of the average apartment in their city, and tenants would pay the difference between the estimated value of their entire apartments and the value of the voucher.

In early 1992, Moscow initiated the plan which entailed the free transfer of housing stock to the possession of tenants (Struyk & Kosareva 1994). By the end of 1994, 32% of the previously state controlled housing units had been privatised, and in the 50 largest cities over 50% of the housing stock was private (Renaud 1995). By the end of 1995, about 35% of all the state housing had been privatised (Struyk & Kosareva 1994), with a higher proportion of the stock sold in Moscow. Moscow is the most commonly used example where significant numbers of publicly owned houses were given away or sold for £1 each. This approach related to the enormous backlog of repair and maintenance and the new regime's desire to offload the burden by passing the responsibility for maintenance and repair to the occupiers of the dwellings. Similar considerations appear to have applied in other east European countries. In Hungary for example (see Murie *et al.* 2005) rents in public housing were traditionally very low and state owned management companies had not carried out any comprehensive maintenance programmes. There was a backlog of disrepair and after 1990 the new government did not want to deal with housing. The ownership of state housing was transferred to local governments without any financial settlement to enable this backlog to be addressed. Consequently local governments could not afford to maintain or repair the rental stock. It made financial sense to dispose of the stock and this was also in line with the philosophy of the transition and the demands of tenants concerned about potential rent increases.

The Right to Buy introduced in Hungary in 1994 applied in all cases except where the building was in a dangerous condition, a decision had been taken to rehabilitate the area, or the building was a listed monument. If none of these circumstances prevailed, the local government had to turn the whole building into a condominium and offer all the flats for sale, even if only one of the tenants had indicated the desire to buy. The prices paid were very low: where the building had not been substantially renovated in the last 15 years it was based on 15% of the market value; and where the building had been substantially renovated in the last 15 years it was based on 30% of the market value. In both cases a further 40% discount was given if the tenant paid in cash. Alternatively, the tenant would not obtain this second discount element but could pay on a fixed 3% interest rate (compared with inflation rates of some 30% per year) over 35 years. A similar pattern has also been reported for Slovenia (Murie *et al.* 2005). In both Hungary and Slovenia the transfer of state housing to local authorities and the establishment of all accommodation as condominiums irrespective of the numbers of dwellings within the building sold meant that the vast majority of the stock was exposed to privatisation. At the same time the proportion of tenants who bought was high and the short window of opportunity to take advantage of the generous Right to Buy terms in these countries persuaded tenants to take up the offer quickly.

East Asia

In China in the period since 1949, public sector housing had been the dominant form of housing. Privately owned properties had often been confiscated in the period of Communist government (Wang 1992). Following 1978 there was a change in emphasis. Private ownership ceased to be so unacceptable and Government began to embark upon programmes designed to reform the economic system and move towards a market system. As part of this, the government housing reform programme began to encourage the sale of public sector houses. The details of these sales programmes are available elsewhere (Wang & Murie 1999; Wang 2004) but an important feature of privatisation in China is the use of a compulsory savings scheme (Housing Provident Fund) to generate the funds and enable lending for individuals to purchase housing under the privatisation programme, with repayments generating funds for others to draw upon for the same purpose. Following the example of Singapore (see Phang 2005) the Chinese approach generated a circulation of capital. While public sector housing, with a flow of rental income (and especially if those rents were extremely low), provided only a trickle of funds to be used to reinvest in the housing sector and to build more houses, a formula based on privatisation with people purchasing houses enabled capital invested in public sector housing to be released quickly and then, crucially, to be reinvested in the housing sector. The Chinese approach has generated funds sufficient to sustain a high level of investment in housing in order to improve housing conditions within the country. This provides an additional rationale for privatisation, adding to the level of home ownership and addressing issues of political stability.

By the end of 1999 home ownership had become the norm in metropolitan China, with up to 70% of all non-migrant households reporting some form of ownership. Davis (2003) commented that, as a result of the policy shifts of 1998 and 1999, the old system of welfare housing became defunct. Subsidised sales continued in some cities through the summer of 2000 but, by December 1999, the bulk of urban housing stock had become fully capitalised alienable individual assets. Urban housing was no longer treated as a decommodified welfare benefit and all owners of urban housing were on the same legal footing, i.e. able to sell properties in the market. Nevertheless Davis argued that:

'. . . the domestic property regime in 2000 is best described as segmented into four groups: owners with full ownership rights, owners with only occupancy and use rights, renters with long term occupancy rights who rent public quarters, and renters with only short-term occupancy rights who rent on the private market. There is a clear hierarchy of property rights: at the bottom are those who rent, above them are those who have purchased use rights but not full property rights, and above them are those with full property rights.'

Davis then added that by 2000, some 60% of non-migrants had purchased full property rights and some 32% had purchased use rights. Very few non-migrants were among those who rented. Migrants were predominantly in the renter category. Wang (2004) stated, 'Home ownership became the most common form of tenure in cities, with over 82% of urban families owning their home.' Davis concluded that:

'by the end of the 1990s housing reforms had commercialised a substantial share of urban real estate and popularised the idea of home ownership in China but, despite the language of market exchange, most buyers had paid less than 15% of market value and the wealthier the family, the higher the absolute value of the subsidies. Housing reforms granted urban residents the full range of housing property rights, but the process through which this commodification was achieved discriminated against blue collar employees. As a result, privatisation of this form of welfare benefit laid the foundation for residential segregation by economic class and undermined the relative equality of lifestyle that had prevailed in earlier years.'

Elsewhere in south and east Asia there has not been the ideological support for state ownership of housing that had dominated Chinese policy from the 1950s to the period of housing reform. In Japan, Korea and Taiwan, for example, a significant state housing sector has not developed. Nevertheless, the state has actively supported the development of home ownership and this has been a central element in the welfare state system emerging in these countries. The welfare state model developed in Singapore placed asset ownership and the appreciating value of property assets at the core of welfare provision (Sherraden 1997). This approach strongly influenced reform in China, involving compulsory savings which encouraged people to invest in property and which directly and indirectly provide resources in older age and in periods of low income.

Catherine Jones (1990) referred to approaches to welfare state provision in Hong Kong, Singapore, South Korea and Taiwan. In each of these cases the pursuit of economic development had been the primary goal of public policy. State housing provision and the release of land were particularly important in Singapore and Hong Kong and were seen as economic drivers rather than social programmes. Jones concluded that the welfare states of the eastern 'tigers' were not characterised by participatory democracy, the promotion of citizen's rights, social obligations or assistance for the poor – indeed they were characterised by the reverse, these east Asian societies reward those who help themselves – according to Jones a 'welfare capitalism that works'. Jones also identified some commonality in the way that state housing services were provided in these countries with large, state run enterprises generally responsible for the direct development of estates, or the supervision of construction under contract. The developments also tended to involve construction of high rise apartments which were individually owned but might be 'managed' by state agencies.

Referring to eight countries in east and south-east Asia, Doling (2002) distinguished between 'strong state providers and developers' (Singapore and Hong Kong) and 'state supported self helpers' (Indonesia, Thailand and Malaysia), with Japan, Korea and Taiwan occupying 'intermediate positions' where selective support had been used to help low income groups meet their housing needs within a market framework.

Reluctant privatisers

There is a significant group of countries with large public or not for profit housing sectors that have avoided any mass sales of properties. Aalbers (2004) has provided an account of this for the Netherlands where the approach to the sale of state built properties has been cautious. The political leadership has never been convinced by the case for privatisation. Perhaps equally importantly housing associations, as the dominant social housing providers, have a different relationship with the state than elsewhere and by the 1990s had become independent of both central and local government.

Some features of the financing of public sector housing in the Netherlands are important to the discussion of privatisation. In this case non-profit housing companies have been able to build up sufficient reserves to fund maintenance and some element of future development programmes. In an environment where sale of properties is not compulsory some associations may choose to sell properties in order to generate capital receipts and, through this, to maintain their development programmes. The same theme runs through the considerations of the Netherlands, Hong Kong, Singapore and China: to see the existing housing stock as a potential source of revenue which can be reinvested within the housing sector and can maintain the development and investment activities of public and non-profit sector bodies.

In the Netherlands prior to the 1990s, the half-hearted attempts to develop sales (Murie *et al.* 2005) had little impact. Following the policy document *Housing in the Nineties* (VROM 1989) some housing associations began to envisage using their greater financial autonomy by including sales of properties in their business plans. Added to this, in the mid 1990s the Dutch Labour Party (PvdA) began to press housing associations to sell one million of their approximately three million social housing units. The original idea of introducing a right to buy was abandoned. It lacked sufficient parliamentary support and fears that a right to buy would lead to British style marginalisation and residualisation were expressed. A more moderate approach was included in the Promotion of Home Ownership Act passed in 2000 and designed to encourage rather than force sale and provide subsidies for low income households to purchase. What has emerged from this is managed sales schemes driven by the landlord who has chosen what to sell. The process has remained under the control of housing associations and there has only been a slow growth in the volume of sales.

The residual case: the USA

Although the United States of America has a very small public housing sector, there has been some experience of the sale of public sector housing there. Public sector housing in the USA originated in the inter-war period as part of the New Deal. Direct Federal construction of housing began in 1934 under the Public Works Administration. It was the Housing Act of 1937 which set up the US Housing Authority and authorised it to make loans for up to 90% of the development costs of public housing projects. The Act included provisions to ensure the housing would be full of families on low income, but at this stage it was seen as a pump priming exercise to boost the economy and as a property programme rather than a social policy. The need for housing for low income groups was less prominent than the problem of unemployment and the desirability of solving it through slum clearance. Public housing production was affected by World War II. The Lanham Act of 1940 provided funds and a new administrative organisation for low income families whose wage earners were engaged in defence or war production and in 1942 the two organisations responsible for public housing under the Acts of 1937 and 1940 were combined into the Federal Public Housing Authority. As a result, the population in public housing became more mixed. Many of those who were unemployed or very low waged but were still capable of paying an economic rent were permitted to remain; at the same time preference in selecting new tenants was given to essential war workers who were not poor and to servicemen's families who often were.

The Housing Act of 1949 still promised a relatively ambitious programme but this was reduced immediately and by 1953 had become very small. There was effectively a reversion back to the Poor Law conception of public housing. This, combined with local politics and racial politics, contributed to the rapid decline of American public housing into a residual sector for the poor, with a much more explicit process of identifying the poor through means testing. Although not all American public housing was unattractive, its reputation was permanently damaged and its stigmatisation established. Public housing had been developed in an environment of rigid restrictions and antagonistic forces (Fuerst 1974) and the same antagonistic forces interpreted the operation of the sector as evidence of the inherent weaknesses and inefficiency of public provision.

Public housing provision in America was established as a small residual sector at a very early stage. It did not go through a process of expansion and did not have a wide social acceptability, or become aspirational housing in the way that existed throughout Europe. The environment of discussion of privatisation was wholly different. The sector was seen as a way station for low income families and not for permanent residence (President's Advisory Committee 1953). It would seem illogical to reward tenants or encourage their continuing residence through a scheme comparable with the Right to Buy. Nonetheless, there were sales schemes and, for example, Rohe and Stegman (1992) reported the evaluation of the public housing home ownership demonstration (PH HOD). Under the National Housing Act of 1974 the US Department of Housing and Urban Development was able to approve sales of public housing to residents at prices determined by local public housing authorities. In 1984, the Reagan administration proposed PH HOD as a way to expand the sale of public housing to tenants and collect useful information for developing regulations. Seventeen demonstration programmes were selected and brought in 1315 units of public housing over a 36 month period. Overall results of the demonstration were disappointing. Only 320 units of public housing were transferred during the 50 month evaluation period – 25% of the units selected. The reason for this disappointing record was considered to be a lack of commitment to the programme, the difficulty of finding public housing tenants who had both the means and the desire to participate in the programme and the difficulty of relocating tenants who did not want to participate in the demonstration. Those who did buy under the scheme had varied benefits due to the differing values of the property and the height to which it was appreciating in different locations. The general conclusion was that only higher income public housing residents participated in the project.

These results were in many ways similar to those in the UK. The small number of units sold meant that there was little impact on the remaining public housing sector. The loss of the highest rent payers and some of the best quality units from the public housing sector was seen as a disadvantage and an expanded sales programme would have had a more dramatic impact on these. The recommendations emerging from the demonstration were to adopt a different approach to focus on replacement housing and the redevelopment of unattractive existing public housing areas; to provide vouchers for public housing replacement; to increase technical assistance and operating assistance and to focus upon different ways of increasing opportunities for home ownership. Subsequent policy energy in the United States has been on these alternative programmes involving housing vouchers and the development of mixed tenure estates.

Outcomes

The final section of this chapter addresses the different consequences or outcomes of privatisation of housing associated with the various countries referred to above. It refers in turn to:

- who benefits;
- residualisation of social and public rented housing; and
- the creation of private markets.

Who benefits

Much of the research literature associated with housing privatisation in different countries has focused on who benefits. While the British literature on this is the most substantial there is some evidence from elsewhere. In Hungary and Slovenia (Murie *et al.* 2005) all tenants except the very poorest participated in Right to Buy schemes. The process has been less socially selective than in the UK and less selective in terms of property types. This is partly because the large post-war mass housing estates in these countries provided some of the best quality and best condition housing, especially when compared with rundown, older properties in cities. Consequently, the attractiveness of state housing is generally higher than in the UK. In Hungary, taking into account that the best public housing units were allocated according to merit in the socialist period, estimates show that 40% of investment value went to households in the top quarter of the income distribution, while only 17% went to the lowest quarter (Hegedüs *et al.* 1996a). In Slovenia, households living in apartments with a high market value benefited the most while the households that lived in restituted dwellings lost out because their right to buy was restricted and most of them continued to live with the threat of eviction (Mandič 1999; Sendi 1995).

In other situations the most important impact of privatisation is the change in ownership and management of estates. In central and eastern Europe it has been common to adopt condominium arrangements, but there are serious questions about how effectively these operate especially in relation to the properties in worst condition and the owners who have fewest resources. In Slovenia, people who were not sitting tenants of the state considered the Right to Buy to be unfair since it only benefitted that small group, while everybody made monthly contributions towards the creation of the public housing stock. Disputes still continue relating to the rights of sitting tenants and the new landlords of restituted dwellings. Coupled with the condominium arrangements and economic changes which left many households with very low incomes, privatisation of housing transformed ownership and management but offered no response to problems associated with dwelling condition, maintenance, repair, improvement or renewal.

When looking at the eastern and central European experience it is important to remember that much of the public sector housing was highly desirable and occupied by higher and middle income groups. Nevertheless it is apparent that the better stock and more affluent tenants have primarily been involved. In spite of the differences in the legacy, the process of privatisation has some similarities to those in the UK.

In relation to China, Wang (2004) stated that the impact of housing reform and development on different social and economic groups varied: it was irrelevant to the large numbers of rural migrants living in the cities and had limited direct impact on people who were traditional home owners not employed in the state sector. Senior employees in the public sector benefited most. What kind of housing people had and what their position in society was at the outset was crucial. Families in good quality housing were able to secure their position. People employed by work units that were not performing well and had not invested in housing ended up living in poor quality housing and 'housing reform reinforced existing inequalities within China'. These conclusions are very similar to those for the UK or central and eastern Europe.

Davis (2003) argued that in China, managers of blue collar workers were much better placed than manual workers to purchase the more attractive properties at the right price. She implied that there had been some manipulation of this process. Production workers were disadvantaged in the workplace and in relation to the purchase of property. She referred to arguments:

'that because market reforms increased managerial autonomy, and redistributed control over collective assets, local leaders had unprecedented freedom to commandeer collective assets for themselves and their relatives and that housing reform was an ideal site for 'cadre abuse' because it allowed the use of power for private gain, which might have been unfair but was not illegal. The recommodification of urban housing stock offered a more widely distributed opportunity for those who were in positions of enterprise authority to reap a personal gain than asset stripping in a steel smelter, or in a workshop of high street weaving machines.'

Wang (2003) reported the findings from social surveys in Shenyang and Chongquing designed to look at the living and housing conditions of low income communities and the social impact of urban reforms. Both cities are located in inland areas of China and the impacts from new high technology and property-led urban development were less than in coastal cities. His survey evidence showed that poor residents tended to live in old traditional houses which were small and lacked exclusive use of toilets and kitchens. They had not experienced significant improvements in their housing and the impact of housing reform on them was very limited. The majority still rented their accommodation and only 12% had bought their house through privatisation. He commented that for the majority of poor residents housing privatisation and subsidy had been irrelevant, although rents in the public sector had increased substantially. Generally, he concluded:

'that economic reform has brought fundamental changes to Chinese cities, and has improved the living conditions of the majority of urban residents. However, while the higher and middle income households now enjoy a lifestyle which was never experienced by ordinary Chinese families in the past, a large group of urban residents has been left behind.'

This new social and economic stratification also has important spatial consequences. Housing played a very important role in the social and spatial reorganisation of Chinese cities. While most government officials, professionals and enterprise managers got their housing either almost free or with a large subsidy from the state, industrial workers and other urban residents who had never secured a good standard home in the old system were trapped in poor traditional housing areas. With the increase in housing prices they could only improve their housing circumstances if they had a substantial amount of money. Property development and urban renewal processes over the last two decades have tended to redevelop the areas with good land value, low population density and simpler land and property ownership, with low compensation costs. The areas left were mainly the poorest communities with a concentration of the lowest income groups.

Residualisation of social and public rented housing

The differential pattern of uptake of Right to Buy schemes has implications for the remaining public or social rented sector. If the privatisation of housing involves the sale of the best housing into home ownership and the retention of the least desirable parts of the stock and if the more affluent and higher social class and status tenants convert to home owners what is left is a less attractive housing stock catering for a more uniformly low income group of households. This is the recipe for welfare housing following the American residual model and is the direction of change in the UK. The effect of this pattern is to further reinforce the distinction between neighbourhoods by adding a tenure label to estates and to lower the reputation and associations with public sector housing.

The creation of private markets

The comparison of the experience of different countries does not only highlight differences in themes and objectives. It also raises questions about the meaning of privatisation. In all of the countries concerned, where housing policy has involved sales to existing tenants, it is arguable that the transfer has been a bureaucratically driven or state sponsored development of the private sector; a process to expand the market and home ownership. As has been argued in Britain the emergence of market processes comes later. Privatisation is different from commodification, and commodification occurs at a later stage when exchanges occur on the open market. However, in some countries these exchanges are likely to take place at a much later date. In China, first there were restrictions and penalties associated with the early sale of welfare housing. The early Chinese legislation initially denied a full property right to purchasers of welfare housing. As their purchase was subsidised and because the housing had been built at a subsidy, they were not deemed to be entitled to sell that property and make a gain from it. Those who did would have to repay the land cost and there would be an adjustment in price before they would be able to enter a market sale. In many cases the nature of this adjustment was not clear.

Even where such penalties did not exist, for example in purchases of low profit or commercially developed housing, it may well be argued that the market in practice does not function in a way that enables households to sell on the open market. There is no developed second hand market and incomes, exchange processes and labour market processes do not make the resale of properties viable. The expectations for their housing market are not ones of exchange and turnover comparable to those in the market systems of Britain, North America, Europe or Australasia.

The same kind of situation exists in some areas within central and eastern Europe. While households may have purchased their properties through state determined processes and are nominally home owners located within a market system, in practice their capacity to sell properties is extremely limited. They do not have the income or the resources to trade-up and other households are not in a position to purchase the dwelling at market price. Privatisation has not automatically created a market system. In most central and eastern European countries the building industry has undergone severe strain and new house building rates have collapsed. While it may be true that in the longer term there will be some convergence of these housing systems, the distinctiveness arising from their different histories and institutional and other legacies will persist. At the same time, the development of lending for house purchase has not been welcomed by the banking system and the development of a second hand market has often been slow. Lending agencies may be extremely reluctant to lend on properties which have uncertain maintenance records and represent poorer security for loans.

This situation has also been apparent in some limited parts of the market for former council houses in Britain. Some forms of local authority flats and particularly non traditional and high rise flats have proved very difficult to resell. They are not regarded as a sound investment by building societies and the uncertainty and potential level of maintenance and repair costs and the relatively high levels of service charges have made them less saleable than houses. These properties may then prove difficult to resell in the open market except at a very low price. Rather than entering a market associated with accumulation and the build up of wealth, the purchase of properties in this case represents the avoidance of a stream of payments associated with rent and therefore the rearrangement of housing costs over time. It does not involve entry into a market system with the ability to realise significant asset values or to trade-up or move within the market system.

Home ownership for these households, in different countries, does not mean accessing a market system, but means changing the package of rights and responsibilities within the existing dwelling and changing the financial regime associated with the use of that dwelling. In these terms privatisation both for the households which purchased and, in many cases, for the governments which sold is associated with a changed financial regime rather than entry to the market as it would be recognised by those who have entered it through other routes or as referred to generally in housing literature. This means properties and people who are not fully embraced within the market as it is generally understood have entered into a hybrid market which retains significant elements of public sector as well as some market sector attributes.

The restructuring of housing finance and new mechanisms to generate sufficient funds to maintain state housing policy goals has produced a hybrid form of tenure which is too easily labelled as private sector. Such an arrangement may be beneficial to all of those concerned and it is not intended to imply that such a hybrid nature is any way second best. For the households concerned the rearrangement of housing costs and the increased security associated with a different form of tenure are significant gains. This is especially the case where the expectation is that the existing occupiers of the dwelling, and perhaps subsequent generations, will not wish to move and the absence of the ability to trade in the market is no significant loss. At the same time, for government the mechanism enables the continued pursuit of housing production and investment goals and the continuing improvement of average housing conditions in the country. The Chinese example illustrates this very strongly with considerable progress being made to raise average housing conditions and in many cases to lift the lowest standard of housing available within cities.

Conclusions

A major theme in the restructuring of housing systems and economies in recent years has been the privatisation of public sector housing. It has become commonplace for countries which have substantial public housing sectors to have embarked upon the process of selling these dwellings. Normally the sale is to the sitting tenant who becomes an owner-occupier but in some cases sales to other agencies are also involved. What emerges from the varied experience of the privatisation of public housing is an emphasis on three elements:

(1) the achievement of home ownership and the political and electoral advantages associated with home ownership;
(2) an agenda associated with maintenance and repair and increasing costs of maintenance and repair;

(3) an agenda associated with circulation and with maintaining a substantial public sector investment programme.

It may be argued that all three of these elements are present to some degree in every situation but the emphasis is very different in different countries.

In Britain and Ireland the emphasis has been very heavily on the first element and the final element has been largely neglected. In China the emphasis has been heavily on the final element. In central and eastern Europe the emphasis has been on the first two elements. In Britain privatisation has been an end in itself, rather than a means to an end. In contrast, in some other countries the purpose of privatisation has been to enable other housing policy activities to take place or to achieve political and economic change.

It has been argued elsewhere that privatisation is facilitated by a number of preconditions. The first of these relates to the state of development of the housing market. It has been argued that in Britain a well developed, mature home ownership market with a high volume of turnover and second hand transactions is a much more appropriate environment for privatisation than a situation in which such market arrangements do not exist. Linked to this are institutional factors related to finance, lending and the legal framework as well as land ownership and exchange. Where these arrangements are well developed and are not a major source of conflict and controversy, privatisation which involves the development of a market is easier to contemplate. In central and eastern Europe the absence of many of these factors has widely been regarded as a barrier. It means that it is possible to change the ownership status of existing households, but this falls far short of creating a market.

While it is appropriate to focus upon preconditions it can also be argued that the process of privatisation is itself intended to create a market and there is an error in regarding privatisation as impossible in a situation where the market does not exist. It does however, mean that the nature of privatisation will be very different. Privatisation will have different effects in each of three possible situations:

- first, where a mature developed market system exists;
- second where no such system exists and the intention is to create such a market through privatisation;
- third, where neither of these situations exists, at least in the short term, and where the aim is purely to change the regime within public sector housing.

In Britain the predominance of single family housing makes the individual sale of dwellings relatively straightforward; more problems have arisen over the sale of flats with complicated arrangements for leaseholds and the management and repair relating not just to common areas but to the fabric of the dwelling itself. In most countries the tradition of public housing has been associated with flat-type accommodation or what is referred to as multi-family dwellings. In this situation the problems of sale of individual properties are arguably much greater. Flat-type dwellings do not lend themselves so easily to individual ownership. In Britain leasehold arrangements automatically apply and these provide a framework for management and maintenance with equal payments being applied in respect of tenants and owners and with the full consultation of owners. However, these arrangements are complex, unfamiliar and likely to give rise to conflicts and confusions. In most countries the framework adopted for sold flats is that of condominium law and this has limitations where owners have low incomes and arrangements for enforcement are unclear.

A further dimension relates to the institutional frameworks surrounding public sector housing. It has been argued that the political independence of quasi-public sector institutions has enabled them to be less subject to privatisation of their housing stock on adverse terms. In Britain unlike most other countries with significant public housing stocks, public housing has been mostly owned by municipalities. Municipalities are products of government in the British system and are open to attack by central Government. They are part of the legitimate arena for political dispute and electoral politics. In contrast the voluntary or independent sector, although it is heavily subsidised, has some degree of insulation from political attack. The evidence to suggest that this is true in Britain lies in the extent to which the housing association movement was able to fend off attempts to include it within legislation relating to council housing in the 1980s.

In the Netherlands, housing associations with a very large not for profit housing stock have a wide base of political support and their financial stability and management continuity are highly regarded by political parties of different complexions. Arguably this has been fundamental to the ability of the Dutch housing companies to fend off potential privatisation programmes. In China with its complex ownership of public sector houses associated with municipalities and work units, the progress of reform required the preparation of privatisation proposals for each of these work units. The fragmented institutional framework affected the speed and nature of privatisation. In central and eastern Europe restitution of land and property further complicated privatisation in some cases.

While not all of the privatisation schemes that have been referred to in this chapter have multiple objectives, it would be appropriate to identify different leading objectives in relation to each. For example the Right to Buy in the UK or Ireland is essentially about expanding an existing established home ownership market, it is enlarging a mainstream home ownership sector which is well established institutionally and financially. In central and eastern Europe, the predominant concern is more of a political one, shock absorbance for political and economic change. In China, the role of housing as an active element in wider economic reform and in generating funds for housing investment is much more evident. The extent to which these different objectives lead to a market system with saleable and transferable commodities, provide for accumulation and exercise of choice in housing and moderate spatial and social segregation varies in relation to the nature of the property and the nature of the local economy. Although all of these arrangements are referred to as privatisation and to some extent they all involve very similar processes, that does not mean that the outcomes are the same, or that the markets that emerge are similar or are likely to converge on one another in future.

12

A Policy Past its Sell-By Date?

A quarter of a century after the introduction of the Right to Buy in Britain, the world is a very different place. In particular the housing system has become more dominated by the owner-occupied sector and substantially changed as a result of the Right to Buy. The structure of society has less clear class divides, demographic trends have led to an older population and the nuclear family is no longer all pervasive. In these revised circumstances it is pertinent to ask whether the Right to Buy is still relevant. In this chapter the cumulative impact of the Right to Buy is reviewed and an assessment is made of the policy in the current context. The chapter summarises much of the findings of the book so far before considering how the Right to Buy has affected different generations. Finally it considers the Government's new housing policy initiatives in the light of its earlier findings.

Historical policy context

The Right to Buy was introduced at a time of some complacency in British housing policy. The massive council house building programme was coming to an end and most of the slum housing areas had been redeveloped. Urban renewal policies had switched from redevelopment to improvement of the housing stock. For the first time in over a century there was not a shortage of housing, at least in numerical terms, and new legislation had recently been introduced to ensure homeless people were entitled to be rehoused in permanent accommodation. The Green Papers of the Labour Government during the latter half of the 1970s lacked any sense of radicalism or a clear vision of the future (DoE 1977a; Scottish Development Department 1977). The Conservative Party manifesto of 1979 made no reference at all to investment in new building, housing improvement, reducing homelessness or housing need.

Over 60 years of investment by local authorities in council housing substantially changed the face of British towns and cities. The image was somewhat tarnished by the urban high rise and medium rise housing of the 1960s and 1970s and by difficult to let estates such as walk up tenement flats built in the 1930s. However, the vast majority of council houses were well built traditional houses that satisfied tenants.

In parallel to the growth of council housing was the even greater rise of owner-occupation (except in Scotland). Home ownership became the dominant and normal tenure, and the 1970s saw growing aspirations by many young people, who would have historically rented, to own their own home. Almost seven out of ten people wanted to be owner-occupiers (see Chapter 6). The private rented sector had declined so far that it was no longer a potential source of tenure transfers to home ownership and for the first time the expansion of both home ownership and council housing were in conflict.

The election of Margaret Thatcher in 1979 brought with it a new political ideology and confirmed the break with any apparent consensus on council housing. The new Government's monetarist macroeconomic stance with its belief in the role of markets and low public spending led to a concerted attempt to reform council house subsidies and reduce the council housing stock. The Right to Buy formed part of a wider attempt to reduce public expenditure through the sale of assets and to facilitate the provision of services through private rather than public capital. The encouragement of low cost home ownership was also stimulated through a variety of special schemes including building for sale, sales of land, improvement for sale, homesteading, mortgage guarantees and shared ownership. However, the Right to Buy was by far the most successful initiative in promoting home ownership.

When it was introduced in 1980 the Right to Buy established a framework for the sale of public sector housing in Britain. Up until this point local authorities had had a discretionary power to sell. The Right to Buy brought about a dramatic increase in the number of sales by providing a high discount to market value for purchasers and by making the scheme universally available to tenants. The scheme has subsequently been endorsed by the Labour Government in England and the devolved administrations in Scotland and Wales. There have been some amendments, notably extending the qualification period prior to purchase and the discount repayment period, and reducing the maximum discount but the essentials are unchanged. However, the aims have been modified under the Labour Government to stress the development of sustainable communities specifically through the promotion of social mix.

Take up of the Right to Buy

The goal of promoting home ownership has probably succeeded well beyond original expectations. More than two million sales have added approximately £40 billion to the national exchequer coffers. Sales, rather than dwindling away as demand is satisfied, continue to occur with the stock depletion rate in the early 2000s higher than a decade earlier, stimulated by the housing market boom. There has proved not to be a finite potential pool of Right to Buy purchasers constrained by some lower income bound. For example some buyers are on state benefits receiving financial assistance from relatives. Together with a continual flow of new tenants and the dynamics of demographic change this means that the Right to Buy still has a long way to run.

The stereotypical purchaser of the 1980s – an older couple over 45 years of age, with grown up children and at least one member in full time employment – has been displaced by a younger generation of purchasers. Today Right to Buy purchasers are most likely to be a two parent family with children at school, although they include a much more eclectic collection of households, more diverse than the buyers in the mid 1990s. Household incomes are generally low and most purchasers are drawn from a social background of the lower middle class and the skilled working class. Many applicants such as single parents and the retired are on state benefits and some depend on relatives for financial support. More than 10% of Right to Buy sales are funded in this way and children offering finance can be a key trigger in the decision to buy. Some of this support is on the understanding of future residency and subsequent ownership/inheritance.

Consequences for social housing

The Right to Buy was presented as a policy to promote home ownership with the belief that this would not have any adverse impact on other tenants or on the operation of the housing market. Yet the policy was the beginning of the end for council housing as perceived in the previous decades. In the 1970s council housing could still be described as the tenure of the working class. Since the initiation of the Right to Buy council housing has been sleep walking without any overt role. Some commentators describe council housing as the tenure of last resort (Whitehead *et al.* 2005), but in many parts of the UK there are social housing shortages and the homeless have to stay lengthy periods in 'temporary' private rented accommodation. This is a direct result of the properties lost to the Right to Buy and the lack of replacement building.

The impact of the Right to Buy on lost lettings did not begin to have any substantive impact until the early 1990s but since then there has been an accumulating effect that has not only reduced access to council housing but has also had a disproportionate impact on the availability of the larger and better council housing stock to existing and new council tenants. As a result there are many people now living in council housing or temporary housing in the private sector that it is too small for their requirements. There is a mismatch between the type of housing available and demand. Overcrowding is on the increase. The majority of vacancies available are in the less desirable estates that have not seen a high incidence of purchase under the Right to Buy.

Socioeconomic factors and demographic trends have changed the composition of the population and have changed the demand for council housing but the Right to Buy has had a clear impact on the sector's role. It means that council housing has become a staging post for many tenants on the way to buying on the open market. Council housing has become a transient stage for many households, similar to that associated with the private rented sector. This is a role associated with providing housing for people at particular stages of their lives and during periods in which they have limited resources. This role for council housing has risen by default without any conscious policy decision and has followed as a consequence of the reduced housing opportunities, for example through the loss of large family units.

There were concerns about residualisation of council housing through the increased concentration of lower income households on council estates in the 1970s. These concerns have been reinforced by the lost tenancies caused by the Right to Buy. Council housing has arguably become almost the exclusive domain of the elderly and the young on low incomes, although it cannot be simply described as welfare housing of the US model. Residualisation has been extended from council estates to council housing as a whole.

The impact on the owner-occupied sector

When the Right to Buy was introduced sitting tenants bought with the intention of staying for the rest of their lives. This began to change in the late 1980s and as resales became more frequent there was a gradual acceptance of former council houses as marketable investments. Resale markets have matured and resales have been integrated into the local housing market in all areas, typically accounting for at least 10% of the market. These houses continue to be sold at a lower price than equivalent housing not built by the public sector, although the negative differential varies across areas. In some places resales are 25% cheaper than equivalent mainstream housing nearby but the differential can be much lower, sometimes almost disappearing, depending on house types and market pressures. Resales have found a niche in the housing market as starter homes and as affordable housing for low income families but former council housing flats in parts of London are readily marketable at prices in excess of £200 000.

The existence of the resale market reinforces and encourages further take up of the Right to Buy: as localised resale markets mature and tenants realise the investment potential of their homes there is in effect a second wave of Right to Buy sales. In areas where resale markets are not established or sustained over time the reverse effect is experienced and Right to Buy sales fall away. There is for example no resale market for multi-storey flats and properties on certain estates. The lack of investment potential of these latter properties has become an effective constraint on the extension of the Right to Buy.

A major proportion of resales are bought by first time purchasers seeking starter homes. Purchasers tend to be at the beginning of the family cycle although they do include pensioners. Many of these younger households intend to move on in the foreseeable future as their family expands. The socioeconomic characteristics of these buyers, particularly of second time buyers, vary depending on local housing market pressures. Where affordability problems are greatest dual income professional families are more often the purchasers of former council housing.

The promotion of the private rented sector

One unexpected development of the Right to Buy has been the promotion of the private rented sector. The sector experienced significant long term decline starting in the early twentieth century. Following the reforms of the 1988 Housing Act that reintroduced market rents and reduced security of tenure, new investment began in the late 1990s and expanded during the subsequent housing boom, especially in London and the south-east of England. The Right to Buy has influenced the sector in three ways. First, the cumulative impact of the Right to Buy on relets is an important factor in reducing the supply of social housing and contributing to a shortage of housing to rent. Second, local authorities faced with record numbers of homeless have had to turn to private sector leasing to resolve their housing deficit. Third, it has contributed to the source of new supply to the sector as some former Right to Buy properties, particularly those that are unattractive or difficult to sell for house purchase because of weak resale markets, represent good value for money to residential landlords.

The 'new tenants' living in former council housing are predominantly young adults in households of three people or less. Outside London they are generally on low incomes. The Right to Buy is indirectly increasing the supply of housing for rent for young people but the rents they are being charged are above those applicable for equivalent council housing. In some cases rents are up to £1000 per month in inner London for former council properties. When these new tenants are receiving housing benefit the state is subsidising higher rents in the private sector having already paid a subsidy through the discount under the Right to Buy. In some cases the new landlord and former council tenant may be the same person. In addition it is unlikely that the private rented sector can replace the public sector in the wider provision of social housing to encompass low income families rather than just young adults. The consequence of the return to renting after the Right to Buy is a 'triple whammy': a reduction in the supply of either affordable housing to buy or affordable social housing to let and increases in the cost of housing to the state.

The Right to Buy and communities

Both Labour and Conservative governments have seen the Right to Buy as supporting neighbourhood sustainability, through a promotion of social mix and meeting the needs and aspirations of existing and future generations. One element in this process is the provision of opportunities to buy affordable homes in areas where people were brought up or currently live. However, Right to Buy resales offer value for money and so attract a range of households not necessarily with local connections, especially in urban areas and rural areas within commuting reach of large employment centres. Even in relatively 'closed' deep rural housing markets, resales are purchased by outsiders, some of whom are retiring or buying a second home. Thus resales on their own are not sufficient to ensure the long term social cohesion and viability of rural areas or balance the loss of social housing supply caused by the Right to Buy.

In urban areas the coincidence of Right to Buy sales and a period of widening social inequality has exacerbated the funnelling of poorer sections of the community or marginalised groups into the least desirable estates. Obtaining a house in these neighbourhoods, whatever condition and quality, demonstrates some elements of social disadvantage by tenants. At the same time the changes in the characteristics of the council tenant population, encouraged by the Right to Buy siphoning off those with financial resources, has meant that the council housing stock is subject to higher turnover. The Right to Buy has therefore destabilised the remaining council housing stock and the least desirable estates in particular. This has inevitably increased social exclusion and economic marginalisation, and reduced the sustainability of communities in these areas. The precise scale of this problem depends on much wider questions about the development of cities and regions and their economies.

In contrast, high sale estates in high demand areas remain relatively stable populations if less so than in 1980. Initially sitting tenant purchasers, who in the main intended to spend the rest of their lives in their homes, formed the backbone of stability on these estates. The initial Right to Buy sale did not increase stability but nor did it reduce stability. As resales become prevalent these properties proved attractive to many households as starter homes and as a result in the longer term this housing will come more regularly on to the market. However, by the mid 1990s turnover in the market sector of these estates was still lower than in the rented sector.

Overall the arguments in favour of the Right to Buy based on social mix are an act of faith. Increased residualisation caused by the Right to Buy means for the poorest sections of the population in an increasingly unequal society greater instability and social exclusion not less. Council estates with both high and low levels of home ownership are more likely to be characterised by higher turnover now than in the past and in the future this higher turnover will increase further. It is unrealistic to believe that but for the Right to Buy the council sector would comprise solely stable working class communities; such a situation never existed. Nonetheless there is reason to believe that the Right to Buy has destabilised some council estate neighbourhoods and damaged the capacity of these areas to function effectively as communities.

Financial issues

From the beginning the finances of the Right to Buy were the subject of controversy. The capital receipts generated ostensibly represent a very substantial contribution to public finances but a full financial appraisal must take into account future lost rents, the capital expenditure on renovation that will no longer be required and the cost of replacement housing where necessary. Financial appraisals must also show substantial subsidies to purchasers. If it were not for the Right to Buy the council housing sector as a whole would have generated huge surpluses and the rise in real rents over the last quarter of a century would not have been necessary. It is therefore questionable who has subsidised the Right to Buy.

A key issue in these financial calculations throughout the life of the Right to Buy has been the cost (incorporating scale and timing) of replacement of the 'lost' housing stock. In the original financial appraisals undertaken by the Government replacement was ignored because surveys suggested Right to Buy purchasers expected to spend the rest of their lives in their home. It is increasingly clear that in areas of high demand for social housing replacement is necessary and the Right to Buy remains a financial drain on the sector. Despite these arguments, in practice very few of the more than two million houses sold have been replaced.

The cumulative impact of the Right to Buy has wrought fundamental changes on decisions by local authorities and individual council tenants. The interaction of tenants and owner-occupiers living on estates has radically revised the management of council housing and increased council housing management costs can be directly attributable to the Right to Buy. The Right to Buy choice facing tenants has evolved over time. It still centres on an assessment of the same financial variables but the emphasis has moved very much away from seeing their home as a consumable good toward seeing it as an investment.

At the outset of the Right to Buy some observers took the view that only a small proportion of households would be able to afford to take it up. These forecasts proved to be severe underestimates. However, the low and variable incomes of purchasers (or their successors) have led to doubts about the maintenance and long term condition of housing sold under the Right to Buy. There is some survey evidence to support these concerns. The Right to Buy has implemented a substantial redistribution of assets from the State to purchasers but it has been the higher income groups who have been most able to utilise this equity by trading up. There is also still a not inconsiderable proportion of households, the poorest, who have been excluded from this wealth redistribution by the State.

Stakeholder outcomes

The historical review of the Right to Buy highlights the intricate and changing outcomes over time of what appears to be a simple policy. These outcomes are interwoven with the changing structure of society, rising real incomes and the increased desire for home ownership, a general move toward a more market-oriented economy and changing housing policy that has sought to harness private capital. It is therefore useful to consider who have been the principal beneficiaries and losers from the policy.

Who benefits, to what extent and in what ways, is a complex set of questions, but there is a final dimension to this which relates to different stakeholders. Again, unlike traditional areas of social policy, privatisation, and in particular the form of privatisation adopted here, creates opportunities not just for individual households or the direct beneficiaries but also for financial institutions such as banks, solicitors, estate agents and other people who provide related services. The best example here is probably builders and firms providing repair and maintenance services. Rather than competing with a direct labour organisation or going through a tendering process to carry out services for the local authority, the expansion of individual home ownership creates a different pattern of activities and opportunities for a variety of companies and individuals working in the housing market.

The Right to Buy changes the shape of the market in relation to management, maintenance, finance and exchange of housing. The shrinking of the local authority sector and explosion of the private sector involves changing the pattern of opportunities for different organisations and individuals. In the long term, what the Right to Buy begins to do is to provide opportunities for businesses in a different form from that which existed previously. It benefits those that are able to provide services successfully for the new home owners, at the expense of those who used to provide services for council tenants. At the extreme point this is a public–private sector split but in reality it is also about the ability of different individuals and companies to respond to changing market opportunities.

For many of those who bought properties in the UK in the early 1980s, the value of the asset 25 years later is much greater, and their individual wealth and family situation are dramatically different. This is not just because of the general rise in prices but also because the development and maturity of resale markets has led to an even greater rise from a very low valuation base. Whether or not people make use of this to move house or whether it benefits the next generation, it is undeniable that there has been a significant change in the financial circumstances and asset holdings of these households.

It is important to acknowledge first that these changes are variable. At one extreme, the Right to Buy purchaser in high demand markets, say in inner London, will have gained wealth in the region of quarter of a million pounds or more. At the other extreme, there are households which purchased an unsaleable property or experienced a change in their circumstances such that they have been unable to benefit at all from having exercised the Right to Buy. Inbetween these two extremes there is a wide variety of experience, although it is important to emphasise that the evidence suggests that it is only a minority of households who will not have benefitted to some extent.

However, this is if we look at only one generation and one cohort. The losers under the Right to Buy are the generation who have not yet graduated to the better quality council tenancies, or to any council tenancy at all. The impact of the Right to Buy is mainly to restrict the likelihood of becoming a tenant, or of becoming a tenant of a desirable home, and therefore to restrict the likelihood of their benefitting from the Right to Buy. People who entered council housing in the post-war period were, by the time the Right to Buy was introduced, at the stage in their housing career and family cycle when they could take maximum advantage of it. Many households in an earlier cohort were too elderly and their incomes were too low to benefit. Many people in a subsequent cohort had not yet been able to access the types of property that would be desirable to buy.

This generational argument should not be overstated. The Right to Buy has benefitted people over a period of 25 years and there still remain significant numbers of properties and households eligible for the Right to Buy. It has been an unusual privatisation in that you did not have to apply by a fixed date, as with the sale of electricity, gas or water, where if you miss the deadline you have missed the opportunity to buy shares in the newly formed company. The Right to Buy has been marked by a continuing flow of opportunities and a continuing recruitment of households able to take advantage of the opportunities it offers. Some of those buying in 2005 were not tenants in 1980, and some of those becoming tenants in 2005 will be in a position to buy over the next few years.

The identification of those who lose out is therefore complex. At one level this simply includes those who are unable to exercise the Right to Buy, but this group comprises at least two distinct categories. There are those who are financially unable or choose not to because the property they are eligible to buy is unattractive; but in many cases they just choose not to. This second group cannot be called losers.

The focus in terms of 'who loses' has consequently tended to be upon applicants for council housing and the potential next occupier of a council house. Because so much property has been sold, these households have a restricted range of choices or a longer waiting time and ultimately there are households who are not able to access high quality housing because of the Right to Buy. This group are much more difficult to identify individually than Right to Buy purchasers. It is difficult to pinpoint exactly 'who loses' because there are so many intermediate processes and in particular the losses may not be absolute, but rather in terms of the quality and location of the housing that people are able to access. This is particularly true in view of the pattern of council housing relets which has applied over the period since the Right to Buy was introduced.

It is further complicated because many of this next generation now aspire to home ownership rather than a council tenancy and Right to Buy resales also offer the opportunity for people to buy value for money housing. In this sense the Right to Buy has helped meet the rising demand for owner-occupation associated with increased real incomes. The problem is that this housing is now allocated by the market so it is not possible to specifically meet local demand. This is a particular problem in rural areas where there tend to be limited housing opportunities and low wages. Second home buyers in tourist areas have been notorious 'beneficiaries'. Would-be local residents in less remote rural areas have also lost out to commuters who themselves may have been rationed out of the nearby urban housing market.

It is undeniable that the opportunities offered by the Right to Buy to different cohorts or groups of households has changed. They change because of the diminution in the size of the council sector, the diminution in its quality and reputation and the changes in policy, which affect discount entitlements. Depending on the state of local resale markets the Right to Buy can indirectly offer the opportunity for low cost home ownership. So what is on offer to different cohorts is different. Further to this what is on offer to the same cohort in different places is different. This is a highly variable policy which provides different benefits in different periods and places. This is an unusual characteristic of social policies which tend to be expected to meet some criteria of fairness or some criteria of redistribution. Ideally one would expect people with similar circumstances to benefit in the same ways or for the pattern of benefit to be consciously skewed in favour of those with lower incomes or greater need. However, in the case of the Right to Buy, considerations of distributional justice have been abandoned.

Key consequences and issues

The Right to Buy has been a driving force of change in the housing system, the most potent housing policy measure in the last quarter of the twentieth century. It represented a sea change in the state's approach to housing policy and it had a symbolic impact beyond the two million plus sales that it achieved. However, it is also important to note that the Right to Buy was swimming with the tide as rising real incomes fuelled the demand for home ownership. Meanwhile for council housing the Right to Buy, combined with low levels of new building, meant the tide had turned and its role began to ebb away. Even so sales continue and the sector has yet to reach its low water mark.

The outcome is a slow strangling of council housing as tenants faced with limited or no choice within the sector opt, if they can, to buy their home as a means to find a home that meets their needs in the private sector. This then reduces even further the opportunities to rent for later generations. The state of much of the housing that remains is increasingly unattractive and council tenancy is dominated by the elderly and the young on low incomes.

The conflict between meeting the aspirations of people to buy their homes and providing good quality social housing for those who cannot afford or do not want to be owner-occupiers was at first minimal. However, as the cumulative impact of the Right to Buy on lettings has grown so has the friction between these goals. This has been exacerbated by the changes to the structure of households, the increasing number of households and the failure of the private house building industry to satisfy the growing demand for house purchase, especially at the bottom of the market. The question of replacement of housing sold under the Right to Buy has come up the political agenda.

The Right to Buy in the current housing policy context

Housing market conditions in the first decade of the twenty-first century are very different from those of the late 1970s. The housing system is under duress with severe affordability problems caused by rising numbers of households, relatively little house building, historically low social housing lettings, record homelessness and high house prices. At the coal face of this crisis are local authorities and others attempting to solve the critical housing problems principally experienced by households on low incomes and those who become unemployed or suffer dramatic losses of earnings.

In 2005, in its five year plan for housing in England, *Sustainable Communities: Homes for all*, the Government accepted this prognosis noting that:

- young families cannot afford to live where they grew up and want to stay;
- first time buyers are priced out of the market;
- more people are forced to stay longer in temporary accommodation or in overcrowded homes.

These problems were attributed to insufficient housing having been built in some parts of the country so the primary policy aim within its strategy was to:

'Make sure that there are enough high-quality homes across the whole spectrum of housing – owner-occupied, social rented and private rented.' (ODPM 2005b)

Beyond this very general 'motherhood and apple pie' aim there were more specific aims including helping more people to own their home and providing for those who need more support to meet their housing needs and aspirations, including halving numbers in temporary accommodation.

The overarching goal of the Government's strategy was summarised under the banner, 'Delivering opportunity and choice for all' (ODPM 2005b). It heralds the fact that over one million more people own their own home than in 1997. Despite the cross tenure perspective of the strategy the Government is principally seeking a private sector solution in partnership with the public sector to these problems, with an emphasis on reforming the planning system, reducing building costs and increasing the land supply. Most of the new housing to be built is in the private sector but the Government plans to invest in 10 000 extra social homes each year in England. This represents an increase in the supply of new social housing units of 50% and compares with approximately 100 000 households in temporary accommodation, the current 400 000 new social housing tenancies a year and annual Right to Buy sales running in the order of 70 000.

At the general election of 2005 the Labour Party, building on the 2004 Housing Act, trumpeted a comprehensive plan for increasing home ownership in England. This included:

- A new Homebuy scheme offering up to 300 000 council and housing association tenants the opportunity to buy part of their home, increasing their equity over time if they wish.

- A first time buyers initiative to help over 15 000 first time buyers who could not own or part-own a home without extra help. It will use surplus public land for new homes, enabling the buyer to take out a mortgage for only the building.
- Strengthening existing home ownership schemes, such as the Key Worker Living scheme and Shared Ownership.

The increased supply and quality of social housing was also reaffirmed to be central to Labour's belief in mixed, sustainable communities.

The emphasis is therefore on stimulating home ownership including an initiative that is an evolution of the Right to Buy designed to target households the policy has not previously been able to reach. By 2010 the Government plans to assist over 80 000 people into home ownership through a new first time buyers initiative, a strengthened key workers support scheme and other existing schemes such as shared ownership and a new version of Homebuy. The extended Homebuy scheme will combine elements of the existing shared ownership scheme to enable social (council and housing association) tenants to buy a share in their own home, with a discount similar to that of the Right to Buy. It was aimed at tenants who could not afford the cost of the Right to Buy and it was anticipated that tenants would buy between half and three-quarters of the equity in their home. The initial plan was that those who bought a three-quarters share would not pay any rent on the other quarter but would be responsible for repairs and maintenance. On resale the Homebuy owner would pay back a quarter of the proceeds to the local authority or housing association. New forms of incentive schemes were also considered to offer tenants in high demand areas the opportunity to buy a home elsewhere with an interest free loan. Altogether these approaches will provide a range of mechanisms for a route to home ownership (ODPM 2005b).

Twenty-five years after the introduction of the Right to Buy it therefore remains an important element of housing policy and the message from the UK Government is that it is not only to continue but in effect it is to be extended. The Government strategy makes no attempt to clarify the role of social housing. Historically a logical solution to the present housing crisis would be a substantial capital expenditure programme on new social housing. Instead the Government states:

'Home ownership, even on a shared basis, is not the right option for everyone at all stages of their lives. For some it is unaffordable. For others the greater flexibility that renting offers makes it a better solution.' (ODPM 2005b)

This statement implicitly accepts the hegemony of promoting home ownership in housing policy but its explicit strategy is simply to offer greater quality, flexibility and choice to those who rent by tackling shortages of social housing, greater capital investment in improving the social housing stock and better management including choice based lettings. There is no discussion about the limits to social housing.

There have been some piecemeal initiatives to redress the negative aspects of the Right to Buy. The Government sought to make it easier for local authorities in England to limit the resale of former council homes in rural areas so that they are reserved for 'local' people. The Scottish Executive has introduced Pressured Area status where the Right to Buy will not apply to new tenancies but few local authorities have applied for this facility and none successfully three years after the legislation was brought into force. It is also obliged to review the Right to Buy in 2005. All UK Governments have reduced the discounts to tenants since 1998 as part of an agenda to achieve value for money and as a means in London and the south-east of England of removing abuses of the policy (Jones 2003). Many other issues remain unaddressed. For example, in view of the position of flats in the debate about the Right to Buy there is no justification for the higher rates of discount on flats.

These developments should be seen in context. The part of the housing market that the Right to Buy applies to in 2005 is smaller, both because of the previous impacts of the policy and because of other privatisations and stock transfers. Recent arguments to restrict or remove the Right to Buy have been voiced more stridently than in the late 1980s and 1990s, although it may be argued that the sector being protected is no longer worthwhile. Governments have so far amended the Right to Buy but have not repealed it; indeed there is a view that it is very difficult to contemplate such repeal without challenge under human rights legislation.

Conclusions

The Right to Buy has been a central if controversial facet of housing policy for more than a generation. It is emblematic of changed aspirations in the housing market from the 1970s onward. In the twenty-first century the promotion of home ownership continues to be the primary tenet of housing policy and the Government in England in 2005 was seeking ways of extending the Right to Buy through a revised Homebuy. There are other proposals to extend the Right to Buy by extending it to housing association tenants whose properties are currently not eligible. Rather than the

Right to Buy being seen by Government as a policy past its sale date the reverse is true.

These initiatives come despite the recognition that the Right to Buy has injured council housing. There is almost a refusal by Government to discuss the detail of the impact of the Right to Buy witnessed to date with virtually no research commissioned by Governments of any persuasion. Similarly there is silence on the role of social housing within the housing system. Instead the Government is set full steam ahead with extending the Right to Buy despite the present difficult housing circumstances and the shortage of social housing. While the Government has changed the Right to Buy, and changing circumstances mean it no longer has the same significance it had in 1980, the new Homebuy proposals can be seen as extending as well as transforming it. The next chapter addresses the underlying philosophical issues of the alternative ways forward.

13

Learning from the Right to Buy

The Right to Buy has contributed to the expansion of home ownership over the period of its operation but its impact on the remaining council sector has often been adverse and it has not improved neighbourhoods and estates in the way that some wishful thinkers suggested. The objective of this chapter is to look at what might be achieved in the future by the Right to Buy and how it might be modified. Any changes to the policy will not reduce the impact of council house sales that have already taken place. Nevertheless, such impacts could be offset and concerns about affordability problems, the modernisation of council housing and residualisation could be addressed. Considerations of equity and value for money could also be included, and changes could be made to ensure that incentives are not all associated with leaving the tenure but could also benefit tenants who choose not to buy.

Against the background set out earlier in this book, it is possible to identify a number of alternative directions for change. It is not appropriate to start with a discussion of whether to continue the Right to Buy or not. There could be a reversion back to discretionary council house sales policies as applied before 1980; there could be a continuation of the Right to Buy in its present form; or there could be a continuation of the Right to Buy in some modified form. This chapter considers how the Right to Buy relates to current areas of policy concern (affordability and modernisation), considerations related to equity, and the pattern of incentives and choices emerging. It then considers the future of the policy itself and reflects on wider debates that connect with the Right to Buy: privatisation as social policy, the nature of the housing market and emerging approaches to the welfare state.

Affordability and modernisation

Reforming the Right to Buy in response to affordability or modernisation agendas is like shutting the door after the horse has bolted. It will not reduce the problems associated with sales which have already taken place. In a period in which affordability problems have come to dominate the housing policy debate and proposals for policy development it is important to acknowledge that the short term impact of halting the Right to Buy on the supply of housing available for rent would be minimal although it would build slowly over time. This is essentially because the adverse effects of the Right to Buy – as discussed in Chapter 5 – emerge at the point when the property would have become available for reletting.

It is possible that some tenants, without the Right to Buy, would relinquish their tenancy in order to buy elsewhere, but such an effect is likely to be small. The evidence suggests that most tenants would not be able to buy a property of equivalent size and quality in the private sector and they would have to be willing to trade-down in order to become a home owner elsewhere. Most tenants will choose to stay where they are. In this sense the more restricted discounts which emerged after 1998 or any suspension of Right to Buy contemplated in the future will save a future flow of vacancies rather than assist in responding to current needs.

In relation to the mainstream housing market, modifying the Right to Buy will have only a long term effect. There is a need for adequate resources to be available to councils to enable acquisition as well as building to meet the existing demand for rented accommodation. Some of this acquisition could be of former Right to Buy properties where these are the types of properties that are in demand and where the prices are appropriate.

On this basis the most logical response to the Right to Buy is to acknowledge its operation and effect and to develop parallel policies which enable regional and local strategies to respond to the housing situation after the Right to Buy. This means that in areas that require modernisation and renewal, the issues of dealing with mixed tenure estates and fragmentation of ownership are addressed. The resources required will need to be sufficient to cover the costs of compulsory purchase or acquisition of former council houses. In this context, the legislative change introduced in 2004 to restrict the Right to Buy in neighbourhoods which are undergoing major refurbishments makes sense. The decisions to provide more opportunity for local authorities to reinvest the proceeds from council house sales are very important and a continuation of this is a key factor in enabling local authorities to adopt appropriate policies to deal with the consequences of the Right to Buy.

Equity

The policy existing in 2005 has a number of exceptions and different rates of discount for different property types and for different regions. These are not just strategic matters, but also raise issues of equity. It makes no sense to have discount rates and discount ceilings that vary regionally: indeed, those who buy properties in a higher priced market are likely to benefit more from asset appreciation and yet they are offered the higher rates of discount. Also, the higher rates of discount act as an encouragement to buy in areas where the loss of rented housing would, in the long run, have the most impact on the supply of affordable housing.

In view of the position of flats in the debate about the Right to Buy there is no justification for the higher rates of discount on flats. If anything the argument would be for lower rates of discount. The argument is strong for reverting back to a common rate of maximum discount across the country and a common formula for calculating discount entitlement irrespective of the property type. The case for a common cash sum rather than the valuation based lottery is also compelling.

There are a number of relatively detailed changes that could be made, consistent with the original intentions of the Right to Buy, that would benefit long established tenants and discourage speculation. These changes would also make it more difficult to abuse the system and would contribute to stabilisation of communities. The obvious options here are to further increase the tenancy qualification, and to extend the period over which the discount would have to be repaid. There would also be a case for excluding certain property types or certain areas, for example rural areas. In these cases an alternative to the Right to Buy that involves a portable purchase grant would be appropriate. These grants are not restricted to use in buying the house a tenant currently lives in but can be used to buy other properties.

If this argument is taken a step further then there is a case for levelling out the advantages associated with different routes into low cost home ownership so that the benefits associated with the Right to Buy are more in line with those associated with the Right to Acquire or Homebuy schemes or shared ownership schemes. In this situation tenants would be given more choice rather than having a disproportionate gain if they exercised the Right to Buy rather than other options. Local strategies to provide choice for council tenants and housing association tenants and to provide routes into home ownership could include a portfolio of policies that provide different opportunities but where the financial incentive associated with each was broadly the same. Under this kind of formula the value of a Right to Buy grant might still be higher than a portable purchase grant in recognition of tenanted market value and to reduce the incentive to move away. This also has the advantage of maintaining a balance between policies that generate a capital receipt and those that generate a vacancy but involve expenditure on the purchase grant.

Incentives and choices

More proportionate discounts and a comparable level of financial incentive for different house purchase schemes address equity issues at one level. However, they leave a fundamental gap. The incentives are still all loaded towards leaving the council or social rented sector. Against this background it is important to consider ways in which a comparable set of incentives can be provided to encourage people to remain as tenants and to achieve other objectives in relation to the management and stability of the social rented sector. In this context there has been a positive debate in recent years about equity stakes for tenants and this appears to have attracted the interest of the Government. It may be that this interest will increase if the gap between owners and tenants is seen as a key source of inequality in an age of failing pensions policies – an inequality in wealth affecting wider life chances and incomes in old age.

The term 'equity stakes' has some difficulties. It conjures up images of a stake in the individual property in which the tenant lives. This could have the same disadvantages as the Right to Buy itself. Properties have different values and appreciate in value at different rates. In some cases there would be an equity stake in an asset of depreciating value. In other cases the asset would increase very rapidly. The equity stakes offered in different parts of the country and different property types would not be equal. Just as the Right to Buy falls down on tests of equity, so would equity stakes linked to the accident of what house someone lives in. This raises a wider issue about the role of housing in personal wealth and the implication that the growth of home ownership has generated greater wealth equality. The debates in this area acknowledge that the expansion of home ownership widens the numbers of households with transferable wealth but also identifies the differential accumulation associated with an uneven housing market as well as the exclusion of those who still remain outside home ownership (see Forrest & Murie 1995; Hamnett 1999).

The Hill *et al.* investigation (2000) of the potential for equity stakes used four illustrative approaches:

(1) a form of shared ownership providing a small share in the real value of the house occupied;
(2) a form that linked the tenants' entitlement to the collective equity in the landlords' stock similar to the stake held by a company shareholder;
(3) a form that linked the stake to the collective equity in an area through a community trust;
(4) tenant asset accounts in which tenants were entitled to an equity stake based on the length of stay in the tenancy and observance of tenancy conditions.

It is the last of these which avoids the potential anomalies referred to above and which seems easiest to introduce and implement. A positive step would be to adopt an equity stake approach. This would involve the tenant building up an entitlement to a share in the equity associated purely with the numbers of years of tenancy or rent payment. It would acknowledge the reality that the market value of the property changes and entitle the tenant as well as the landlord to benefit from this without requiring the tenant to buy the property in order to benefit. It could provide the opportunity to make withdrawals at identified periods if the tenant had a clear rent record and the implication would be that there would be a payment available at the point when someone left their tenancy. To some extent this would acknowledge the value associated with the tenancy itself and would provide an opportunity for saving but this would not be based upon the accidents of asset value and appreciation.

If this argument is taken one step further it focuses upon what bonuses are available to the long-term tenant and tenants who consistently pay their rent throughout their lives. The present situation offers no reward at all to these households and the message is that if you want to benefit you should exit the sector. A logical approach is to rebuild the advantages associated with remaining as a tenant in the social rented sector so that they compare with the advantages which are on offer to those who leave the sector. Some of these would be advantages about the quality of accommodation and service. Others could be about entitlements to periodic repayments. Others could be about entitlements to revert to lower rent levels, perhaps associated with people in older age or with longer periods of tenancy. The implication of this approach is that long term tenants are rewarded rather than encouraged to move out. The benefits in terms of neighbourhood stability and management should not be overstated but there are benefits in terms of equity and choice as well.

Repeal or reinvest?

All of these issues address concerns about the equity and choice associated with the Right to Buy and wider strategic agendas related to the provision of affordable housing and residualisation. These are not likely to be effectively or sufficiently addressed in the short term through amendment of the Right to Buy. These agendas require resources in their own right and the suspension or removal of the Right to Buy will make very little impact in the short term. Arguably, the resources associated with the sale of properties under the Right to Buy, if they could be reinvested in housing, would provide a more effective way of ensuring that rented housing provision is available than would suspension or termination of the Right to Buy. Suspension and termination do nothing to address the issues arising from the decimation of the social rented sector over 25 years. What is needed is a policy for investment and it may be that the best way of achieving this is to maintain the Right to Buy but ring fence the proceeds from sales for investment in the social rented sector.

The key calculation here relates to the rate at which Right to Buy properties would have become available for reletting had they remained in the rented stock. If the reletting rate was 8% a year then 100 properties would generate 8 vacancies. If the reinvestment of the proceeds from the sale of 100 properties funded more than 8 replacement properties then there would be a short term gain to tenants and applicants. For example, a replacement rate of one for every ten properties sold would generate 25% more vacancies than if they remained in the rented stock. On this basis, continuing sales would generate a greater supply of lettings of rented housing than would be achieved through termination or suspension of the Right to Buy, at least in the short and medium term. A higher rate of replacement could be expected in many places. It is reasonably argued that the lead time and land availability for replacement through new construction do not always make this a realistic proposition. If this is the case acquisition of existing dwellings by the council must be seen as an effective alternative. It is also an alternative that could be effective in achieving objectives related to dwelling size and location.

These considerations suggest that the key issue in relation to the wider strategic agendas associated with affordability and residualisation are not best addressed through the suspension of the Right to Buy if this would adversely affect the flow of funds for capital investment in housing. The logical step is to ensure that there is adequate funding to address these issues, but this is only logical or supportable if any capital receipts generated through Right to Buy activity are reinvested in social housing. This refers to decisions at both central and local level. If it can be demonstrated that there is no local need then the investment should take place in social housing elsewhere.

The implications of this are that the Right to Buy itself should be subjected to a series of tests related to choice, equity and impact, and that the problems faced in the social housing sector in relation to modernisation and renewal, the shortage of affordable housing or residualisation need to be addressed head on. These considerations translate into questions about the appropriateness of existing rules relating to the qualification for purchase, the level of discounts, the repayment of discount and the disproportionate rate of discount on flats. They also raise questions about exclusions and local discretion and the identification of Pressured Areas. There remains a dilemma – the Scottish approach to Pressured Areas enables local authorities to suspend the Right to Buy, but the analysis in this book suggests that suspension of the Right to Buy will have next to zero impact on the flow of relets and the supply of housing for those wanting to rent. They would have a better chance of finding housing if there was an active investment programme that could be financed through the receipts from sales. The policy agenda needs to balance the concern to protect the existing stock with a concern to generate investment.

Scepticism about how local authorities used discretionary powers influenced the introduction of the Right to Buy and the monitoring and enforcement of the policy in the early 1980s. However, in the drive to modernise local government, there is a new emphasis on giving local authorities flexibility in how they invest money and deal with housing markets in their areas. It would, therefore, be an appropriate time to confer greater flexibility on local authorities in relation to how they operate the Right to Buy alongside their plans to modernise and invest in social rented housing.

It may be that, in the environment of 25 years after the policy's introduction, with different inspection systems and a greater acceptance of evidence-based approaches and strategic thinking, the replacement of the Right to Buy with a discretionary sales scheme would not lead to decisions in this area being based purely on a political judgement.

Equity, choice and value for money considerations provide the clearest basis for modification of the Right to Buy. They suggest that the less generous approach which has emerged is correct and it is appropriate to have a scheme which provides advantages that are more proportionate to other incentives to move to buy a property and to rewards available to people who choose to stay as tenants. A less generous Right to Buy scheme, based on these equity, choice and value for money considerations could also form an appropriate part of a package of measures designed to address strategic issues of affordability and residualisation. The arguments for different treatment of different areas or for exemptions in addition to those already applying are less compelling. They are bound to create anomalies and the need for them is not evident if the overall scheme is less generous and backed by commitments to reinvest.

Reforming the Right to Buy in the expectation of making a major immediate difference to affordability problems or residualisation is misplaced. In relation to these agendas reform of the Right to Buy would only be effective as part of a wider policy and might not prove to be an essential element of such an agenda. In contrast, the reform of the Right to Buy does appear to be worth consideration if issues about equity and the modernisation of the council and social rented sector are the key objectives.

At the same time it is apparent that any significant alteration to the rights of tenants under the Right to Buy presents major problems of equity. Why should one cohort benefit and a slightly later cohort not have the same entitlement? The threat or actual withdrawal of the Right to Buy would trigger a major rush to exercise the right before it is withdrawn, perhaps leading some people into unwise decisions or encouraging some of the abuses which have been identified in the operation of the policy.

Privatisation as social policy

This book has reflected upon a varied body of evidence about the sale of council housing and the particular form of privatisation associated with the Right to Buy. While housing policies have been a feature of social and economic policy for 100 years or more, privatisation is still a relatively new term in public policy debates. It is most strongly associated with the transfer of state-owned enterprises and public utilities to private ownership: gas, electricity, water, telephones and manufacturing. It is often associated with the New Right or the transformation of state socialist economic systems and, in the British context, it has been associated with the period of government of Margaret Thatcher. In contemporary debate, it is associated with notions of choice and extending citizenship rights in the market and empowering citizens by equipping them to act independently in the market place, exercising their own preferences and choices. It is an assertion of the rights of the user and the consumer against the interests of the producer of services or the state bureaucracy.

In all of this, privatisation can be seen as part of an agenda to move from paternalistic welfare capitalism, where producer interests dominate, to individual consumer sovereignty. In regard to housing this relates to four key elements:

- creating a market and bringing people into that market;
- providing choice and mobility;
- providing opportunities for accumulation;
- developing a housing market which assists in the operation of the general economy through mobility, labour and in other ways.

This book has focused upon the privatisation of public or state housing and it has been acknowledged that this is only one element of privatisation in relation to housing policy, and housing privatisation is only one element in wider privatisation. Other housing related privatisations include moving rents to market levels, adopting a contracting culture, the cessation of new public sector building to create the opportunities for the private sector to build, the introduction of private finance to replace public expenditure, and various direct encouragements of home ownership and deregulation of private renting. These are all about creating more space for the market. Arguably, the sale and transfer of state housing provides the most direct intervention to change ownership and control and to alter the regimes of finance and management and the package of rights associated with housing.

In relation to the privatisation of state housing there is a fundamental pre-condition: that there is a state housing sector. Although in some cases – and the USA is the most obvious example – the development of state housing was restricted, most of the advanced industrial economies and many others have significant state and 'not for profit' housing sectors. The formation of these sectors was often associated with periods of emergency or reconstruction and replanning especially after wars and the political coalitions which supported them have varied. Different countries have different sizes of public housing sectors with different qualities and characteristics. In some cases the state housing includes high quality, high demand housing; in others, it is mixed. Privatisation of state housing can only occur when there is a significant state housing sector, and the nature and impact of privatisation will depend upon the quality and size of this sector and its desirability.

As has been emphasised throughout this book, privatisation is path-dependent. It reflects what was there before, as well as the particular process of privatisation that is adopted. In practice, the Right to Buy in the UK and privatisations elsewhere have involved very favourable terms of sale and have created a privileged category of citizens who, by accidents of time and place, are able to buy properties they could not otherwise have afforded. The nature and terms of sale mean that they are able to take advantage of these accidents and benefit to different extents. They benefit initially by buying properties for discounted prices, and avoiding a pattern of rising rents. In some cases in the UK this has meant that within a very short time, they were paying less for their housing than they would have been had they continued as tenants. They had become responsible for the costs of maintenance and repair, but where the properties were in good condition at the outset, such costs could be limited, at least in the short term. Certainly purchasers changed their pattern of housing payments over their lifetime. They concentrated housing expenditures in the years in which they were in employment rather than continuing to incur such costs into older age. In most cases, they also had increased choice and opportunities to move to other housing, especially to other housing in the private sector in other parts of the country. Such opportunities would be less likely to have been available to them if they had remained as tenants.

In this sense there is an acknowledgement that housing policy has never had the same pattern of objectives or benefits as social security policies, or health service provision. State intervention in housing has produced varied products, which have contributed to patterns of stratification within societies. The competition to gain access to council housing within the UK in the 1960s was identified by Rex and Moore (1967) as a key element of urban competition. The quality and status of state housing in central and eastern Europe or in China and Hong Kong are evident by the extent to which key groups of workers, the political cadre or the 'nomenclatura' were most likely to be allocated to state housing. The building of high quality public sector housing created an opportunity for some individuals to improve their housing and living environment enormously, but it was never able to deliver this for all households, and in most countries, it consciously contributed to patterns of exclusion and inclusion. Privatisation of state housing has only begun to do the same thing.

However, it is also true that housing does not simply provide benefits and opportunities to individuals and their families. Housing policy is about the competitiveness of cities, the attractiveness of neighbourhoods and the performance of economies. Decisions to invest in state housing have been made with judgement about the reproduction of labour – providing good housing for a workforce where it was needed – and about the performance of the economy as a whole. Similarly, it may be argued that privatisation has been seen as part of a modernisation process for housing, and reorganisation varies between countries.

All of this suggests that there are different elements for privatisation, and different forms of privatisation. In the cases, such as the UK, where the privatisation of state housing has made a considerable addition to the private sector, what has been created is a private housing market shaped by the building activities of the state and the bureaucratic transfer to the private sector. Some owner-occupied housing has never been exchanged on the open market, although arguably it will be at some point in the future, but the process of privatisation is a bureaucratic state sponsored action not a market exchange.

Integration with the housing market

Even after 25 years of the Right to Buy it is not clear to what extent this distinctive part of the housing market will be fully absorbed into the market. Will former council properties always be distinguishable? And compared with other properties of the same size and type, will they command a different price? Will the fact that a property is on a former council estate always be an attribute that affects its marketability and price? The evidence from Chapter 6 is that resales have integrated into the local housing market although in most areas they sell at a lower price than equivalent housing not built by the public sector. In some places resales are 25% cheaper than their mainstream equivalent but the differential can be much smaller, particularly where housing demand pressures are highest.

Taken one step further, will there be some parts of the market where lenders and financial institutions will continue to be reluctant to provide mortgages, or where the purchasers will always have to pay more than they would do for a comparable property elsewhere? There is still evidence that financial institutions in Britain are unenthusiastic about lending on certain types of non-traditionally built properties and flats with more than five storeys and there is some suspicion that these policies are really ways of avoiding lending on properties located within council estates.

At its extreme then, some households may be entering a market that is not associated with accumulation and the build-up of wealth seen in the housing market in general. They are entering a different housing finance regime, avoiding a stream of payments associated with rent and rearranging their housing costs over time, but they are not really entering a market system with the ability to achieve significant asset values, to trade up or to move on. Households in this situation may have a very different experience from households in the most expensive, most high status parts of the owner-occupied sector. Privatisation begins to change the nature, location and status of owner-occupation and contribute to stratification within that tenure.

Privatisation also contributes to changes in council housing neighbourhoods, and in the status and role of social housing. In this context it is still relevant to look at the American experience and the problems of creating a social rented sector which is unattractive to most people, except those with no choice. The social rented sector in the UK has changed significantly from its status before the Right to Buy was introduced. It has become more individualised; it is no longer associated with the affluent working class, but rather with the homeless and households on the margins of the labour market, those with high dependency on benefits, and the elderly.

The big issue facing UK governments in relation to the social rented sector and privatisation is about whether they go further along the American route towards an even more residual sector, or whether the capital receipts from selling council housing are saved and recycled so that the social rented sector can be reinvented and reinvigorated. This would help to sustain a flow of new, high quality properties, and would provide people with more choice. These households are then more likely to choose to stay even when their circumstances improve. Just as plausibly a reinvigorated public housing sector could provide opportunities for people to enter good quality housing and, as their circumstances improve, to buy that property. The proceeds released through that sale could then be used to create an opportunity for another household. Recycling of receipts and the creation of a *flow* of housing opportunities may be more appropriate than resisting the sale of properties altogether.

Unequal opportunities

Discussion of the Right to Buy raises some important issues for the evaluation of social policies. It naturally falls into a debate about distributional consequences of policy interventions, the kinds of debate headlined in terms of 'who benefits' and 'who loses'. However it also highlights the danger of one-dimensional approaches to these kinds of questions. 'Who benefits' and 'who loses' can be set out in terms of the characteristics of households, i.e. incomes or social class, but housing provides a flow of services over a lifetime and housing situation can provide a platform or a pathway for opportunities elsewhere. Therefore it may be argued that we need to be looking not just at income or social class at a particular point in time, but at lifetime earnings and employment. The Right to Buy, by providing access to home ownership and to opportunities for wealth creation and for investment in housing, is much more complex to analyse in terms of 'who benefits' and 'who loses' than an adjustment in the housing benefit system or a change in pensions policy. Because housing situation may itself become a resource that determines future life chances, the nature of the benefits is also more complex.

There are additional factors which increase complexity. For example a lot of distributional evaluations take no account of where people live. The social security system in the UK is designed as a national system and applies the same criteria irrespective of where people live – entitlement to benefits is not affected by the location of home or work. However, under the Right to Buy, where people live, and what they live in, has a fundamental effect on the quality of the opportunity offered by the Right to Buy and financial or other advantages. Accidents of place have been emphasised throughout this book. Analysis of distributional impacts only related to income or employment neglects the fundamental issue of where people live.

Households in a given income range in one city may benefit to a much greater extent than a household in the same income range in another city because the flow of benefits associated with the purchase of a property and the appreciation in value of the property may be very different. There is a body of literature that suggests accidents of place have also been important in other areas of social policy (see Davies 1968). The quality of health or social services, or the quantity of domiciliary services that are available varies according to where people live. However, these kinds of analyses have been less prominent in the literature than national evaluations, which inevitably understate the importance of where people live. Evaluation of social policy that takes account of lifetime and life cycle factors and of where people live becomes much more complex.

There are also a number of difficult qualitative issues. At one level, ignoring the financial dimension, households live in the same property and the same neighbourhood the day before they exercise the Right to Buy as they do the day after. Is there any change in terms other than a formal label and the financial implications flowing from it? Saunders (1990) among others has argued that there is a change in terms of ontological security or people's sense of having control and autonomy over their own lives, independent from other agencies, but this is very difficult to establish. In some situations, the purchase of a particular type of property generates certain qualitative gains whereas in others there is a much less clear flow of benefits.

Do purchasers of flats who continue to pay leasehold charges experience the same change in the sense of control over their lives as those who buy freehold houses? Do people who begin to find difficulties with meeting housing costs or with repairs and improvements feel the same benefits? Do people whose household circumstances change through loss of employment or the breakdown of relationships feel more secure or less secure in this situation because they are owner-occupiers? Evidence on these things is not easy to generate and, as with the discussion on house condition, the results are likely to be much more tentative than those related to the financial benefits flowing from exercising the Right to Buy.

It is not helpful to fall back into a morass of complexity and argue that everything is more difficult to identify than we might hope. However it is clear that the simple headlines of 'who gains' and 'who loses' – the purchasers of good quality houses and the cohort of applicants who are unable to access such good quality houses – only provides part of the story. The perspective that suggests that households which had gained privileged positions through the welfare state and had graduated to the best housing are those which did best out of the Right to Buy and those which have been unable to access these opportunities have done worse is undeniably true, but is only part of the story. Perhaps most fundamental in terms of debates about the welfare state is the extent to which the Right to Buy has suspended ideas about equity, fairness and citizenship rights that were seen to have underpinned the welfare state. As well as considering 'who benefits' and 'who loses' it is important to acknowledge the great variation of benefits associated with the provision of council houses and the operation of the Right to Buy.

Where the state has not provided a monopoly service but has provided housing that is significantly better than much of the housing available in the private sector, then it has provided a privileged status to a minority of households that have managed to negotiate access to that housing. The extent to which the standing of council tenant represented a privileged status depends fundamentally on what housing people occupied and where. Adding on top of this the inequalities associated with the Right to Buy can only lead to the conclusion that the combination of the provision of council housing and the privatisation of that council housing has provided considerable, but unequal opportunities to households. It has provided some real opportunities for accumulation and the exercise of choice.

Just as some of the early analyses of the welfare state suggested, council housing had a primarily redistributive effect, so it may be argued that it has had a significant effect in restratifying society, through its provision, its privatisation and its subsequent commodification. By providing an exceptional route for a selected minority of households to gain access to private wealth and to exercise mobility and choice about where they live, the state has benefited a specific part of a cohort of households. These are households whose social class and economic position made them more likely to graduate to council housing and who accessed this benefit. Because of the importance of accidents of time and place, the pattern of redistribution of opportunities is less systematically about social class or income than would otherwise be the case. Nevertheless the whole story is one where major interventions by the state through the decommodification and subsequent privatisation of housing has significantly affected the life chances of a group of households.

Is this a cause for celebration or for concern? Inevitably the issues of equity and unequal treatment offend some of the principles underpinning welfare state provision, and it is doubtful whether a government embarking upon a programme that suggested such a poorly targeted pattern of benefit would win much support. However, looked at from another perspective, this is a success story. It is an example where state intervention does change life chances, both through the provision of council housing and through privatisation.

Home ownership and the new welfare state

There have been attempts to place the Right to Buy within broader theoretical frameworks. First, it has been linked with debates about commodification and modernisation. Council housing is seen as a classic case of decommodification where households were not charged the rents that would have been demanded in the market place, but were able to access a much better quality of provision because of this decommodification. There was a real redistribution of housing opportunity as a result. It has been argued that privatisation is a 'halfway house' between this decommodified status and housing being treated as a commodity on the open market (Forrest & Murie 1995). This is because the price paid under the Right to Buy was not a market price, but included an enormous discount or grant to assist purchase, and also because the only potential purchaser certainly under the Right to Buy was the sitting tenant household. True commodification would not involve a subsidy and might involve bidding between a number of potential purchasers. This is what happens on resale – at the point when the Right to Buy purchaser chooses to sell, they will sell through normal market processes at market prices. Although these prices may be below those of similar properties that have a different history, or are in different neighbourhoods, the transaction becomes fully commodified.

Goodlad and Atkinson (2004) have contributed to this debate in a different way. They emphasise that the privatisation of housing through the Right to Buy should not be seen purely in terms of the rolling back of the state and Government's attempts to recommodify state services, but rather it is part of a process of reconstructing the welfare state to reflect a new pattern of rights and interests. This kind of perspective is more compatible with the arguments about home ownership as a state sponsored tenure, and the expansion of home ownership being a deliberate act by the Government to change the relationship between the state and the citizen and to promote particular kinds of property ownership on a large scale. This framework does not refer to the withdrawal of the state, but rather the state repositioning itself in its relationship to citizens and their property circumstances.

The promotion of home ownership can be seen as part of a process of creating a property owning democracy and establishing an interest for the individual household in existing political and organisational structures. This process also relates to the modernisation of a post-industrial world as the strength of workplace and employment based solidarity is weakened; the restratification of society in which position in relation to employment becomes less important than position in relation to the consumption of key goods and services, including housing. Restratification in terms of sociospatial inequalities means that where people live becomes much more important than where people work; territorial and generational differences are much more significant, and the role of the state is much less about providing citizenship rights on an equal basis to all citizens, but is about appealing to the different interests of different cohorts of the population in different places.

In all of this it is important to reflect upon the difference between analyses of the Right to Buy, and processes of reorganisation associated with it, that are inward looking from those which are outward looking. The inward looking analyses will focus upon the Right to Buy itself: 'who benefits' and 'who loses'; the restructuring and reshaping of housing policy with the increasing promotion of owner-occupation; the development of a more complex owner-occupied market and the links between this and neighbourhood differences; and the status differences associated with where you live. However, these are all still looking close to home, close to the Right to Buy, and close to the housing market.

The alternative is to see the Right to Buy and the restructuring of housing in a bigger picture concerned with the global influences on the development of the welfare state and the economy, the reproduction of labour, and the dynamics of cities, regions and subregions. In this kind of outward looking approach, decommodified housing and rented housing provided by the state are no longer key elements of developing the competitiveness of cities and regions, or developing a welfare state that meets the demands of modern competitive economies in a globalised economic system. The form of decommodified housing provision that was appropriate for an earlier phase in the development of the economy and political discourse is not appropriate 100 years later, or 60 years later.

Issues of choice and mobility are not just issues for individual households but relate to the functioning of the economy as a whole. Certainly by the beginning of the twenty-first century the damaged reputation of decommodified housing in the UK (and elsewhere in the world) suggested that maintaining that model was unlikely to meet the expectations and aspirations of individual households or the needs of the economy as a whole. It is not surprising that in this context Government has become increasingly interested in issues about asset ownership and arguments about equity stakes related to other parts of the not for profit housing sector in the UK. A modern economy with an ambitious workforce looking for opportunities for social mobility and more likely to take responsibility for their future in terms of pensions provision and insurance against the risks faced by everyone is more compatible with a widespread ownership of property and the creation of opportunities for people to better themselves. This is essentially the conventional wisdom for the new model welfare state: encouraging people to build personal asset ownership and to develop household strategies to increase their wealth.

This agenda differs from a simple decommodification or dismantling of the welfare state model in one fundamental respect – that is that the state has a continuing role in improving the range of households or the likelihood of all households accessing the opportunity for individual wealth ownership and accumulation. This is what has been done, largely through the Right to Buy. The state has created a pathway to home ownership which is accessible to households which, in some cases at least, would not otherwise have accessed home ownership. It therefore has increased the scope of the property owning welfare state. The crucial question then for a government which wishes to continue to build a new model welfare state upon individual property ownership is about whether it can continue to do this successfully without creating similar pathways.

Government has partly begun to articulate this position in relation to debates about providing equity stakes and opportunities for children to build wealth through savings. One mechanism that has already worked is for the state to act as a developer, to build high quality housing which it allocates on need and subsequently sell this housing at a discounted rate. The state then enhances the quality and quantity of housing available and addresses issues of housing shortage, at the same time influencing access to this housing and in turn to home ownership. If this is a process that works at least for a significant section of the population how can the state maintain the flow of benefit for others? It can only do this if it continues to provide the flow of opportunities associated with high quality council housing.

In this logic, a continuing component of the new model welfare state built around individual asset ownership and property ownership would be a programme to build high quality council housing with the expectation that this would be available to tenants buying in the future, so providing a pathway to home ownership rather than a permanent tenantry. Recycling of capital receipts would be one mechanism for achieving this. If the Right to Buy has worked in enabling people to access home ownership and a wider set of opportunities in a way that is more compatible with the needs of a modern economy, then the lesson should be to continue to provide state housing in order to maintain that route into home ownership. Rather than the Right to Buy being seen as the end of state housing provision it would then be seen as a continuing necessity for the modern welfare state.

Throughout the period since the Right to Buy was introduced, commentators have consistently highlighted the extent to which this has contributed to the residualisation of social rented housing. The British public sector has increasingly been referred to as a social rented sector, because it was developing a clearer social welfare role as well as because the term embraced council housing and housing association property. The British social rented sector has changed from a sector marked by considerable social and income mix, to one which caters disproportionately for the non-working poor and those on benefits. It has moved much more towards the American model, although it falls far short of it. Recent data shows that the British social rented sector is more skewed towards lower income groups than is true in other European countries – in France, Germany, the Netherlands or Scandinavia for example.

It is important to acknowledge that, while the UK system is targeted at the lowest income groups, other larger providers of social rented housing are experiencing a process of residualisation. As home ownership expands in these countries, middle and higher income groups are disproportionately attracted to home ownership and the consequences are that the households remaining in the not for profit sector – state built housing and social rented housing – are disproportionately older, or on lower incomes. The Right to Buy has sped up and deepened the residualisation process but not created it. Without the Right to Buy the consequences of residualisation would have been delayed and moderated significantly and the problems within the local authority sector and the attitudes towards it would have been significantly moderated.

Conclusions

The Right to Buy has now been in existence for 25 years. The housing circumstances which apply today are very different from those that applied at its introduction and the major concerns of Government in relation to the modernisation of housing and the provision of choice are very different from those of the 1970s. If in 1980 the Right to Buy was a policy for its time, by 2005 it was a policy beyond its sell-by date.

There are very different strategic considerations today relating to meeting people's housing requirements than there were in 1980. The Right to Buy itself has changed patterns of access and affordability and this has contributed to the housing problems faced today as well as having benefited a significant section of the population. In addition, the situation facing tenants is much more complex today than it was 20 years ago. There are a greater variety of rights depending upon when people became tenants, of which landlord and of which property. In the future the Right to Buy is more likely to be exercised by younger tenants with shorter periods of tenancy. The demographic profile of the council and social rented sector has changed and the middle age group which has made so much use of the Right to Buy is no longer so large a part of the sector and is not likely to be in the future. The tenants who are able to buy in the future will not be tenants who have paid rent for years and seen no return for it – the households that the Right to Buy was originally aimed at.

At the same time the home ownership sector has also changed. Deregulation and the development of a wide range of financial products for house purchase have improved access to the sector. A range of policies have provided new routes into home ownership for different sections of the community. The cohort of tenants that the Right to Buy was targeted at has now largely benefited from the policy. The nature of council housing and the perspectives of many new tenants are quite different from those of the tenants of more than 20 years ago.

If the Right to Buy continues to operate in broadly its existing form it will continue to have a major impact on what happens to council estates and on the development of owner-occupation. In considering the position of the Right to Buy it is important to acknowledge the greater variety of rights than was the case 20 years ago. The apparent simplicity of the Right to Buy when it was introduced in 1980 no longer exists and the case for simplifying and clarifying the policy alongside tenancy law in general is strong. At the same time there have been changes in relation to the Right to Buy in Scotland with extension to housing associations. There is a case for considering whether changes along these lines would be appropriate for England, Wales and Northern Ireland.

There is a case for consolidating policies concerned with the encouragement of home ownership to provide alternatives to households but alternatives which are proportionate and offer similar levels of grant or support. This also makes more sense in terms of concerns about value for money. The discounts associated with council house sales in the past have not always provided value for money for Government and have been much higher than was necessary to encourage people to exercise the Right to Buy. This is an argument not for abolishing the Right to Buy but for bringing the incentives associated with it more into line with what is defensible in terms of value for money and more into line with the incentives offered by other policies providing options to move into home ownership, such as the Homebuy scheme, starter home and key worker housing schemes and a variety of other incentive schemes.

This approach is also more compatible with concerns about the strategic development of housing policy. This has been recognised by the ability to deny the Right to Buy in estates undergoing major renewal or rehabilitation. While in these situations tenants would not have the option of the Right to Buy they continue to have the option of other policies that would give them the equivalent grant to move into the owner-occupied sector if they so wished.

The logic of this approach is that there should also be some proportionate advantage associated with people who remain as tenants. There are important short and long term benefits of a social rented sector that is a sector of choice and the stability and opportunity associated with this. If all of the incentives are to buy or to move out then there are consequences in terms of a tenure which will not be associated with choice but with short term residence and high turnover. No amount of choice-based letting schemes will generate a tenure that offers long term choice against this background. There is a case, therefore, for developing some sort of equity stake or repayment or differential rent structure which rewards longer term tenants.

Against this direction of change there is a further debate about the role of asset ownership or equity stakes in future policy. In a new model welfare state home ownership is a key element in taking individual responsibility for changing needs over the course of the family cycle. The Right to Buy was conceived as part of the dismantling of a previous municipal welfare state system which only partly embraced housing provision. It has bridged a period in which the role of housing in a new welfare state has become more clearly articulated. It has now been absorbed into an approach involving more comprehensive planning for asset ownership and routes into home ownership.

References

Aalbers, M.B. (2004) Promoting home ownership in a social-rented city: policies, practices and pitfalls. *Housing Studies* **19** (3), 483–496.

Association of London Government (2003) *The Impact of the Right to Buy – A Report*. Association of London Government, London.

Association of Residential Letting Agents (2004) *The ARLA Review & Index, Third Quarter, 2004*. ARLA, Amersham, Buckinghamshire.

Association of Residential Letting Agents (2005a) *ARLA Members Survey of the Buy to Let Sector, First Quarter, 2005*. ARLA, Leeds.

Association of Residential Letting Agents (2005b) *ARLA Members Survey: Source & Tenure of Property in the Residential Rental Market, First Quarter, 2005*. ARLA, Leeds.

Atkinson, R. & Kintrea, K. (1998) *Research Report 61, Reconnecting Excluded Communities: The neighbourhood impacts of owner occupation*. Scottish Homes, Edinburgh.

Atkinson, R. & Kintrea, K. (2000) Owner-occupation, social mix and neighbourhood impacts. *Policy and Politics*, **28**, 93–108.

Barker, K. (2004) *Review of Housing Supply – Delivering Stability: Securing our future needs – Final Report: Recommendations*. Office of the Deputy Prime Minister, London.

Baross, P. & Struyk, R. (1993) Housing transition in Eastern Europe. *Cities*. August 1993, pp. 179–188.

Bramley, G. (2003) *Report 21: Housing Need and Affordability Model for Scotland*. Communities Scotland, Edinburgh.

Butler, D.E. & King, A. (1965) *The British General Election of 1964*. Macmillan, Oxford.

Butler, D.E. & King, A. (1966) *The British General Election of 1966*. Macmillan, Oxford.

Clapham, D. & Kintrea, K. (1996) Analysing housing privatization. In: Clapham, D., Hegedüs, J., Kintrea, K., Tosics, I. & Kay, H. (eds) *Housing Privatisation in Eastern Europe*. Greenwood Press.

Communities Scotland (2005) *Housing and Disrepair in Scotland: Analysis of the 2002 Scottish House Condition Survey, Working Paper 3*. Communities Scotland, Edinburgh.

Comptroller and Auditor General (1981) Financial consequences of the sale of council houses. In: *Second Report of the Environment Committee, Council House Sales, Vol. III*. Her Majesty's Stationery Office, London.

Conservative Party (1949) *The Right Road for Britain*. Conservative Political Centre.

Conservative Party (1979) *Conservative Party Manifesto 1979*. Conservative Central Office, London.

Conservative Party (1967) *Annual Conservative Conference, Verbatim Report*. The Conservative Party.

Conservative Party (1970) *A Better Tomorrow*. The Conservative Party.

Conservative Party (1971) *Annual Conference Report*. The Conservative Party.

Conservative Party (1972) *Annual Conference Report*. The Conservative Party.

Conservative Party (1973) *Annual Conference Report*. The Conservative Party.

Cooney, E.W. (1974) High flats in local authority housing in England and Wales since 1945. In: Sutcliffe, A. (ed) *Multi-Storey Living*. Croom Helm.

Cowans, J. (1999) The role of low cost home ownership in tackling exclusion: findings of the Joseph Rowntree Foundation Inquiry. In: Cowans, J. (ed) *Inclusive Housing: the role of low cost home ownership.* Joseph Rowntree Foundation, York.

Davies, B.P. (1968) *Social Needs and Resources in Local Services.* Michael Joseph, London.

Davis, D.S. (2003) From welfare benefit to capitalised asset: the recommodification of residential space in urban China. In: Forrest, R. & Lee, J. (eds) *Housing and Social Change: East-West Perspectives.* Routledge, London and New York.

Department of the Environment (1977a) *Housing Policy: A Consultative Document, Cmnd 6851.* HMSO, London.

Department of the Environment (1977b) *Housing Policy: Technical Volume Part 1, Cmnd 6851.* HMSO, London.

Department of the Environment (1980) *Appraisal of the Financial Effects of Council House Sales.* DoE, London.

Department of the Environment (1996) *An Evaluation of Six Early Estate Action Schemes.* HMSO, London.

Department of the Environment for Northern Ireland (1995) *Building on Success.* Department of the Environment for Northern Ireland, Belfast.

Department of Environment Transport and Regions (1998a) *Secure Tenants Right to Buy: A consultation paper.* DETR, London.

Department of Environment Transport and Regions (1998b) *Buying Back Ex-Council Flats and Houses: A consultation paper.* DETR, London.

Doling, J. (2002) The south and east Asian housing policy model. In: Agus, M.R., Doling, J. & Lee, D.S. (eds) *Housing Policy Systems in South and East Asia.* Palgrave Macmillan, Basingstoke.

Dunn, R., Forrest, R. & Murie, A. (1987) The geography of council house sales in England, 1979–85. *Urban Studies,* **24,** 47–59.

English, J. (1979) Access and deprivation in local authority housing. In: Jones, C. (ed) *Urban Deprivation and the Inner City.* Croom Helm, London.

Forrest, R. & Murie, A. (1976) *Social Segregation, Housing Need and the Sale of Council Houses.* University of Birmingham.

Forrest, R. & Murie, A. (1984a) *Right to Buy? Issues of Need, Equity and Polarization in the Sale of Council Houses.* School for Advanced Urban Studies, University of Bristol.

Forrest, R. & Murie, A. (1984b) *Monitoring the Right to Buy.* SAUS, University of Bristol.

Forrest, R. & Murie, A. (1990a) *Selling the Welfare State,* 2nd edn. Routledge, London.

Forrest, R. & Murie, A. (1990b) *Moving the Housing Market.* Avebury, Aldershot.

Forrest, R. & Murie, A. (1995) From privatisation to commodification: tenure conversion and new zones of transition in the city. *International Journal of Urban and Regional Research,* **19** (3), 407–422.

Forrest, R., Murie, A. & Gordon, D. (1995a) *Leaseholders and Service Charges in Former Local Authority Flats.* HMSO, London.

Forrest, R., Murie, A. & Gordon, D. (1995b) *The Resale of Former Council Dwellings in England.* HMSO, London.

Foulis, M. (1985) *Council House Sales in Scotland.* Central Research Unit, Scottish Office, Edinburgh.

Foulis, M. (1987) The effects of sales on the public sector in Scotland. In: Clapham, D. & English, J. (eds) *Public Housing: Current Trends and Future Development.* Crown, London.

Fuerst, J.S. (1974) Public housing in the United States. In: Fuerst, J.S. (ed) *Public Housing in Europe and America*. Croom Helm.

Gilbert, B.B. (1970) *British Social Policy 1914–1939*. Batsford, London.

Goodlad, R. & Atkinson, R. (2004) Sacred cows, rational debates and the politics of the Right to Buy after devolution. *Housing Studies*, **19** (3), 447–463.

Groves, R., Middleton, A., Murie, A. & Broughton, K. (2003) *Neighbourhoods that Work: A Study of the Bournville Estate, Birmingham*. The Policy Press, Bristol.

Hamnett, C. (1999) *Winners and Losers*. UCL Press, London.

Hargreaves, J. (2002) *Does the Right to Buy make Business Sense?* Chartered Institute of Housing, London.

Harloe, M. (1995) *The People's Home? Social Rented Housing in Europe and America*. Blackwell, Oxford.

Harloe, M. (1999) Cities in the transition. In: Andrusz, G., Harloe, M. & Seleigny, I. *Cities After Socialism*. Blackwell, Oxford.

Harris, N. (1973) *Competition and the Corporate Society*. Methuen.

Hegedüs, J., Mark, K., Sárkány, C. & Tosics, I. (1996a) Hungary. In: Clapham, D., Hegedüs, J., Kintrea, K., Tosics, I. & Kay, H. (eds) *Housing Privatization in Eastern Europe*. Greenwood Press.

Hegedüs, J., Mayo, S.K. & Tosics, I. (1996b) *Transition of the Housing Sector in the East-Central European Countries*. Metropolitan Research Institute, Budapest.

Hill, S., Lupton, M., Moody, G. & Regan, S. (2002) *A Stake Worth Having*. Chartered Institute of Housing and Institute of Public Policy Research, London.

Hoffman, J.D. (1964) *The Conservative Party in Opposition 1945–51*. MacGibbon & Kee.

Holmans, A. (1993) The changing employment circumstances of council tenants. In: *Department of the Environment Housing in England*. HMSO, London.

House of Commons (1980) *First Report from the Environment Committee, Session 1979–80. Enquiry into Implications of the Government's Expenditure Plans 1980–81 to 1983–84 for the Housing Policies of the Department of the Environment*. HC 714, HMSO, London.

House of Commons (1981) *Second Report of the Environment Committee, Council House Sales, Vol I Report*. HMSO, London.

House of Commons Debates 1945–46, vol. 414, col. 1222; vol. 427, col. 1423.

House of Commons Debates 1947–48, vol. 445, col. 1167.

House of Commons Debates 1948–49, vol. 468, col. 186.

House of Commons Debates 1950–51, vol. 489, col. 2132.

House of Commons Debates 1951, cols. 2227–2354; vol. 493, col. 846–7.

House of Commons Debates 1953, vol. 513, col. 642; vol. 522, col. 191–2.

House of Commons Debates 1955–56, vol. 543, col. 83; vol. 544, col. 204.

House of Commons Debates 1958, vol. 591, col. 997.

House of Commons Debates 1958–59, vol. 604, col. 26–7; vol. 610, col. 25.

House of Commons Debates 1965, vol. 715, col. 39.

House of Commons Debates 1967, vol. 740, col. 1336; vol. 743, col. 203; vol. 748, col. 1397; vol. 755, col. 214; vol. 967, col. 79–80; vol. 967, col. 407.

House of Commons Debates 1970, vol. 803, col. 1340–1; vol. 806, col. 404.

House of Commons Debates 1973, vol. 859, col. 1499.

Howe, G. (1965) The waiting-list society. In: *The Conservative Opportunity*. Batsford in conjunction with Conservative Political Centre.

Jones, C. (1982) The demand for home ownership. In: English, J. (ed) *The Future of Council Housing*. Croom Helm, London.

Jones, C. (2002) The definition of housing market areas and strategic planning. *Urban Studies*, **39** (3), 549–564.

Jones, C. (2003) *Exploitation of the Right to Buy Scheme by Companies*. ODPM, London.

Jones, C. & Brown, J. (2002) The establishment of markets for owner occupation within public sector communities. *European Journal of Housing Policy*, **2** (3), 265–292.

Jones, C. & Leishman, C. (2001) The extent, spatial pattern and causes of homelessness. In: Jones, C. & Robson, P. (eds) *Health of Scottish Housing*. Ashgate, Aldershot.

Jones, C. & Murie, A. (1999) *Reviewing the Right to Buy*. Centre For Urban And Regional Studies, University of Birmingham.

Jones, C., Leishman, C. & Watkins, C. (2004) Housing market processes, urban housing submarkets and planning policy. *Housing Studies*, **19** (2), 269–283.

Jones, Catherine (1990) Hong Kong, Singapore, South Korea and Taiwan: Oikonomic welfare states. *Government and Opposition*, **25**, 446–62.

Kerr, M. (1988) *The Right To Buy: A national survey of tenants and buyers of former council houses*. HMSO, London.

Kilroy, B. (1982) The financial and economic implications of council house sales. In: English, J. (ed) *The Future of Council Housing*. Croom Helm, London.

Kingsley, G.T., Tajcman, P. & Wines, S.W. (1993) Housing Reform in Czechoslovakia. *Cities*. August 1993, pp. 224–236.

Kintrea, K. & Morgan, J. (2005) *Evaluation of Housing Policy 1975–2000, Theme 3: Housing Quality and Neighbourhood Quality*. ODPM, London.

Labour Party (1967) *Report of the Annual Conference*. Labour Party.

Leather, P. & Anderson, K. (1999) *The Condition of Former Right to Buy Properties and Innovative Approaches to the Management and Financing of Repair Work*. Scottish Homes, Edinburgh.

Lynn, P. (1991) *The Right To Buy: A national follow-up survey of tenants of council homes in England*. HMSO, London.

MacGregor, J. (1965) Strategy for housing. In: *The Conservative Opportunity*. Batsford in conjunction with Conservative Political Centre.

MacLennan, D. (1983) Housing in Scotland. In: Smith, M.E.H. *Guide to Housing*. Housing Centre Trust.

MacLennan, D., Munro, M. & Lamont, D. (1987) New owner occupied housing. In: Donnison, D. & Middleton, A. (eds) *Regenerating the Inner City: Glasgow's Experience*. Routledge & Kegan Paul, London.

MacLennan, D., O'Sullivan, A. & MacIntyre, C. (2000) *Evolving the Right to Buy: evidence for Scotland*. Scottish Executive, Edinburgh.

MacLeod, I. & Maude, A. (1950) *One Nation*. Conservative Political Centre.

McGreal, S., Berry, J., Adair, A. & Murie, A. (2004) *The House Sales Scheme and the Housing Market*. NIHE, Belfast.

Mandič, S. (1999) *Impacts of privatisation and restitution on housing estates*. Paper presented at International Conference on Twentieth Century Urbanisation and Urbanism, Urban Planning Institute, Ljubljana.

Merrett, S. (1979) *State Housing in Britain*. Routledge & Kegan Paul, London.

Merrett, S. (1982) *Owner Occupation in Britain*. Routledge & Kegan Paul, London.

Ministry of Housing and Local Government (1953) *Houses: The Next Step. Cmnd. 8996*. HMSO, London.

Munro, M., Pawson, H. & Monk, S. (2005) *Evaluation of Housing Policy 1975–2000, Theme 4: Widening Choice.* ODPM, London.

Murie, A. (1975) *The Sale of Council Housing.* University of Birmingham.

Murie, A. (1994) Privatising state owned housing. In: Clarke, C. *International Privatisation Strategies and Practices.* Walter de Gruyter, Berlin.

Murie, A. (1997) The social rented sector, housing and the welfare state in the UK. *Housing Studies,* **12** (4), 437–462.

Murie, A. (1998) Segregation, exclusion and housing in the divided city. In: Musterd, S. & Ostendorf, W. (eds) *Urban Segregation and the Welfare State, Inequality and Exclusion in Western Cities.* Routledge, London and New York.

Murie, A. (2002) *Public sector landlords and Right to Buy leaseholders.* Unpublished paper, CURS, School of Public Policy, University of Birmingham, Birmingham.

Murie, A. & Leather, P. (2000) *A Profile of Housing Executive Sold Properties in Northern Ireland.* CURS, Birmingham.

Murie, A., Niner, P. & Watson, C. (1976) *Housing Policy and the Housing System.* Allen and Unwin, London.

Murie, A., Tosics, I., Aalbers, M., Sendl, R. & Mali, B.C. (2005) Privatisation and after. In: Hall, S., van Kempen, R., Tosics, I. & Dekker, K. (eds) *Restructuring Large Housing Estates in Europe.* Policy Press, Bristol.

Murie, A. & Wang, Y.P. (1992) *The Sales of Public Sector Dwellings in Scotland 1979–91.* School of Planning and Housing, Edinburgh College of Art/Heriot-Watt University.

Niner, P. (1976) *Local Housing Policy and Practice.* University of Birmingham.

Niner, P. (1998) *The Right to Buy and Housing Associations.* CURS, University of Birmingham.

National Economic Development Office (1977) *BMRB Housing Consumer Survey.* HMSO, London.

Northern Ireland Housing Executive Research Unit (1992) *House Sales Review.* NIHE, Belfast.

Northern Ireland Housing Executive (2003) *The Northern Ireland Housing Market: Review and Perspectives, 2004–2007.* NIHE, Belfast.

Obrinsky, M.H. & Meron, J. (2002) *Housing Affordability: the apartment universe.* National Multi Housing Council, Washington D.C.

Office of the Deputy Prime Minister (2003) *Sustainable Communities: building for the future.* ODPM, London.

Office of the Deputy Prime Minister (2004) *The Egan Review: skills for sustainable communities.* ODPM, London.

Office of the Deputy Prime Minister (2005a) *Sustainable Communities: settled homes; changing lives.* ODPM, London.

Office of the Deputy Prime Minister (2005b) *Sustainable Communities: homes for all,* Cm 6424. HMSO, London.

Ormerod, P. (1997) Stopping crime spreading. *New Economy,* **4** (2), 83–88.

Page, D. (1993) *Building for Communities.* Joseph Rowntree Foundation, York.

Page, D. & Broughton, R. (1997) *Mixed Tenure Housing Estates.* Notting Hill Housing Association, London.

Paris, C. (ed) (2001) *Housing in Northern Ireland.* CIOH, London.

Pawson, H. & Bramley, G. (2000) Understanding recent trends in residential mobility in council housing in England. *Urban Studies,* **37** (8), 1231–1259.

Pawson, H., Satsangi, M., Jones, C. & Leishman, C. (2002) *Assessing and Predicting the Long-Run Impact of the Right to Buy.* Communities Scotland, Edinburgh.

Pawson, H., Watkins, C. & Morgan, J. (1997) *Right to Buy Resales in Scotland*. The Scottish Office Central Research Unit, Edinburgh.

Phang, S.-Y. (2005) The Singapore model of housing and the welfare state. In: Groves, R., Murie, A. & Watson, C. *Housing and the New Welfare State*. Ashgate, Aldershot.

Pinto, R.R. (1993) *The Estate Action Initiative*. Avebury, Aldershot.

Power, A. & Tunstall, R. (1995) *Swimming Against the Tide*. Joseph Rowntree Foundation, York.

President's Advisory Committee (1953) *Report on Government Housing Policies and Progress*. United States Government Printing Office, Washington D.C.

Renaud, B. (1995) The real estate economy and the design of Russian housing reforms Part 2. *Urban Studies*, **32** (9), 1437–1451.

Rex, J. & Moore, R. (1967) *Race Community and Conflict. A Study of Sparkbrook*. Oxford University Press, London.

Rodger, R. (1992) Scotland. In: Pooley, C.G. (ed) *Housing Strategies in Europe, 1880–1930*. Leicester University Press, Leicester.

Rohe, W.M. & Stegman, M.A. (1992) Public housing home-ownership. *Journal of the American Planning Association*, **58** (2), 144–158.

Rosenburg, L. (2001) *Right to Buy Resale Market in East Lothian*. East Lothian Council, Haddington.

Samuel, R., Kincaid, J. & Slater, E. (1962) But nothing happens. *New Left Review*, 13–14.

Satsangi, M., Higgins, M., Pawson, H., Rosenburg, L., Hague, C., Bramley, G. & Storey, C. (2001) *Factors Affecting Land Supply for Affordable Housing in Rural Areas*. Scottish Executive Central Research Unit, Edinburgh.

Saunders, P. (1990) *A Nation of Home Owners*. Routledge, London.

Scottish Development Department (1977) *Scottish Housing: A Consultative Document. Cmnd 6852*. HMSO, Edinburgh.

Scottish Executive (1999) *Better Homes for Scotland's Communities: the Executive's proposals for the Housing Bill*. Scottish Executive, Edinburgh.

Scottish Homes (1996) *Sales of Public Sector Dwellings in Scotland 1980–95*. Scottish Homes, Edinburgh.

Scottish Office (1993) *Progress in Partnership*. Scottish Office, Edinburgh.

Sendi, R. (1995) Housing reform and housing conflict: the privatisation and denationalisation of public housing in the republic of Slovenia in practice. *International Journal of Urban and Regional Research*, **19**, 435–446.

Shelter (2005) *Generation Squalor: Shelter's national investigation into the housing crisis*. Shelter, London.

Sherraden, M. (1997) Provident funds and social protection. The case of Singapore. In: Midgely, J. & Sherraden, M. (eds) *Alternatives to Social Security*. Alborne House, Connecticut.

Struyk, R.J. (ed) (1996) *Economic Restructuring of the Former Soviet Bloc. The case of housing*. The Urban Institute Press, Washington.

Struyk, R. & Kosareva, N. (1994) *The Russian Housing Market in Transition*. Moscow Urban Institute Technical Co-operation Project.

Tanninen, T., Ambrose, I. & Siksio, O. (eds) (1994) *Transitional Housing Systems. East-West Dialogue on the New Roles of Actors in Changing Housing Policies*. Dessau, Bauhaus.

Taylor, M. (1995) *Unleashing the Potential*. Joseph Rowntree Foundation, York.

Tosics, I. (2001) The mass give-away. Lessons learnt from the privatization of housing in central and eastern Europe. *Eurocities Magazine*, **14**, Autumn 2001.

Twine, F. & Williams, N. (1993) *The Resale of Public Sector Houses in Rural Scotland*. Scottish Homes, Edinburgh.

[Ministerie van] Volkshuisvesting, Ruimtelijke Ordening en Milieubeheer (VROM) (1989) *Nota Volkshuisvesting in de jaren negentig* [Memorandum Housing in the 1990s]. The Hague (Sdu Uitgevers).

Wang, Y.P. (1992) Private sector housing in urban China since 1949: the case of Xian. *Housing Studies*, **7** (2), 119–37.

Wang, Y.P. (2003) Urban reform and low income communities in Chinese cities. In: Forrest, R. & Lee, J. (eds) *Housing and Social Change: East-West perspectives*. Routledge, London and New York.

Wang, Y.P. (2004) *Urban Poverty, Housing and Social Change in China*. Routledge, Abingdon.

Wang, Y.P. & Murie, A. (1999) *Housing Policy and Practice in China*. Macmillan, London.

Webster, D. (1981) *Second Report of the Environment Committee, Council House Sales, Vol III, Memorandum of Evidence, House of Commons*. HMSO, London.

Whitehead, C., Gibb, K. & Stephens, M. (2005) *Evaluation of Housing Policy 1975–2000, Theme 2: Finance and Affordability*. ODPM, London.

Wilcox, S. (various) *UK Housing Review*. Chartered Institute of Housing/Council of Mortgage Lenders, London.

Williams, G. (1996) *Renewing, re-generating and re-imaging the urban neighbourhood – the case of HULME, Manchester*. Paper presented to the ACSP-AESOP International Congress, Toronto, Canada.

Young, M. & Lemos, G. (1997) *The Communities we have Lost and can Regain*. Lemos and Crane, London.

Index

Lightning Source UK Ltd.
Milton Keynes UK
UKOW02f1538150114

224672UK00002B/7/P